HUNGARY
ON THE ROAD TO
THE EUROPEAN UNION

HUNGARY
ON THE ROAD TO
THE EUROPEAN UNION
Transition in Blue

László Andor

Westport, Connecticut
London

Library of Congress Cataloging-in-Publication Data

Andor, László.
  Hungary on the road to the European Union : transition in blue /
László Andor.
    p. cm.
  Includes bibliographical references and index.
  ISBN 0–275–96394–2 (alk. paper)
    1. European Union—Hungary. 2. Hungary—Economic integration.
  3. Hungary—Economic conditions—1989– 4. Hungary—Social
  conditions—1989– I. Title.
  HC240.25.H9A5 2000
  337.43904—dc21   99–43101

British Library Cataloguing in Publication Data is available.

Library of Congress Catalog Card Number: 99–43101
ISBN: 0–275–96394–2

First published in 2000

Praeger Publishers, 88 Post Road West, Westport, CT 06881
An imprint of Greenwood Publishing Group, Inc.
www.praeger.com

Printed in the United States of America

The paper used in this book complies with the
Permanent Paper Standard issued by the National
Information Standards Organization (Z39.48-1984).

10 9 8 7 6 5 4 3 2 1

To the memory of my father

Contents

Acknowledgments

This book was written when the author was a Visiting Fulbright Scholar at Rutgers, The State University of New Jersey. The text is largely based on two courses taught at Rutgers: *Hungary and the European Union*, and *Transition Policies in Hungary*. In addition to the course materials, the text reflects upon consultations with colleagues at Rutgers and other East Coast universities, and it was also shaped by questions raised by the American press and public life. The discussions within the circles of the Hungarians of New Jersey also helped immensely to pinpoint the relevant issues and directions of analysis.

The final version of the book was prepared in Budapest, where facts, data and arguments were updated to the level possible in 1999. The intention was to provide a comprehensive and critical view on the so-called transition and integration process of the 1990s and to create a volume that can be useful for foreign experts, students, researchers and visitors to Hungary, and also for courses in history, political science, sociology, economics, as well as international relations.

The author is indebted to the colleagues at the Institute of Hungarian Studies and the Department of Political Science at Rutgers, as well as the Fulbright Commission that made this work possible in the United States. I am also grateful to Philip Rawlinson, Béla Gedeon, Gergely Csorba and László Domokos for their contribution to the finalization of the text.

HUNGARY
ON THE ROAD TO
THE EUROPEAN UNION

1

Prologue:
A Heritage of Extremes

In April 1998, the European Union (EU) officially started accession negotiations with the Czech Republic, Cyprus, Estonia, Hungary, Poland and Slovenia. The beginning of these talks was a significant milestone on the long road of European reintegration that had formally begun immediately after the collapse of the Berlin wall in 1989.

A TURNING POINT IN HISTORY

When the Polish and the Hungarian national roundtable negotiations opened the way for democratization in Eastern Europe in 1989, the European Community (EC) offered financial and political assistance for the reforms in the transition countries. Former socialist countries (FSCs) first began to make association agreements with the European Community in 1991, and the European Council announced at the Copenhagen summit of 1993 that these association agreements would eventually lead to full membership in the European Union. From that point on, the question was not "if" but "when" some FSCs would become part of the European Union.

The accession of Hungary and other FSCs, however, will not be the same as previous enlargements of the European Community (more recently the European Union). For these countries, European integration has been a part of a broader project—the transition from state socialism to some form of capitalism. The prevailing political forces of the 1990s portrayed this process as a historic victory that will return the nations of East-Central Europe to a more natural path of development and bring them close to the West European nations, not just in an institutional and organizational context but also in terms of living standards.

When it happens, the accession of Hungary to the European Union will be the crowning of the so-called "transition project." Beyond that, however, it is also expected to provide compensation for those who perceive themselves as losers as a result of the changes that began in 1989, after the collapse of communist rule. The main losers in the transition were not the political elites at the top of the old communist parties. Some of them, of course, lost their political power and suffered material setbacks and some form of public humiliation as a result. But the real losers in the wake of the changes that enfolded after 1989 are the workers of these countries, who lost their jobs and suffered massive losses in their real wages and overall living standards while benefiting very little from the new political freedoms.

It is, however, not only the outright losers of the transition for whom the European Union appears to be the last hope—the promised land awaiting for us beyond the vale of tears. Most of the new entrepreneurs have not been satisfied by the economic opportunities provided by the new regime. For many of them, the gigantic marketplace of Europe represents the promise of business fortunes. For most Hungarians, the costs of the transition appear to be the investment into the European integration. Thus, the legitimacy of the transition itself depends on the success of EU accession.

In the early 1990s, the public discourse was dominated by the enthusiastic slogans about Hungary's "return to Europe." "Things can only get better" was the prevailing feeling surrounding the dismantling of the state socialist system and the construction of the new parliamentary democracy. From the very early years of transition, however, Hungarians faced large-scale and unexpected hardships in their livelihood, which made them the most disappointed nation in Eastern Europe by 1993 (see White 1993: 14).

In the second half of the 1990s, the policies of the Socialist–Liberal coalition, and particularly the positive developments in the enlargement process of the North Atlantic Treaty Organization (NATO) and the European Union, restored the belief in a rapid and successful accession to the major Western economic and security organizations. In a referendum on 16 November 1997, Hungarians voted in favor of membership of the country in NATO.[1] According to foreign minister László Kovács, a rejection of NATO would have prevented Hungary from joining the European Union rapidly and without difficulties. Hungarian citizens may thus assume that membership in the European Union will now come automatically and that it will be, by definition, a good thing.

Nevertheless, we may assume, with good reason, that the beginning of actual negotiations about entry into the European Union is just the beginning of the difficulties arising in both the economic and the political fields. These difficulties have not been sufficiently made clear by the experts studying and running the accession and dominating the public relations of the integration area. The professional discourse about the conditions of EU accession is usually overwhelmed by technicalities that are barely understandable for the nonprofessional public, despite the fact that EU documents—ever since the 1993 Copenhagen summit—have made it clear that the main criteria for accession are to have a democratic political system and a functioning market economy. The question then becomes: what are the criteria for a democratic political system and a functioning market economy?

Establishing a democratic polity and a market economy was the goal of the dual transformation (Bartlett 1997) that began in Hungary, as in the rest of the FSCs, in 1989. However, the nature and direction of this process has always been rather vague for most of its promoters, observers and participants. The uncertainty has been expressed in alternative descriptions of the era.

The word "transition" became the most widespread name for the recent changes in Eastern Europe in social science internationally, though not without rivals. "Transition" has been a favorite expression in political science and economics, while sociologists, with more affinity to the time requirements of such a process, have preferred talking about "transformation."

In Hungary, the most widely used phrase is "systemic change" [*rendszer-váltás*]. This phrase appeared to be able to express a contrast with "reform," which can cover the mildest changes within the state socialist system as well, or "model change," which was in fashion for a while when Gorbachevian tendencies became dominant temporarily in Hungarian politics.

Both transition and systemic change imply that for the actors in the process it is clear from where and to where this move is taking place. Even the late József Antall, the first prime minister of "free" Hungary, acknowledged, however, that "horses in front of the stagecoach can be changed, but a new social system can only evolve." It soon became clear for everyone after 1989 that simply taking over West European or North American patterns was not an option after the disintegration of the Soviet block. Politics and the social sciences, however, remained within the terminological framework that had emerged in the 1989 euphoria and thus had to struggle to preserve some relevance in relation to the reality of the 1990s.

From Where?

It was not only the changes of the 1990s but also the pre-1989 regime that continues to be called by alternative names. During the cold war, "communism" was officially used in the West, despite the fact that the Soviet Union and its allies never described their countries as "communist." The ruling parties claimed that they were building a socialist system or at best a communist system, but they never proclaimed that that latter objective would be accomplished.

For describing the political and social system of Hungary between the late 1940s and the late 1980s, we will use the term "state socialism" instead of communism or other possible alternatives. The word "communism" should be reserved for the revolutionary tendency within the socialist movement, or for a classless social system that was not even approached in Eastern Europe in the twentieth century. State socialism, however, is an appropriate phrase to describe an era when the largely egalitarian objectives of socialism were pursued by using the state as a major instrument for promoting social progress. Statism has been an essential feature of the East European systems, but calling them simply "statist" would lose the necessary distinction from certain capitalist regimes that, after the end of laissez-faire, also used the state as the main vehicle of modernization.

The state socialist regimes of Eastern Europe have also been called "Stalinist," which can be right in certain cases but can be misleading in others. The Stalinist model of state socialism can be characterized by central planning in the economy, the reign of terror in politics, and a dogmatic Marxism–Leninism and the cult of personality in culture. In reality, a number of state socialist regimes existed without these characteristics. Tito's Yugoslavia and Kádár's Hungary were clearly different from this model. The Soviet Union in the mid-1920s and Poland in the 1970s were countries with a good many democratic rights and cultural pluralism as well. True, such tendencies were often reversed or precipitated the breakdown of state socialist institutions; nevertheless, they provide evidence that Stalinist rule was neither an archetype of the socialist system nor the objective of the communist movement.

In order to consolidate the position of the Soviet Union in a hostile international environment, Stalin created an amalgam of the socialist revolution and the imperial Russian tradition. He did not produce a classical model of the socialist system, as Kornai (1993) and others suggest—rather, he gave up the long-term objectives of socialism and made a painful compromise with the ancient regime. Of course, he did not bring back the Romanovs or the boyars, but he created his own court and political nobility and ruled as only the most ruthless tsars had done before. Whenever tension in the international environment mitigated, the domestic tyranny of state socialist regimes was relaxed. Nevertheless, the Stalinist experience has caused substantial damage to the credibility of socialist movements, not just in Eastern Europe, but all around the world.

In order to distance themselves from the crimes of Stalin and his pupils, all different types of socialists, social democrats and communists also used the term "state capitalism." Indeed, the state in a state socialist regime functioned as a collective capitalist one from a purely economic point of view. It took care of accumulation and used the necessary political and ideological instruments to enforce the targeted results of accumulation until the period of terminal crisis. However, state and society had important features that distinguished them from their capitalist counterparts. There were serious restraints on the private appropriation of the economic output, the institutions of public welfare were established, and—particularly in the first decades of these systems—a high level of social mobility was achieved.

The regimes of Cold War Eastern Europe were also called "totalitarian," which was a phrase that—following Hannah Arendt's contribution—brought Russian state socialism and German national socialism to a common denominator. Despite the fact that manipulative elements of Arendt's analysis have since been discovered, the phrase remained in use and helped to obscure the picture of European and global politics instead of clarifying it. George Orwell's *1984*—a novel that was written at the same time as Arendt's notorious book—was also instrumental in picturing the Soviet system as a totalitarian nightmare and the worst of all possible worlds.

In political science, totalitarianism is a form of rule whereby the autonomy of the civil society is abolished by an omnipotent and omnicompetent state apparatus. Talking about civil society as such, however, hides the actual cleavages within that society that result in the emergence of such an aggressive form of government. The advocates of totalitarianism theory have not been able to face the fact that the social revolutions in the first half of the twentieth century were not *coup d'états* organized by small groups of bolsheviks, but large-scale movements toward ends like peace, progress, justice, liberty and equality. Hence, Leon Trotsky and most of his followers called the Soviet Union a degenerated workers' state.

Even if there are reservations, all theories of twentieth-century East European socialism (Stalinism, state socialism, state capitalism, totalitarianism, degenerated workers' state etc.) supply some relevant critique of the Soviet-type systems. None of these critiques can be perfectly placed and balanced, however, if they ignore the international context of East European history. It must be noted, for example, that any deterioration in international relations provides an impetus to the militarization of society, and the latter enhances the totalitarian elements in the organization of the government, regardless of the patterns of ownership. Sometimes the lack of statistics makes it difficult to reach a proper balance sheet. For all these reasons, the horror of state socialism has been largely overstated in the political discourse of the postcommunist era. It is also often forgotten that Stalinism was not the only horror of this region in the twentieth century.

The peoples of Central and Eastern Europe were oppressed by the political regime and impoverished by the economic mechanism of peripheral capitalism. This was a region where absolutist monarchies survived much longer than in Western Europe, and the attempt to democratize capitalism collapsed and fascism emerged instead. Between World Wars I and II, the territory between France and the Soviet Union became the crisis zone of Europe. The reason Eric Hobsbawm could call the twentieth century "the age of extremes" was largely due to the developments in Central and Eastern Europe.[2]

However appealing Hobsbawm's phraseology is, it needs mentioning that the identification of fascism and state socialism under the terminology of "extremes" is a most misleading feature of contemporary social science. Notwithstanding the remarkable similarities in the forms of rule, from an analytical point of view, state socialism did not represent an opposite extreme to the totalitarian capitalist systems, and certainly not under its most totalitarian period, Stalinism. While fascism was indeed the most reactionary form of twentieth-century capitalism, Stalinism was certainly not the most progressive form of socialism, or even state socialism. The initiatives of communist leaders like Gorbachev, Kádár, Tito or Dubček were appreciated by Western social democrats and moderate right-wing politicians as well. While preserving some rigid Stalinist institutions, state socialism also became a world of experiments.

Within the Soviet bloc, Hungary distinguished itself in a number of significant features. These specificities derived predominantly from the 1956 uprising and the subsequent economic reforms introduced by János Kádár, leader of the country for 32 years. These reforms came very close to establishing a socialist system "with a human face," to use a popular Western expression of the time.[3] They distanced the political and economic system of Hungary from Stalinist theory and practice.

In Hungary, the Stalinist system was built up under the leadership of Mátyás Rákosi, who even called himself Stalin's best pupil. In 1956, he was forced into exile and lived in the Soviet Union until he died there in 1971. Rákosi's regime was undermined by the 20th Congress of the Communist Party of the Soviet Union, which condemned the Stalinist form of rule in February 1956. Their conclusions triggered off a crisis within the leadership of the Hungarian Party of Labor (MDP), as the ruling party was called at the time. In order to improve the public acceptance of the party, reformist politicians like Imre Nagy were brought into the leadership in October. For Nagy it was a return to premiership, since he had already been prime minister between 1953 and 1955, as a result of Soviet recommendations following Stalin's death and the Berlin uprising.

As a result of revelations of serious political crimes committed by communist politicians, and also in response to the civil unrest in Poland, a giant demonstration took place in Budapest on October 23, to demand a correction of the socialist system. Western influence, through Radio Free Europe and heavy intelligence activity, turned the popular movement into an armed anti-Soviet and anticommunist struggle. Noncommunist parties were revived, and a coalition government was formed by Imre Nagy. In the meantime, the Soviet leadership decided to stop the uprising through military intervention and thus prevent further radicalization. The U.S. administration, being involved in the simultaneous crisis in the Suez, provided tacit consent. Various East European leaders, including Tito of Yugoslavia, supported Khruschev's initiative as a second-best solution to the crisis.

The reformist politicians of the communist party faced a dilemma. They either had to turn against the Soviet intervention and side with the radicalizing street fighters, or turn against the popular uprising and side with the very unpopular Soviet intervention. Imre Nagy opted for the first, while his minister János Kádár chose the second. His decision was made in the Soviet Union, where he was invited by Khruschev in secret, and the secretary general of the CPSU offered him the leadership of the ruling party and of the country in the following period.

Thus, the legitimacy of Kádár and the Hungarian Socialist Workers' Party (MSZMP)—which was formed during the uprising—was primarily based upon the condemnation of the 1956 events as a "counterrevolution."

Kádár strengthened the legitimacy of his regime by implementing economic reforms that raised the living standards of the working people. He also allowed a limited private sphere to emerge. By the early 1960s, the regime ceased to be totalitarian, though the centralizing, authoritarian and sometimes autocratic tendencies survived until the very end. Despite the fact that the MSZMP maintained a monopoly of state power, it managed to construct a humanized version of state socialism, which was recognized and even supported by most Western leaders as well. The popular names "goulash communism" and "fridge socialism" referred to the fact that, unlike the models of many other state socialist countries, this was a dictatorship that satisfied most of the basic needs of the people, and the leadership gained a tacit consensus for its rule. The best evidence for this is that in December 1999 a media survey found János Kádár at No. 3 (after King Stephen I and Count István Széchenyi) in the race for being the Person of the Millennium in Hungary.

However, not even the most humanistic form of state socialism could be made legitimate in the political process, and the financial crises of the 1980s undermined its economic legitimacy too. The rule of Communist parties was challenged in various countries in different periods, but the collapse of the whole block occurred only when the Soviet Union under Gorbachev allowed its satellite countries to go their own ways without the least restrictions. An historic earthquake began that buried not only the Communist parties of Central Eastern Europe but eventually the Soviet Union too.

To Where?

Most of the Communist parties of the former Soviet block included factions that were prepared to implement the inevitable reforms and thus to remain in charge of the changes even in a post-Soviet era. They claimed that all reasonable changes could be introduced within the framework of socialism, including the creation of a market economy as well. When, however, privatization was named among the necessary and sufficient ingredients of the transition to market economy, it became clear that what was being spoken about was the restoration of capitalism in Eastern Europe. A socialist market economy with the dominance of various forms of public ownership would not qualify.

At the end of the 1980s, it was not politically correct to speak about the return of the capitalist system. Politicians and intellectuals understood that the socialist propaganda—and, as a matter of fact, progressive social science—were successful in leaving bad connotations for this phrase in the minds of the people. Therefore, it was much more popular to talk about a transition to a market economy, the arrival of the information society, or—to give a geographical dimension to the expected good developments—a return to Europe.

By the mid-1990s, it became widely accepted that "market economy" was in reality a maiden name for capitalism. Some social scientists—in Hungary Miklós Almási and Tibor Dessewfy—suggested that the new system was not going to be the same as the old capitalism, and they initiated the use of the expression, "new capitalism" [*újkapitalizmus*]. Of course, on the eve of the twenty-first century, we are witnessing a number of new tendencies in world capitalism; however, that was the case after World War II and now, at the turn of the century, too, when major technological innovations coincide with institutional change and the emergence of a new political practice.

Some other recently popularized terms refer to the failure of the transition project. Amsden, Kochanowicz and Taylor write about "pseudocapitalism" that emerged after the destruction of pseudosocialism (Amsden et al. 1994: 1), while the Berlin political economist Elmar Altvater suggests that a kind of "hybrid capitalism" emerged in the former Soviet bloc. Capturing the crisis of postcommunist societies in terminology is indeed important, but it cannot be ignored that capitalist systems have never been pure even in the most prosperous times of the most advanced capitalist states. Capitalism has always and everywhere included either remnants of feudalism and slavery or the seeds of socialism or both.

In Hungary, some intellectuals and political leaders were conscious of the procapitalist tendencies of the events in 1989, but such slogans could not have provided a basis for wide social and political coalitions. Neither in 1956 nor in 1989 did the Hungarian people support a transition to a free-market capitalist system, and Hungarian society preserved its scepticism in the 1990s too. At the general elections of 1990, 1994 and 1998, the decisive majority of the Hungarian electorate voted for parties that appeared less enthusiastic about dismantling the socialist institutions and pursuing neoliberal economic policies.

As a matter of fact, the doubts of the Hungarian people proved right in the first decade of postcommunist transition. None of the great promises and expectations toward the "free economy" had been fulfilled by the time the nation entered the new millennium. The new system was supposed to become more democratic, free, fair, productive, affluent, decentralized and prosperous. In reality, with the creation of some "new" forms of democracy, some other forms of democracy have been abolished. Freedom and fairness are seen as jokes by millions struggling to prevent their complete social degradation. The new economic system reached the output level of the old after just ten years of adjustment, and the management of the new economy requires as much centralization as did the reformed state socialist model of the 1980s, though in different forms. A major criticism of state socialism suggested that it was a system that experimented with people. In the 1990s, we have been witnessing another experiment that required a similarly high social cost.

As Bruszt and Stark claim, "postsocialist societies can be seen as an extraordinary laboratory to test existing social theories" (Bruszt and Stark 1998: 2). Western "experts" did not hesitate to launch their small- and large-scale experiments in Eastern Europe, even if their models and policies had already failed in other parts of the world. Sometimes it was apparent at the very first glance that the proposed solutions would not work as claimed, but local knowledge and initiative were systematically swept away to give way to blueprints supported by Western political, economic and ideological circles.

The promise of independence became perhaps the least relevant among the slogans of the transition. Within the emerging structures of pluralism and representative democracy, the policy agenda of postcommunist countries has been controlled by narrow circles of government technocrats supported by East European departments of Western governments, multilateral organizations and transnational corporations. Local and national interest groups could to some extent influence government policies, but whenever different objectives came to conflict with each other, it was usually the goal of capitalist reconstruction that prevailed.

Of course, it was assumed by the new hegemonic ideology that the emergence of capitalism goes hand in hand not just with democracy but also with an improving standard of living for almost everybody. When, however, it was noticed that the arrival of these goods is not perfectly synchronized, to say the least, the reply was that "we cannot expect the benefits of the market to manifest themselves immediately." The need for the reduction of consumption was explained almost the same way as by Rákosi in the 1950: "We must not eat the hen that lays golden eggs." When the casualties of austerity were mentioned, the arrogant reply of the reformer technocrats echoed Stalin's aphorism: "Where trees are chopped, splinters are flying."

It has never been sufficiently explained why such a massive destruction in living standards was a precondition for the market to produce the slightest appreciable improvement. Some social scientists, like Attila Ágh, have tried to save the record of the new system by calling this initial destruction "creative" in a Schumpeterian sense of the word, but the creativeness of this destructive chaos has displayed itself very slowly and rather selectively.

The outcome of the transition has partly been the manifestation of domestic interest, partly the consequence of policy mismanagement; however, a large amount of arrogant expertise also appeared among the inputs into the process. As soon as Gorbachev gave consent to the disintegration of the Soviet block, and the newly elected politicians believed that they could follow Frank Sinatra by going their own way, the International Monetary Fund (IMF), Jeffrey Sachs, Anders Aslund and others arrived and claimed that there was only one "highway" to the transition and all other—locally designed—blueprints would only lead to "byways" (see also Kornai, 1995).

Most transition advisors advocated rapid change (usually called "shock therapy") in order to exclude the possibility of the reversal of the transformation. This argument, however, reveals an awareness of the fact that the suggested change would not benefit most of those going through it, and the millions of losers could be drawn into the process if decisions were to be made and implemented before the subjects could even think about it.

A shock against inflation should have been distinguished from a shock for transition. Based on the rules of financial psychology, it is hard to doubt that hyperinflation in a country can only be defeated by a comprehensive and consequent shock therapy implemented by the government. When, however, the transformation of the institutions of society and economy is on the agenda of the government, the advocates of shock simply deny the relevance of democracy in deciding the future of the country. Such advice is even more ironic when the subject countries are going through a period of alleged democratization.

The neoliberal advisors who have dominated the field in postcommunist Eastern Europe claimed that no debate was necessary about the means and ends of the transition, since the only rational action is to establish a full-blooded free-market capitalist system; and an institutional shock could rapidly bring these countries to their goals. In their view and that of their followers, any talk about a third way was irrelevant and even irrational, despite the fact that in 1989, in their own ways, such internationally renowned social scientists as Ágnes Heller, Iván Szelényi and János Kornai argued for a third way as an alternative to the neoliberal shock.

Ideal types do exist and function in theory, but in reality there are only "third ways"—that is, mixtures of various systems and institutions that might be elements of those ideal typical models. A policy debate that targets ideal types is inevitably misleading, since practical policies can only target mixed systems or "third ways." The East European transition debate that rejected the idea that a new mix of institutions should be found, instead of a general rejection of the involvement of the state, has been greatly undemocratic. Those who exclude the discussion of alternatives apparently pursue special interests or some other kind of hidden agenda.

The view presented in this book thus suggests that the so-called transition process in Eastern Europe has been largely misguided and thus unable to fulfill the expectations created during the destruction of the state socialist regimes. Despite being relatively successful in crisis management, Hungary has been no exception from this rule. The promise of EU accession has become a second edition of false promises. Similarly to the transition project, the enlargement of the European Union will be unable to achieve what was claimed by its promoters. Nevertheless, as a project of international cooperation and regional unification, the eastward enlargement of the European Union should be seen as a vital and immediate task for the states and societies of the continent, even if it cannot satisfy half of the euphoric expectations of the late 1980s and early 1990s.

NOTES

1. Half of the electorate participated in the referendum, and a convincing majority (85% of the participants, or 3.3 million people) voted in favor of joining NATO.

2. In his book, Hobsbawm mentions that the phrase "the age of extremes" originates from the Hungarian economic historian at UCLA, Iván T. Berend.

3. An appreciation of the Hungarian reforms can be found in Nove (1983).

2

Away from Eastern Europe: The Crisis of State Socialism

The collapse of state socialist regimes took many observers by surprise. Most of the supporters of the regimes believed that the system would last for eternity, and most of its opponents had long abandoned the hope of witnessing its fall. The apparently sudden meltdown of the Soviet bloc was particularly surprising because the economic and military performance of the Soviet Union did indeed impress two generations not so long before. Despite widespread critique of the political controversies of the Soviet system and the Soviet dominance of other socialist countries, the social achievements of state socialism were appreciated worldwide, and the Soviet Union was able to match the power of the United States in all major strategic areas.

Indeed, it took a landslide to destroy the East European state socialist systems at the end of the 1980s. This landslide, however, was precipitated by two major changes in the spheres of domestic economics and international politics. First, the capacity of the state socialist institutions to facilitate technological progress vanished as the industrialization of the East European countries was accomplished. Once the human and environmental resources of these underdeveloped economies were fully mobilized, the system was unable to increase productivity without questioning some of its fundamental features.

Second, the renewal of the Cold War in the late 1970s and the early 1980s challenged the capacities of the Soviet bloc in a period when syndromes of crisis were arising in any case. Whenever the destruction of East European state socialism became a major objective of the United States and other major Western powers, they increased their complex pressure in cases where the crisis had already been sharpened for other reasons. Under the intensified arms race and the accompanying economic and ideological warfare, the system that had been struggling with more and more internal problems disintegrated within the space of a decade.

The "dependent dictatorships" of Eastern Europe were thus destroyed by a combination of a few major causes. These were the inherent crises of their economic systems, the crisis of their main patron, the Soviet Union, the disintegration of their ruling elites, the constant pressure from the West, and also the activities of their domestic opposition movements. The balance of these causes varied, country by country. In Poland, the domestic popular movements played a greater role than anywhere else. For East Germany, the Western pressure in all its various forms was greater than anywhere else. The specificity of the Hungarian transformation is its gradualism, which can be explained by the fact that the ruling elite of Hungary was the most prepared to distance itself from the Marxist–Leninist paradigm; this invited Western attention and encouraged opposition activities alike.

THE RULERS: FROM FINANCIAL TO POLITICAL CRISIS

From the mid-1960s on, the keyword of Hungarian politics was "reform." From the late 1970s on, however, the system came to a crisis that demanded far-reaching changes from the political elite, going far beyond the original design of socialist economic reform. The rhetoric did not change, but in essence there emerged an ever deepening and, as we now know, terminal crisis of the system. The way from controlled reforms to a self-inducing crisis could also be observed in foreign policies and domestic economic policies.

Kádár's "Westpolitik"

With the preparation and introduction of the a New Economic Mechanism (NEM) in Hungary in 1968, the leadership of the MSZMP not only shifted toward a mixed economy—between state socialism and market capitalism—but also opened the way toward a reorientation of foreign policy. An increased international competition was part of the stimulation framework of NEM, and an improved supply of consumption goods was part of Kádár's "goulash communism." For all these reasons, from the late 1960s on, Hungary was seeking the opportunities of Western cooperation, though within certain limits.

The most favorable development in the West that facilitated such a change in Hungary and some other countries of the region was the emergence of Chancellor Willy Brandt's *Ostpolitik*—that is, the new Eastern policy of Germany. Brandt's initiative was aimed at improving Germany's Eastern relations; this required the breaking down of certain restrictions imposed on Germany after World War II. Brandt, who was himself in exile during the war, asked for historical forgiveness and promised mutual benefits from enhanced trade between Germany and the East European countries. The reception was favorable, and he was able to develop friendly connections with certain communist leaders. Kádár became perhaps the best Eastern partner of the German Chancellor, as was the case when Helmut Schmidt occupied that position a few years later.

The designers of NEM in Hungary demanded stronger Western links to make the system work, and these links included membership in the IMF, the World Bank (IBRD), and the GATT as well. However, in those times the influence of Moscow was still so strong that the preparations of the accession talks with the IMF and the World Bank were halted. Finance was seen as a political threat, but this was not the case with trade. Hungary was allowed to join GATT in 1973, and thus another step was made toward a normalization of trade relations with capitalist countries. GATT membership brought some advantages for Hungary, but it did not prevent the trade embargo of the COCOM and various other sanctions when the Cold War intensified again at the end of the 1970s.

A most important aspect of Kádár's Western policy was to take advantage of the improving relationship between the two major economic associations of Europe. The relations between the European Community and the Council of Mutual Economic Assistance (CMEA or COMECON) had a long history, from nonrecognition in the 1960s to applications for membership in the 1990s.[1]

During the Cold War, a frozen relationship prevailed in the contacts between East and West. The CMEA, like many other Eastern organizations, wore the features of the time of its birth. It was a semimilitarized system centered around the Soviet Union, and it remained immensely bureaucratic for the duration of its existence. A major shortcoming of the CMEA was that its member countries displayed very weak performances in the production and supply of consumption goods; this enabled the rise of a relatively large sector of illegal (black) and semilegal (grey) activities.

In their relations with other organizations, the member states remained captives of the CMEA, which considered the EC an organization whose main objective was to provide economic support for NATO in Western Europe. Apart from this political judgment, the CMEA insisted on the doctrine of state sovereignty, and it did not want to recognize the EEC and later the EC as a full negotiating partner because it was seen as a derivative subject of international law.

In the 1960s and 1970s, Hungary, Poland and Romania displayed a greater level of flexibility toward East–West relations, including their respective attitudes toward the EC. They were still unable to go as far as recognizing the EC as a subject of international law, though they could take certain advantages of the Common Agricultural Policy (CAP) of the EC for improving the import conditions of food.

The changes in CMEA–EC relations began when, in 1972, Leonid Brezhnev declared that "we have to accept the existence of the EEC." A new approach developed along the principles of the so-called Helsinki process, leading up to the Conference on Security and Co-operation on Europe (CSCE). Bilateral agreements were made between the member states of the two organizations. The relevance of the EC concerning these agreements was limited to the provision of a general legal background for the talks and contracts.

The main fields of import from West to East under the first agreements were consumption and investment goods. It soon became clear that East–West technological cooperation was vital for the further development of state socialist economies. The first major precedent of such agreements on long-term economic, industrial and technological cooperation was one between France and the Soviet Union, which was followed by similar agreements between other EC and CMEA member countries. In 1974, East–West relations came to a crisis because of the Middle East war, though this did not have a direct impact on the ongoing bilateral cooperation.

The first attempt to normalize EC–CMEA relations at the top level also took place in the period 1973–81. High-level EC officials visited Moscow and exchanged blueprints for cooperation between the two organizations. CMEA leaders proved even more ambitious about the possibilities of cooperation; however, the two parties were unable to bridge the legal difficulties. Further disagreements remained on the forms and areas of cooperation too. In 1977–78, top-level negotiations continued in Brussels, Moscow and Geneva, but they were still unable to eliminate the remaining disagreements. Finally, the EC rejected further consideration of the CMEA position, and the negotiations disappeared among the waves of the reviving Cold War.

The increasing Western opportunities and the repulsiveness of the Soviet Union's "advanced socialism" generated a major investment that became perhaps the most misunderstood project of the Kádár era. In 1989, most of the policy debate revolved around a grand project called the Gabcikovo–Nagymaros dam, but most of the observers failed to grasp its real political profundity. Some commentators refer to the dam as the most notorious of the "costly international projects aimed at currying favor with Hungary's allies in the Warsaw Pact." What they do not pay attention to is that the idea of the dam was revived as a result of the oil price shock, when Kádár and the Hungarian government wanted to reduce the reliance of the Hungarian economy on oil and, more precisely, on Soviet oil. Kádár disliked the Brezhnevite Soviet Union, and he wanted to build up Western ties in order to counterbalance the influence of the ailing Moscow leadership. The dam was a part of this project, not just as an alternative source of energy but also as a necessity for improving waterways toward Germany, the Benelux countries and France through the Main and Rhine rivers. Another example of this West-orientated foreign policy component in large-scale investments was the Adriatic pipeline, which was also built in the late 1970s but never used until the collapse of the Soviet Union. The irony of history is that these projects of undercover Westernization later became symbols of "Stalinist gigantomania" and waste.

It was, however, not only with economic links that the Hungarian leadership attempted to normalize and improve East–West relations in the 1970s. For Kádár, the settlement of the disputes with the Vatican was also very important. Hungary had had great problems with the Catholic Church ever since the 1940s, when Cardinal József Mindszenty was arrested and convicted on criminal charges. He left his house arrest in 1956, and, following a short but powerful radio speech during the uprising, he found refuge in the U.S. Embassy building in Budapest. He was allowed to leave the country fifteen years later, when the Hungarian Catholics had been leaderless for more than two decades. In an attempt to improve the public relations of the party and the human rights record of the country, Kádár visited Pope Paul VI in the Vatican. The relations between the MSZMP and the Catholic Church improved significantly, and this had an impact on the conditions of other churches and their followers as well.

The cultural dimension of Westernization was represented not only by the Vatican connection. Hungary became increasingly open to Western popular culture and consumerism. *Cats* became a most successful musical in Budapest. *Dire Straits* and later *Queen* came to give rock concerts in Hungary. Formula 1 races were imported, the first (and only) example in the socialist camp, and Hungary kept on renewing the right to organize the races despite the immense loss they caused to the national budget. The legendary soccer player Ferenc Puskás was allowed to return to Hungary after 25 years in exile and was welcomed by leading politicians in addition to being celebrated as a national hero by millions of Hungarians.[2]

During the new round of the Cold War, in the 1980s, it was not so self-evident that the opening up of Hungary toward the West could be continued, but the Hungarian leadership indeed went ahead with this project. This period brought membership in the IMF and the World Bank as well as visits by Prime Minister Margaret Thatcher and Vice-President George Bush. From this phase on, however, the debt crisis became the main driving force of foreign policy reforms (discussed later in this chapter).

Nevertheless, Kádár worked successfully to promote *détente* even during the new Cold War. He kept expressing the hope that "the tensions that came into being between the two superpowers are of a temporary nature." Austro–Hungarian relations in the 1970s and 1980s were regarded as a model for relations between Western and socialist countries. Since Kádár's group demonstrated their unconditional dedication to the Soviet cause in 1956, their cautious moves to improve Western relations and promote domestic reform did not have to face frequent objections or challenges from Moscow (Heinrich 1986: 176).

In the years 1984–88, a second attempt began to normalize EC–CMEA relations. In this period, however, the conditions of the talks were quite different from those in the 1970s. An apparent economic crisis was torturing the Eastern economies while the role of East–West trade was already relatively important. The EC had an import surplus with the Soviet Union, Poland and Romania and an export surplus with Hungary and Bulgaria. The share of Central-Eastern European countries in EC trade was nevertheless declining, but the share of Soviet trade increased in the EC countries in total. The oil crisis caused severe financial problems for the smaller CMEA members, and they were falling behind in technological development too.

A CMEA declaration initiated a revival of negotiations at the highest level. More precisely, the new initiative targeted a "parallel dialogue," which was meant to address and resolve the previous legal disagreements between the two sides. The reply was positive. Hungary had already started to settle its EC relations by making adjustments in foreign policy and calling attention to the changing principles of economic regulation. Only Romania, out of the CMEA countries, was faster and more eager to strengthen EC trade and cooperation in those years.

Under the improving international circumstances, EC–CMEA negotiations were carried out in Geneva, and a Joint Declaration was reached in 1988. In the same year, Hungary was the first of the CMEA member states to sign a trade and cooperation agreement with the EC. The agreement was preceded by a visit by deputy prime minister József Marjai to the Commission of the EC in February 1987 and a meeting between János Kádár and Commission leader Jacques Delors in November 1987. Hungary's ambassador arrived at the Brussels headquarters of the EC in January 1989. The rest of the CMEA member states, with the exception of the Soviet Union and the German Democratic Republic (GDR), followed Hungary's example in 1989 and 1990.

Hungary was leading the state socialist countries not only on the way toward the establishment of closer links with the West but also toward reform of the CMEA. A major initiative of the late 1980s was to introduce dollar terms in international trade within the CMEA. At first the Soviet Union opposed the idea, but once the Soviets started to calculate how much they would gain from it, they became as enthusiastic as the Hungarians, who were expected to lose billions of dollars but supported the idea for political and ideological considerations.

The fourth phase of EC–CMEA convergence started only after the fall of the state socialist regimes and concluded in association agreements and eventually in applications for full membership of the European Union. This phase is discussed further on in greater detail. A very important conclusion can already be drawn about the first three phases. From the evolution of Hungary's Western relations, it can be seen that when the crisis came, it did not cause any spiritual conflict for the leadership of the MSZMP to reply to the emerging economic crisis by increased international openness and by building up even more Western ties instead of some kind of isolation (which was the case in some other state socialist countries).

The Debt Crisis and the New Path of Growth

From the 1970s on, most East European countries became affected by the international debt crisis. Throughout the 1980s, the foreign exchange positions of several East European countries showed many similarities with less developed countries (LDCs). Hungary, Poland, Romania, Yugoslavia and the GDR joined the group of severely indebted middle-income countries (SIMICs), in the company of the Philippines, Mexico, Peru, and others. With the exception of the GDR, the management of foreign debts also tended to follow the LDC pattern. Multilateral financial institutions (MFIs) gained increasing influence over economic policies in the region.

Researchers of the debt crisis have always been cautious about including Eastern Europe in their studies, given the tremendous political specificities of the region as compared to Latin America or Sub-Saharan Africa (which were the typical groups of countries mired in critical indebtedness in the 1980s). Similarly, researchers of Eastern Europe have always been cautious about mentioning the debt crisis in their analyses, because often it would have interfered with their favorite theories about Communism or State Socialism or Stalinism or State Capitalism or Transitional Society, and so on. It is, however, only a parallel analysis that can lead us to a full understanding of the final crisis of East European state socialism. This is particularly the case with Hungary—a country the economic reforms of which have been deeply studied and one that since the late 1970s has been considered one of the most indebted countries in Europe. The relationship between the two factors has, however, seldom been displayed. The analysis here tries to assess how the geopolitical features of the country have provided special conditions for Hungary's debt management and, on the other hand, how the debt problem contributed to political changes of different magnitudes in certain periods over the last decade of East European state socialism.

The precondition for Hungary's indebtedness in Western capital markets was a slow but certain opening of the economy toward the capitalist economies. This took place after the reforms of the late 1960s. The motivation of the leadership in connection with the reforms was to provide an improvement in the consumption standards of the population.[3] As early as the early 1970s, however—that is, before the first oil price shock—it turned out that keeping the current account in balance would not be so easy if the inflow of Western goods was to be maintained. The impact of the first oil price shock was significantly mitigated by the CMEA price mechanism, and the advisors of the leadership suggested that the cheap availability of foreign loans would allow the government to go for growth. This decision resulted in the greatest investment boom in Hungarian history, and it took place between 1976 and 1978.

The planners were not totally ignorant about the future need to repay debts in foreign exchange, but the 40 billion forint export development fund fell short of what was later demanded by the international markets.[4] In 1978 economists from the National Bank alarmed the leadership with a report about the scale and consequences of foreign indebtedness. At the end of the year, this resulted in a resolution of the Central Committee (CC) of the MSZMP to slow growth and to try to balance the current account, while only maintaining the existing living standards of the people.[5] Leading politicians opposing this "New Path of Growth" were replaced. Since the change in the economic policy was belated, and the second oil price shock as well as the interest rate shock struck soon afterwards, by the end of 1981 a serious liquidity crisis began to take shape. This situation led the CC to decide to join the IMF and the IBRD.

The speedy financial arrangements with the IMF and the Bank of International Settlements (BIS) helped the country to survive the critical year of 1982.

The loans to Hungary reflected a traditional BIS connection, and were crucial in maintaining that country's liquidity. Hungary lost some US$1,200 million of reserves between December 1981 and March 1982, with a fall from US$1.6 billion to US$460 million, thought to be as a result of the Soviet Union and others taking funds out of that country. The quick action of the BIS, lightly referred to as the reincarnation of the Austro–Hungarian empire, given its support from Austria, as well as Switzerland and Germany, was exceptionally helpful to Hungary in that situation. [Lomax 1986: 94]

In the 1982 Hungarian financial crisis, the IMF did not prescribe a conventional stabilization program with tough requirements about demand contraction. Launching a second phase of institutional reforms was enough to gain support and confidence. The fact is that the pressure of debt decreased in the following two years as a result of a heavily centralized ("manual") foreign exchange management. A favorable trade agreement with the Soviet Union, which allowed Hungary to earn dollars for surplus in the "meat and wheat for oil" deal, also contributed to the relatively successful consolidation. Finally, hard-currency earnings were boosted by the increase in "transit trade," when oil, cement and other goods imported from the East were simply resold on Western markets.

In order to overcome the financial crisis, Hungary joined the Bank and the Fund in 1982, in the middle of a period of virtual insolvency. This was a time of a new round of the Cold War and of a gradual foreign policy reorientation in Hungary. The question of the day for the international community was whether the Soviet Union was able and willing to provide substantial support or—as it was called then—an "umbrella" for its allies. Though Hungary and some other countries enjoyed the benefits of certain cooperation agreements with the USSR, such a comprehensive salvation project did not occur. The lack of the financial life belt from the East resulted in all five East European countries attempting to strengthen their links with the West, though all of them did that in their own respective ways.

Romania demonstrated its independence from Moscow using various tactics, including participation in the Los Angeles Olympic Games, boycotted by the Soviet Union and by all countries loyal to Moscow. Nicolae Ceaucescu was celebrated in the West despite the fact that he used the temporary benevolence to consolidate his neo-Stalinist dictatorship. East Germany developed a "special relationship" with West Germany and saved herself from IMF intervention by taking advantage of intra-German trade relations in this period. Due to the martial law in effect there, Poland became a pariah in international politics. Nevertheless, the Polish government was able to secure agreements with the IMF and came to the assistance of Margaret Thatcher's troubled government by delivering coal to Britain during the miner's strike in 1985.

The Hungarian leadership also developed Western links. Apart from joining the MFIs, it maintained intimate relations with the right-wing governments of Britain and Germany. In order to be more convincing about the seriousness of its Western orientation, it gave way to a new wave of political and economic reforms in Hungary.

Some politicians raised doubts concerning the necessity and the consequences of joining the two multilateral financial agencies. Imre Pozsgay, then Minister of Education, was one of them. He was soon dismissed from his cabinet job and appointed to be secretary general of the Patriotic People's Front (HNF). This relatively insignificant position was meant to be a kind of exile for Pozsgay, but he managed to turn the HNF into a forum of popular consultation and started to prepare his return from the political rim. He surrounded himself by some innovative experts and enthusiastic activists and turned himself into the key figure of political reform in Hungary.

Political Reforms and Disintegration

The economic crisis management resulted in various changes in society and politics in the early 1980s. Due to the halt in economic growth, rising unemployment was feared among the political leadership. A logical step to offset the pressure for redundancies was to introduce the five-day working week—that is, to make Saturdays free for most of the working population. This measure was politically wise, as it helped to defuse Polish-type demands for improving labor conditions.

The extension of the sphere of legalized entrepreneurship was another important step in the early 1980s, more precisely in 1982. The new policy allowed significantly more private enterprise and encouraged new forms of intrafirm enterprise in state companies too. Interestingly enough, the respective decisions and analyses of small entrepreneurship and the second economy never really belonged to the agenda of economic policy. Instead, they always constituted a part of the "social policy" [*társadalompolitika*] discourse.

Perhaps the most significant political consequence of the economic crisis was a reform in the electoral system that introduced a significant amount of competition and openness into the state socialist polity. The most important change in the new electoral system—tried first and last in 1985—was that in every single constituency at least two candidates had to run for a seat in parliament. In addition, the candidates had to be introduced and nominated at open conventions. This very fact represented an immense change in comparison with the previous mechanism, in which the HNF nominated all candidates, one for each constituency, and no public debate was possible to challenge the official nomination.

Of course, the HNF did not forget to nominate two candidates with the consent of the local MSZMP organization. They were either both party members or, in a small number of cases, both nonpartisans (so as not to give voters a chance to beat a party member by voting for a nonpartisan so easily). There were, however, a number of cases where third and fourth candidates were nominated at the open conventions, and s'ome of those "independent" candidates became members of parliament. The challenge and possible failure were predictable parts of the new system. Therefore, the HNF set aside a national list of 25 seats for leading MSZMP politicians, as well as representatives of the churches, the arts and science.

Kádár himself always felt uneasy about political reform, particularly after Gorbachev launched his *perestroika* and encouraged rejuvenation in the ruling parties of the Soviet bloc. When asked about the possibility of more or faster reforms, he answered that the Soviet Union might be faster with reform in the political system but Hungary has gone much further in economic reform. In the second half of the 1980s, however, he lost his grip on political change and proved unable to prevent a complete meltdown of the system.

After 1985, due to an ill-conceived attempt to return to growth after seven years of stagnation and partly to adverse changes in exchange rates, the gross debt stock doubled again within three years.[6] The only invention in structural change in the 1980s was the development of Western tourism, which resulted in an increase in the related hard-currency earnings from U.S.$180 million in 1980 to U.S.$540 million in 1987 (van Zon 1991: 60). This, however, was far from enough to counterbalance the yawning trade deficit. Hungary remained in the cluster of "severely indebted middle-income countries" and had the highest per capita debt in Eastern Europe in the second half of the 1980s.[7] The country moved toward the limits of its debt-carrying capacity, and the problem became acute with the decline in Hungarian creditworthiness on the international financial markets.

While the leadership was puzzled by the new round of run-away indebtedness, in autumn 1986 a pamphlet (*Turn and Reform*) by neoliberal economists rocked intellectual and political circles. Soon afterward, a CC adopted an alarmist mood with regard to the necessity of structural adjustment but did not explicitly spell out what the fundamental problem was. At the end of the year, top economic ministers (the President of the National Planning Office and the Minister of Finance) were replaced, apparently as scapegoats. The following summer, however, further deterioration in the national finances ended the 12-year premiership of György Lázár. The ambitious party bureaucrat Károly Grósz took office as Prime Minister, presenting the image of a devoted reformer. He was welcomed by the West, the most striking evidence of which was his visit to Chancellor Helmut Kohl, who presented him with a DEM 1 billion loan package as well as a BMW car.

In September 1987, soon after Grósz announced his government program (tailored to the taste of the IMF), the first opposition organization, the Hungarian Democratic Forum (MDF), was formed. The semidissident founders of the Forum were encouraged to come out by the rhetoric of Mikhail Gorbachev, and they launched their organization to facilitate discussion about the questions of national fate. The doors of the MDF were open to anyone regardless of party membership. The proclamation of the MDF, dominated by nationalist and populist slogans, was published in a daily newspaper (*Magyar Nemzet*) with the help of Imre Pozsgay.

Beyond a major reshuffle, Grósz introduced changes in the system of governance in 1987. He made the policy process quicker and more efficient. The ironic situation was that the one-party communist regime included too much consociational negotiation, bargaining relationships and articulation of competing interests for the liking of the World Bank and the IMF. According to Henderson, "the consociational system's reliance upon compensation-based consensus-building frustrated IMF pressure for rapid adjustment" (Henderson, 1992: 251). Adjustment policies had often been delayed, not just because the original programs were sometimes lost in the endless bargaining process, but also because the promoters of the adjustment policies had to take care of Hungary's image as "a most successful country of market reforms" in the eyes of the rest of the Soviet bloc.

Under Grósz, Turn and Reform economists became influential advisors of the government. Major market reform measures were prepared, including a new tax system—value added tax (VAT) and personal income tax (PIT)—abolition of state subsidies, and a massive liberalization of foreign trade. The way to privatization and to an increased role of monetary policy was opened up. Having gained the confidence and support of the party and state apparatus for fundamental reforms, Grósz took over the party leadership from János Kádár in May 1988, when more than half of the Politburo and the CC were also replaced in a national party conference. By coincidence, a standby agreement was also signed with the IMF in May, which was followed by a change in personnel at the top of the National Bank too. The long-serving Mátyás Tímár was replaced by the younger technocrat, Ferenc Bartha.

A year later, as marketization rapidly increased the power of the business lobby, Grósz was already classified as conservative. His brave performances— like the one on his U.S. tour in the summer of 1988, when he said that he would not object to as much as 25% foreign ownership in Hungary—were quickly forgotten. It is a surviving feature of communist studies to divide East European politicians into proreform and antireform camps. Thus, instead of an insight about the dynamics of the evolution of economic ideology and policy, we end up with a black-and-white picture of reformers and conservatives. This simplification makes the analysis more confused instead of clearer. For instance, Károly Grósz, the secretary general of MSZMP after Kádár, is often described as head of the hard-line faction of the party and an enemy of reforms. This is wrong. When Grósz died early in 1996, he was hailed by the international press as "the Gorbachev of Hungary," which is closer to reality. As prime minister in 1987 he was determined to implement stabilization and adjustment policies prescribed by the IMF and much opposed by the real hard-liners of the party. He was in favor of economic reform, though up to a certain point (early 1989) he was indeed against political pluralism. This latter, however, should not hide his commitment to market reforms, nor the fact that Hungarian politics, and East European politics in general, has always been more complicated than simply describing it in terms of the two poles of reform and conservatism.

The lack of popular trust in those who were allegedly obstructing vital reforms was displayed by a three-day capital flight in April 1989, when Hungarian families left hundreds of millions of dollars in the shopping malls of Vienna, in exchange for video equipment, TV sets, freezers, and cars.[8] As a result of such events, the young PM Miklós Németh, who took over the premiership from Grósz in November 1988, changed his style and policies.[9] In order to regain the creditors' confidence, he started to speak about the need for a "market economy without adjectives," as opposed to a "socialist market economy."

All these developments indicated that the Hungarian leadership did not have the intellectual courage and political power, let alone the unity, to achieve stabilization and economic renewal on a socialist basis. The collapse of the MSZMP in October 1989 was a logical outcome of this process, even without the popular unrest on the scale of the Velvet Revolution in the then Czechoslovakia.

In a school program on the transformation in Hungary, Channel 4 of Britain pointed out the crucial relationship between indebtedness and political crisis with the following sentence: "In 1989, weighed down by debt, the Hungarian government simply collapsed" (Channel 4, 1992). Indeed, the evolution of the debt crisis in Hungary accelerated the erosion of one-party communist rule and cleared the way for the fundamental political transformation of 1989, followed in 1990 by the first multiparty elections after 43 years. Some analysts speak about the direct role of the IMF and the IBRD in bringing about democracy. However, several facts indicate that the main concern of the financial institutions was not necessarily democratization but to help those forces into power which did not have so many reservations with regard to their neoliberal policies.

THE OPPOSITION:
THE SHORT HISTORY OF CENTRAL EUROPE

The 1980s was the final decade of a system that had gone through a number of crises during its lifetime. Some commentators even say that the system had been in a crisis from its birth, since it was a product of a rape against history. The Russian revolution was often identified with such a crime, particularly in countries where state socialism had arrived as a system imported from the Soviet Union. In those countries, this was not only a matter of a different social system in the same country, but the country itself being dragged into another and apparently unnatural geographical zone: Eastern Europe. The Yalta conference of 1945 was seen as an unfortunate event that locked Poland, Czechoslovakia, Hungary and other countries into the orbit of Moscow, and these countries soon became isolated from the West by the imaginary iron curtain. The opposition to

Stalinist rule in these countries, based at home or abroad, was thus not simply, and not even necessarily, a challenge to socialist principles. The more fundamental and comprehensive aspect of their critique was found in the dimension of geography, by claiming back the rights of Poles, Hungarians and others to be Central Europeans or sometimes simply Europeans. Historical justification thus played a crucial ideological role in the "long revolution against the Yalta system," as Ferenc Fehér called the four-decade-long struggle against the division of Europe and the hegemony of Moscow.

Politics, History and Geography

Those who did not feel comfortable with being in the Soviet bloc of a divided Europe looked for a different regional and national identity. These efforts intensified as the crisis of East European state socialism became apparent and acute. Thus, in the 1980s, political geography proved to be a central area of discourse for those who were preparing a collective escape from the Soviet bloc. They claimed that for Hungary, Poland, and others, there was a "natural" place or a historically determined region in Europe other than Eastern Europe.

The politicization of geography was by no means a new phenomenon in Hungary in the 1980s. There was, for instance, a similar debate in 1940 in the daily paper *Magyar Nemzet*, where the advocates of "Eastern Europe" and "Carpathian Europe" crossed swords. The representatives of the first suggested that Eastern Europe was divided by the Carpathian Mountains into two regions. The first, the northern region, belonged to the authority of Polish statehood, and the second, the southern region, stretching between the Adriatic, the Black and the Mediterranean Seas, constituted a zone of interest for the Hungarian state. According to the latter opinion, Hungarians as a people and Hungary as a state were surrounded by the Carpathian mountains, and Hungarians could only become dominant over their territory if they were to accept the continental dominance of others. Consequently, the "Carpathian Europeans" favored an Anglo–French orientation in the emerging war and designated a counterbalancing role for Carpathian Europe between and against Germany and Russia with the support of the Atlantic Europeans, whereas the "Eastern Europeans" rejected this approach. It was, however, not only a debate about military alliances. The "East Europeans" were critics of capitalist culture and did not believe that Hungary would belong to the bourgeois culture of the West, while the other camp looked down on East Europeanness and claimed a place for Hungary in the bourgeois culture and politics of Western Europe.

The learned contemporary communist commentator József Révai criticized both sides of the debate by describing the "science" of geopolitics as "the geographical mystification of imperialism." Révai wrote:

The science of "geopolitics" aims at presenting certain temporary laws of *historical* development, which derived from the social and historical relations of a certain era, as *geographical* laws that derive from the natural conditions of the "landscape" and which therefore are eternal and unchangeable. [Révai 1966: 299]

It is hard to disagree with this view. In 1940, it was the needs of the imperialism of a certain country that determined in what geographical region it wanted to find its natural living space. In the 1980s, it was also the feeling of superiority that made Hungarian, Polish and Czechoslovak intellectuals think very hard about a natural region for their countries other than the Soviet-dominated Eastern Europe.

During the decades of the Cold War, the imaginary iron curtain divided Europe into two halves, these halves dominated respectively by the two world superpowers: the United States and the Soviet Union. Accordingly, Western Europe was a political region that included the U.S.-led capitalist countries of the continent, and Eastern Europe was a synonym for a group of state socialist countries under Soviet leadership. Political geography did not entirely match geometry; Finland and Greece were "Western" countries even if they could be found in the north or the southeast, while Prague and Berlin became East European capitals despite being located much to the west of capitalist Vienna.

Under the Cold War classification, Hungary clearly belonged to Eastern Europe, which was seen as a geopolitical reality rather than some kind of natural and desirable place for the country. Some party ideologues tried to collect historical justification for this classification, without too much success. Instead, similarly to the entire socialist project, Soviet-centered East Europeanness tried to justify itself by references to the future. The Soviet bloc was explained to be a community of peoples building the social system of the future through economic cooperation in a political and military alliance.

Not even the most influential historians of the Kádár era advocated a natural place for Hungary in a homogeneous Eastern Europe. The prevailing scientific theory of the time suggested that Hungary was part of a region called Central-Eastern Europe, which had emerged in the sixteenth century as a by-product of the emerging world capitalism. Hungary had manifestly been just as much part of the overall European game before 1945 as England, Portugal, Denmark or Austria. However, the emerging Marxist school of history suggested that the boundaries of the international division of labor constituted much stronger and more lasting divisions in Europe than did the more visible political borders and military alliances. Economic historians Zsigmond Pál Pach, Iván T. Berend and György Ránki explained in various works that Hungary was in essence a peripheral economy, even as a part of the Austro–Hungarian Monarchy.

According to Pach and his school, the dividing line between Eastern and Western Europe along the rivers Elbe, Saale and Leitha emerged as early as the seventh century. The territories between these rivers and the Ural mountains constituted an area that became a meeting ground for, and a peculiar combination of, the West with Asia. In the Middle Ages, feudalism became a dominant mode of production in these areas too, but the patterns of land ownership and nobility were not the same as in Western Europe.

It was not only Marxist historians who recognized that in the late Middle Ages Hungary had fallen behind the mainstream of Western development, for this condition was largely the result of an era of Tartar and Turkish invasion and occupation. Pach and his students argued, however, that it was not primarily foreign occupation but the unequal international division of labor, which emerged in the sixteenth century, that produced the sharpest dividing line between East and West. This was an impact of early colonization, and it facilitated rapid commercialization and industrialization in the West, while turning Eastern Europe into a supplier of raw materials and agricultural products for the industrializing Western Europe. The social structures of feudalism were restored as a result, and political modernization was prevented.

When the advantage of Western powers over Eastern ones became more and more apparent, particularly after the "double revolution" of the late eighteenth century, catching up with the West became a major motive for East Europeans who saw the increasing European divide threatening their social and material standards. Monarchs who saw their empires crumbling because of industrial weakness thus often became the leaders of such campaigns, which explains why "enlightened absolutism" emerged as a typically Central and East European phenomenon. Due to the survival of strong feudalistic interests and the hostile attitude of foreign rivals, such modernization exercises were usually aborted. By the twentieth century, a semimodernized system with a dual economy and a dual society had emerged.

Within the Hapsburg Empire, Western regions—primarily Austria and Bohemia—were allowed to undergo industrial development, as West-European countries did, while Eastern parts of the Empire, including Hungary, were preserved in their position as agricultural and raw-material producers. It was only in the five decades after the compromise between the Austrian and the Hungarian elites (1867) that substantial industrialization took place in Hungary, although leaving vast areas of the country without any trace of the new manufacturing sectors.

The disintegration of the Monarchy as an economic unit left Hungary with no other options but to become a peripheral supplier of raw materials—this time for Italy, Austria and Germany. The exploitation by the latter during World War II reached unspeakable levels. After the war, German companies were taken over by the Soviet Union, and conventional opinion sometimes suggests that Hungary's subordination was the same as, or worse than, that to Germany. This judgement, however, requires qualification. Politically speaking, the subjugation was ruthless indeed, particularly in the first period. From an economic point of view, however, it was the Soviet Union that undertook the most peripheral roles in that most of its exports to Hungary—and other satellite countries—were crude oil and various raw materials, while the satellites supplied manufactured goods such as buses and cranes. The political control over prices, however, blocked the full exploitation of this division of labor.

Berend, who became the politically most influential historian in the 1970s and 1980s, argued that the Yalta system did not violate any historical rules, since it simply reproduced the dividing line that had already existed between Western and Eastern Europe for about fourteen centuries. Nevertheless, he claimed a somewhat intermediate position for historical Poland and Hungary.

It is at least as important to distinguish the essential differences within the vast area from the Elbe to the Urals as it is to recognize developmental affinities there. Russian East Europe and the Balkans differ from Central East Europe substantially; at the same time these subregions display similarities in economic, social, and political development which must be kept in mind if one is to understand the history of the region. [Berend 1986: 157]

The Central East European subregion was defined as part of the largely backward East, which was also a legacy of Byzantine statism; however, the frequent and sometimes successful modernization campaigns, as well as Western political and cultural connections, were also recognized. As another distinguished and similar-minded historian, Emil Niederhauser, put it: this zone has been "a part of Eastern Europe which always wanted to belong to Western Europe" (Niederhauser 1989: 191).

The Meanings of Central Europe

The most powerful alternative concept to the respective definitions of Eastern Europe and Central-Eastern Europe was the hypothesis that Hungary belonged to Central Europe. This alternative interpretation of geopolitical realities and possibilities was internationally popularized by some famous writers of the region: eminently, Milan Kundera, Vaclav Havel, Adam Michnik, Czeslaw Milosz and György Konrád. These authors supported their hypothesis primarily with evidence from cultural history—an experience shared by Poles, Czechs, Slovaks and Hungarians. Central Europe was a region where the legacies of both the Roman and the Byzantine empires were to be found. Thus this region was seen as an intermediate territory between East and West, stretching from the Baltic Sea to the Adriatic, with a relevance of about 2000 years. Furthermore, this in-between position had been reconfirmed by the impact of the Hapsburg empire and the Austro–Hungarian Monarchy, entities that included most of the territories of the alleged Central Europe.

The Central Europe of writers was predominantly constituted by cultural factors, or perhaps even feelings. Very few scholarly works of history supported their classification, which, nevertheless, became politically very powerful. One of the few well-known historians close to such a concept of Central Europe was Péter Hanák, a social and cultural historian of the Austro–Hungarian Monarchy.[10] Another paradigm very close to that of the writers was Jenő Szücs's contribution. In 1981, Szücs published a monumental study about the three historical regions of Europe, claiming that these three regions had their own specific features of development, and these had emerged over the last two thousand years—thus giving them a right to maintain these distinct features. The anti-Soviet message of the "three historical regions" had great intellectual and political power, though it must be mentioned that the intermediate region between the Baltic and Adriatic Seas was still called Central-Eastern Europe by Szücs.

The political importance of Central Europeanization was revealed by a special edition of the student journal *Századvég*, which invited contributions from dozens of social scientists, including Attila Ágh, Csaba Gombár, Pál Szalai, Géza Jeszenszky and Timothy Garton Ash. "Do we need Central Europe?" the editors asked, and the scholars answered by explaining their different attitudes to the phrase but almost unanimously recognizing the fact that Hungary belongs to a region that is different from Russia and does not resemble the West either. Only one of the contributors argued that Hungary by any standards naturally belongs to Western Europe. That was Géza Jeszenszky, a professor of history of diplomacy. For all the others, the question was still not how to highlight similarities between Hungary and the West but how to distinguish the country from the East and how to use the concept of Central Europe for that purpose. Timothy Garton Ash, the leading British student of the region, wrote: "If for nothing else, the concept of Central Europe can be useful to help Westerners to understand that Siberia does not begin at Checkpoint Charlie" (Ash 1989: 58).

Pál Szalai, an author and activist in the Democratic Opposition, was one of those who expressed concern about the revival of the phrase "Central Europe," since Hungary, as a Central European country, had experienced the period when the name of the region was pronounced in German as *Mitteleuropa*. Within that Central Europe, which was a part of the continent that consisted of Germany and some countries under German hegemony, Hungary belonged to East-Central Europe (ECE), a name that was revived when the transition began in 1989. The partners of Hungary in this cluster were similar to the previous Central Europe: Poland and Czechoslovakia, the state socialist countries of the Balkans, and perhaps even the three Baltic states.

From this angle, Central Europe was clearly a twentieth-century story and could be identified with the "German problem." The phrase *"Mitteleuropa"* was introduced by a German liberal author, Friedrich Naumann, in 1915 as an expression of the new directions of the German imperial endeavor. The first actual organizational framework of the new regional arrangements was the Central-European Economic Union (1904), which would have included the Austro–Hungarian Monarchy in addition to Germany. At the turn of the century, Germany was an emerging great power, and the objective of the Central European initiative was to gain dominance over the territories between Britain and

Russia. France was apparently already written off in these blueprints (which went wrong after Germany was defeated in World War I).

After the war, Germany was restricted from exercising direct influence on its Eastern neighbors, and France appeared to be strongest in deciding the future of Central Europe. The French attitude, however, resulted in economic chaos and the rise of import-substituting development policies that turned out to be economically damaging and paved the way toward a nightmare in politics. By the end of the 1920s, the idea of Central Europe was revived in Germany, and a customs union with Austria was proposed. The French premier Tardieu put forward an alternative plan to create an alliance of five countries, which would have excluded Germany and required British financial support. Both turned out to be an illusion.

When Hitler came to power in Germany, the Central European ideas of Naumann's time returned in a most aggressive form. Hitler's economic mentor, the Reichsbank leader Hjalmar Schacht, presented his *Neuer Plan* (1934), which aimed at incorporating "south-east Europe" into Germany's *Lebensraum* [living space]. Germany was defeated again in World War II, partitioned into two by the anti-Nazi powers, and its Eastern neighbors became even more isolated than in the 1920s. West Germany became an integral part of the American-dominated Western Europe, while East-Central Europe, as it was then called by the Polish historian Oscar Halecki and others, was incorporated into the Soviet zone of influence.

While Soviet influence on Hungarian politics and economics was strong until the last moment of the socialist period, exposure to the West increased slowly too. During the late 1960s, Hungary was already buying large quantities of capital and consumption goods from the West, primarily from Germany, and became slowly dependent on that supply. It was, nevertheless, foreign indebtedness more than anything else that represented a major factor in a new peripheralization over the past two decades.

In the late 1960s, Willy Brandt's *Ostpolitik* was understood as an attempt to revive *Mitteleuropa* with a human face. Germany regretted its historic crimes and promised economic cooperation with mutual advantages. Indeed, economic relations rapidly improved in the 1970s. During that decade, German trade with Poland, Czechoslovakia and Hungary tripled. In the 1980s, economic partnership with the two German states and Austria was already as important for Hungary as the links with the Soviet Union. Nevertheless, the role of the Hungarian economy in the new division of labor was different. In the *Mitteleuropa* paradigm, Central Europeanness allowed Hungary to come to be on a German economic periphery instead of on a Soviet military periphery, though this notion of the phrase was not popularized at the end of the 1980s.

There was, however, a tradition of Central Europeanness in Hungary that was suspicious of and objected to the possibility of Western dominance. This tradition was linked to a search for a confederation of the small nations of the region. Such an idea had been popularized by Lajos Kossuth (the leader of the 1848–49 revolution and war of independence) when, in exile, he proposed an alternative to the compromise with the Hapsburgs in the 1860s. When the crisis of the Austro–Hungarian Monarchy became apparent, particularly during World War I, the radical politician Oszkár Jászi revived the idea of a new federation, to be organized along the river Danube. Unlike their predecessors, the liberals and radicals of the late 1980s did not contemplate the idea of federalism, particularly not in a framework that would have included Slavic nations or the Romanians. The question of the day was how to separate Hungary from East European nations with whom it shared economic and military communities.

The concept of Central Europe played a crucial role in Hungary by helping politically active people to imagine regional arrangements other than the sharp East–West division of Europe. Just like any other regional classifications used in the geopolitical debate, Central Europeanism mirrored various expectations, in addition to relating itself to historical experience. It shared the common problem of all such exercises by claiming a "natural" place for the country and thus ignoring historical dynamics and the possibility of making progress or falling behind in development. It also shared a feature with the Central–Eastern European paradigm of the 1980s—namely, that they not only sought an intermediate geopolitical position for certain countries between the Soviet Union and the North Atlantic bloc, but they also favored socioeconomic models other than pure statism or the free market. In Hungary, they fell into the tradition of thinking about a "third way."

Losing the "Third Way"

For all those discussing geopolitics in the 1980s and suggesting anything other than Eastern Europe or Western Europe, the concept of a Third Way between or beyond state socialism and market capitalism was a popular idea. In fact, the idea of the Third Way provided common ground for different tendencies advocating and promoting reform in Hungary. This common ground was encapsulated in the term "democratic socialism" and personalized by the outstanding intellectual István Bibó.

István Bibó was a highly erudite author from southeast Hungary who became politically active in the National Peasant Party in the postwar years, when he crossed swords in a press debate with Georg Lukács, the leading scholar in the Communist party. In the Rákosi era, Bibó was silenced, but he returned to active politics in 1956 when, along with his counterpart Lukács, he became a minister without portfolio in Imre Nagy's government. He issued some appeals in defence of the uprising even when the Soviet army was already invading Budapest.

Despite all that, Bibó was not antisocialist. He was indeed against Stalinism and any forms of communist dictatorship, but he did not oppose public ownership. He was critical of capitalism and did not believe that the objective of the 1956 events was a return to the precommunist system. He knew that dictatorship could be imposed by big business too. He was in favor of multiparty politics, but he also demanded constitutional protection for public ownership, which could not have been challenged by the rival political parties of his imagined pluralism. That was his democratic socialist ideal, and he thought that Hungary's location in Central Europe—between Stalinist Russia and the capitalist West—could become a conducive circumstance to such a system.

In the mid-1970s, Bibó's following included those who tried to preserve the memory of 1956, who opposed the suppression of the Czech reforms in 1968 and who saw the New Economic Mechanism as a departure toward a socialism with a human face in Hungary. Bibó died in 1979, but just a few years later his followers wrote and edited a memorial book commemorating his contribution to Hungarian thinking about politics. The volume did not reach official publicity but became a classic for all different currents of the reform movement. Jenő Szücs, one of the contributors to the Bibó memorial volume, believed himself to be deriving his regional typology from Bibó despite the fact that Bibó himself usually talked about "Central and Eastern Europe" and considered Poland, Bohemia and Hungary as East European countries. The liberal-minded law students of the 1980s called their society István Bibó College. This institution was one of the cradles of the Alliance of Young Democrats (Fidesz) and a workshop of the whole opposition movement in general.

While the reform movement was small and weak, unity was easily preserved. It did not matter if some, like László Lengyel, Csaba Gombár or Mihály Bihari, were members of MSZMP, while others, like István Eörsi or István Csurka, belonged to a circle of writers marginalized and sometimes even banned by the cultural policy of the party. However hard it may be to believe it now, one or two decades later, but their demand for "democratic socialism" gave the impression of honesty and radicalism.

The cult of Bibó and the program of democratic socialism survived for a few years after the reform movement had started to split into various camps. The party members wanted to incorporate Bibó's legacy into the ideological framework of MSZMP and prepared an official edition of Bibó's collected works in three thick volumes. The populist tendency that organized the famous Lakitelek meeting in September 1987 continued to frame its demands under the headline of democratic socialism. So did the liberal group, which in 1987 still criticized the undercover blueprints of the MSZMP leadership to pursue some kind of South Korean type of economic development. Tamás Bauer, a leading economist in the liberal reform tendency, advocated workers' self-management in the mid-1980s. He and his supporters did not challenge the existing structure of public ownership until the end of 1988.[11] The formation of the youth organization that eventually called itself Alliance of Young Democrats (Fidesz) was initiated by Bertalan Diczházi, an engineering student, who wanted to include democratic socialism in the manifesto of the group, which kept on attracting social democratic and ecologist youth until 1990.

The discourse about the Third Way had an impact on the names of opposition organizations too. One of the reasons they did not include the word "party" in their names was that it was for a while uncertain how far the MSZMP would tolerate the emergence of rivals. The other reason, however, was indeed that they were also critical toward the Western bourgeois political institutions and saw how alienated the political parties and governments of the West could be from the ordinary people. They wanted something more democratic than West European pluralism, let alone the American version, which explains the application of names like alliance, forum or movement. When, for example, the liberal Democratic Opposition was turning itself into a tighter organization, they became the Network of Free Initiatives. When the majority of the Network later decided to turn the organization into a party named Alliance of Free Democrats (SZDSZ) to contest elections, some well-known members like Erzsébet Szalai and Ferenc Miszlivetz left the organization. Similarly to the Free Democrats, the Alliance of Young Democrats and the Hungarian Democratic Forum also declared themselves parties whose aim was to contest general elections in a later phase, when the so-called "historical" parties of Hungary had already been revived.

The revived historical parties constituted the second type of political party for the new Hungarian democracy. They main historical parties were the Independent Smallholder's Party (FKGP) and the Social Democratic Party of Hungary (MSZDP)—two major players in the postwar coalition period. The newly formed Hungarian People's Party declared itself a successor of the precommunist National Peasant Party (NPP), and the Christian Democratic People's Party (KDNP) traced its origins to the Democratic People's Party (DNP) of the same period. Despite their diverse political characters, a common feature of these parties was the advanced age of their members, who had learned and experienced the basics of multiparty politics in their youth in the 1940s. In 1989, none of these parties was able to display too much power to determine the course of events, though their presence was important in legitimizing the emerging system from a historical point of view.

With the broadening of the reform movement and the weakening of the power of the ruling MSZMP, the democratic socialist consensus of the opposition started to disintegrate. Diversification and radicalization became possible. As Gáspár Miklós Tamás, a well-known philosopher and at the time liberal tendency activist, declared: "the Bibóite era of the opposition came to an end." It was first and most of all the liberal tendency, then already organized in the Alliance of Free Democrats, that went beyond the framework and limits of democratic socialism in Hungary. They announced in their 1989 manifesto "the program of systemic change," and through their initiative for a national referendum undermined a tacit compromise between the reform wing of MSZMP and the more populist and nationalist circles of the opposition (primarily MDF).

When the discussion about Central Europe and the Third Way died away, "joining Europe" became a major slogan of systemic change in Hungary. The implication in this slogan was that integration into the West European and Atlantic organizations would be an obvious and relatively easy step once Hungary had got rid of the Soviet influence. It was also implied by many that entry into the European Union and NATO would automatically insert the ex-socialist countries into the core of the world system, thus raising the development level of the country to West European standards. Any contributions that sent out warnings about the obstacles facing such an optimistic scenario were silenced, stigmatized and marginalized (despite the fact that some internationally recognized scholars had explained in detail what it meant to be part of the periphery of world capitalism).

Early on in this process, Professor Tamás Szentes (1972) explained to his Hungarian readership a few main features of the nature of a peripheral status. It means, first of all, that from an economic point of view the peripheral country becomes dependent on alien capitalist powers of the world system. A dual structure of the economy takes shape due to the role the country is given in the international division of labor. The dual economy gives rise to a dual society. Finally, the country suffers permanent losses of income via various forms of international exploitation. The symptoms emphasized by Szentes were used to understand the characteristics of distant developing countries on other continents; however, it was unbelievable for many people in 1989 that these characteristics could easily be observed in Hungary's own national framework. To be more accurate, they had to be observed *again*, since Hungary had been on the periphery of the capitalist system before the socialist period.

In the euphoria of 1989, however, most of those who became active in bringing about political change in the country did not want to hear these warnings. They only wanted to hear about the great future that would follow the destruction of state socialism. This sentiment manifested itself in the great and small decisions of 1989.[12]

NOTES

1. The founding members of the CMEA were the Soviet Union, Poland, Czechoslovakia, Hungary, Romania, Bulgaria and Albania.

2. Soccer has been the most popular and politically most important sport in Hungary. Puskás has been the most outstanding of all Hungarian players, and the most successful scorer in the world history of soccer. Together with other national players, he left the country in 1956 and was treated by the authorities as a deserter because he had played for the club of the army. His return in 1981 was a sign of intended reconciliation between the Kádárist leadership and the Hungarian emigrants. He was temporarily appointed coach of the national team in 1992—an even stronger signal in the same direction from József Antall's right-wing government. (For more details see Taylor and Jamrich, 1997.)

3. The word "leadership" refers to the top decision-making circles of the so-called communist system. It is definitely not concrete enough, but using Politburo or government would be equally misleading in the case of a system that operated largely through informal connections.

4. In the mid-1970s, 40 Hungarian forints (HUF) equaled 1 U.S. dollar. In 1995, the exchange rate was 120, and at the end of 1998 it was 220.

5. Between November 1956 and October 1989, "Hungarian Socialist Workers' Party" was the official name of the ruling Communist Party in Hungary.

6. A highly controversial issue in the story of Hungarian debt management is that of the wrong arbitrage strategy. By the mid-1980s, the chief bankers had restructured most of the foreign debts into Japanese yen and German marks, while most of the exports remained denominated in U.S. dollars. Hence, the depreciation of the dollar by some 40% following the Plaza Agreement of 1985 caused Hungary to lose some U.S.$4 billion.

7. SIMICs are those countries in which GNP per capita was more than U.S.$480 and less than U.S.$6,000 in 1987, and in which three of the four key debt ratios are above critical levels. These ratios and their critical levels are debt to GNP (50%), debt to exports of goods and all services (275%), accrued debt service to exports (30%), and accrued interest to exports (20%). In 1990, the countries in this group were: Argentina, Bolivia, Brazil, Chile, Congo, Costa Rica, Cote d'Ivoire, Ecuador, Honduras, Hungary, Mexico, Morocco, Nicaragua, Peru, Philippines, Poland, Senegal, Uruguay and Venezuela.

8. Contrary to popular Western belief based on Orwellian images, most Hungarians were already free to travel to the West before 1989. What was officially restrained was, and in fact still is, the access to hard currency. Hungarian citizens were allowed to buy a certain amount of hard currency every third year. Many people bought regularly but did not use these amounts, and also many bought hard currency illegally from tourists or other visitors. The authorities were ambivalent about this; sometimes they acted against cases of illegal currency trade, but mostly they tolerated it because they wanted the people to develop an interest in tourism, which brought hard currency to a country heavily in debt. By the late 1980s, entire shopping networks had been built up in and around Vienna especially for Hungarians, who went there for goods available in a much greater assortment and sometimes even cheaper than at home. The panic of April 1989 was caused by leaked information about the plans of the government to increase tariffs on personal imports in order to reduce the amount of hard currency leaving the country. The bank holiday on 4 April gave an opportunity for consumer-minded families to make a quick one-day trip to Vienna and bring home trendy electronics (as well as tons of cans, plastic bags and other rubbish on the roadside) in exchange for an enormous sum of cash.

9. Grósz stepped down as PM in November 1988, saying that he wanted to concentrate his efforts on leading the party. He did not consider either the premiership or the personality of Németh a possible rival. Németh was about 40 years old, Harvard-educated, and a representative of the technocrats in the political leadership. As a regular tennis partner of U.S. ambassador Mark Palmer, he soon joined the reform platform initiated by Imre Pozsgay and Rezső Nyers and turned against his mentor (Grósz) during the spring of 1989.

10. Professor Hanák later became head of the department of history at the Central European University, the newly established private institution financed by George Soros.

11. The turning point in the assessment of public ownership appeared in an article by Márton Tardos in *Közgazdasági Szemle* in December 1988.

12. One such "small decision" concerned two social scientists cited in this chapter. At the University of Economic Sciences, the race between Géza Jeszenszky and Tamás Szentes for deanship of the social science faculty was won by the former by a significant margin.

3

Transition Politics: Running the New Democracy

In 1989, the reformers of the Communist party and the politicians of the new parties created a political system that would approach West European standards. The new elites of Hungary were optimistic, though many observers—and particularly foreign observers—were still doubtful about the stability of the new regimes. Indeed, the new democratic systems of Eastern Europe have since gone through a number of tests with varying success. As a result of such challenges, it is not just the preservation of the new democracy that has been on the agenda, but also its gradual adjustment.

In the 1990s, one of the most interesting features of Hungarian political developments has been the frequent swing in the political opinion of the population. This swinging opinion has reflected a political and economic agenda that has turned out to be very different from early expectations. The speedy disappointment with liberal politics and free-market economics boosted nationalism and conservatism, and the disintegration of the latter gave rise to an East European version of social democratic politics.

It was, however, not only domestic factors that made a difference in Hungary but particularly the international environment and the influence of foreign governments and multilateral agencies. Some elements of the political agenda, like macroeconomic stabilization and structural adjustment, were imported from the experience of developing countries. Some others, like cultural restoration or the fight against large-scale corruption, are related to the historical legacies of the region.

Thus, in the 1990s Hungary built up and preserved a democratic system comparable to those of Western Europe, but the actual politics within this polity has had a completely different agenda from countries at the core of world capitalism. This difference can be explained by the fact that in the last decade of the twentieth century Hungary appeared to be an emerging capitalist society with a still underdeveloped economy; all this falls very far short of the expectations of the 1980s and the promises of 1989.

LIBERALISM:
CREATING PLURALISM AND A MARKET ECONOMY

In the first half of 1989 there was an apparent political crisis in Hungary, and in the second half of that year a chain reaction brought down the communist regimes of Eastern Europe from the Baltics to the Black Sea. New political movements and leaders emerged. In Hungary, as in other countries of the region, these new actors of politics represented a liberal philosophy, regardless of their actual party membership. In most decisions made in 1989, there was a consensus on the establishment of political pluralism and a free-market economy. Wherever a debate emerged, liberal arguments usually won in politics and economics alike. In Hungary, the actual membership of the liberal political organizations was small, but their influence in 1989 was overwhelming. This influence and consensus lasted until fundamental decisions were made about the shape of the political system and the break with the state socialist economic arrangements. Once the country came to deal with practical questions of governance, the liberal hour was over.

The End of History in Hungary

In 1989, the political discourse in Hungary, as on the international scene, was dominated by a famous article written by Francis Fukuyama. The American political analyst's interpretation of the East European changes, and particularly of the reforms initiated by Soviet leader Mikhail Gorbachev, suggested that it was not only the 40-year Cold War that was coming to an end, but history itself. In a neo-Hegelian style, he argued that history came to an end whenever nations committed themselves to liberalism and free markets. In the United States and France it happened at the end of the eighteenth century, in other countries later. The last phase of this process was the termination of the communist experiment in Eastern Europe and particularly in the Soviet Union.

When Fukuyama wrote and published his article, communist-led states in Eastern Europe were still standing and there was no sign of the fall of the Soviet Union, though some analysts might have expected such an outcome of the crises and reforms of the 1980s. What made Fukuyama draw a conclusion that apparently surprised most observers was the degree to which Mikhail Gorbachev diverted from mainstream communist ideology and the previously prevailing Marxism–Leninism. He absorbed the idea of pluralism as well as the inevitability of a market economy even under a socialist system. For analysts, this ideological conversion simply meant the surrender of the socialist system itself, with the exception of its name.

In Hungary, the dominant forces of the MSZMP absorbed the ideas of pluralism and the market economy gradually and reluctantly. Reformist tendencies within the party had always demanded a greater role for the institutions of pluralism and the market, but their influence on mainstream party politics had not been constant. The year 1989, however, began with a fundamental breakthrough in the official ideology and political strategy of MSZMP. The party declared its commitment to the liberal institutions of politics and claimed a leading role in the changes that were to lead to their establishment.

The sudden breakthrough was provoked by Imre Pozsgay, the most popular reformist in the leadership of the party. In a radio interview at the end of January 1989, he announced that, according to a group of historians—headed by Berend—commissioned by the Central Committee to investigate the past four decades, the events of October 1956 could not be characterized as a counterrevolution—rather, "popular uprising" would be the appropriate phrase. The relevance of such a renaming might look minor, but it was of enormous importance for the cohesion of the MSZMP, since the whole legitimacy of Kádár and his party was based upon the condemnation of the 1956 events as a "counterrevolution."

In January 1989, Kádár was no longer effective as leader of the MSZMP. He had no power to prevent the changes that questioned his 33-year political performance. An extraordinary meeting of the Central Committee was called. Pozsgay's interview was on the agenda, and most of the members thought that what had already been said could not and should not be withdrawn. Furthermore, the Central Committee understood that a more positive evaluation of 1956 would shift power into the hands of those who, just like the late Imre Nagy, would be open to cooperation with noncommunist political parties and to a mitigation of Soviet influence in Hungary. At the end of the debate, the Central Committee declared that the party would initiate the establishment of a multiparty system in Hungary.

Previously, ever since the May 1988 national party conference, the MSZMP had represented the idea of "socialist pluralism" and "socialist market economy." The adjective "socialist" in these phrases was meant to represent a few key commitments that were not to be given up under any circumstances. It meant that the dominance of public ownership in the economy must be preserved, the dominance of the MSZMP over the state should not be challenged, and the loyalty of Hungary to the Soviet Union could not be questioned. Indeed, an informal definition of "the enemy" by the Politburo of the MSZMP said in spring 1988 that the enemies are those who want large-scale privatization, view the multiparty system as a fetish and question the relationship of Hungary with the Soviet Union. In that sense, the mainstream party line did not change as a result of the May 1988 party conference, though alternative approaches were represented inside the party with greater voice and publicity than ever before.

Though the adjective "socialist" was predominantly interpreted as a restriction in the late 1980s, socialist pluralism did have a certain content, which was basically the promotion of a partnership between the ruling party and nongovernmental interest organizations. The basis of such social partners could be profession, regional or national origin, gender or age, religious orientation or even hobby. Most of these organizations had already been in existence under the guidance of the MSZMP. The party preferred to run public affairs in cooperation with networks of such organizations instead of engaging in open debates on public policy with rival political parties. Nevertheless, following the 1988 May party conference, certain circles and bodies of the MSZMP became more open to extra-MSZMP groupings, demanding the abolition of restrictions that could be summarized by the word "socialist."

Socialism indeed lost its remaining appeal because it was associated with restrictions instead of some kind of positive development. Even if a positive surplus did exist in many areas, the focus on political restrictions destroyed their credibility. Prime minister Miklós Németh soon declared that a "market economy without adjectives" would be the objective of his government, which basically meant that he was going to neglect the previous political constraints over economic policy. Just a year earlier, Németh had been seen as a nonstarter in national politics. By summer 1989 he was an all-powerful prime minister on the reform platform, and he also became more and more influential in party politics. He absorbed and popularized the liberal ideas of politics and economics and adjusted the policies and the personnel of his government to the demands of the opposition and some powerful foreign actors, like his regular tennis partner Mark Palmer, the ambassador of the United States.

The change in the attitude of the MSZMP leadership opened up the way toward peaceful political change in the country. They started to negotiate with the Opposition Round Table (EKA), which was a provisional coalition of a dozen new or revived political organizations, with the assistance of the Independent Lawyers' Forum. By the summer, a National Round Table (NKA) was formed to negotiate the details of the democratic transition. Interestingly enough, NKA had three sides. Apart from the MSZMP and EKA, it included a group of social organizations, most of which had been supporters of the "socialist pluralism" favored by the MSZMP.

The peacefulness of the changes did not mean that mass demonstrations were completely absent from the scene. March 15, the anniversary of the 1848 revolution, which had always seen spontaneous demonstrations, became the day of an unprecedented march. In 1848 the revolutionary youth had taken possession of the printing press on behalf of the people, and the radicals of 1989 claimed rights over the national television on behalf of the people too. Mass demonstrations took place to express solidarity with the Hungarian minority in Romania and to oppose the construction of the Gabcikovo–Nagymaros Dam on the Danube. However, the greatest events of all were two funerals in the summer of 1989— those of Imre Nagy and János Kádár.

Imre Nagy was buried on the 16th of June—the 31st anniversary of his execution. For more than three decades, his body and those of three of his colleagues had laid in unmarked graves in a peripheral Budapest cemetery. In early 1989, the bodies were exhumed and identified by state-of-the-art biochemical methods. The funeral was staged at Heroes' Square and became a mass political demonstration that attracted thousands of emigrants in addition to the domestic supporters of opposition organizations. Despite the fact that all four politicians celebrated that day were communists, the funeral was turned into an anticommunist rally, partly by adding a fifth coffin in memory of the unknown heroes of 1956.

Soon after the Nagy funeral, János Kádár passed away. During the last six months of his life, his mental condition had deteriorated rapidly. His last speech before the Central Committee in February 1989 provided a distressed text for writers and psychoanalysts. Despite the fact that the summer of 1989 saw Kádár's political achievements denied and evaporating, his body was visited by tens of thousands of people from all around the country, even if they had to queue for hours in burning sunshine. His funeral was also attended by a huge crowd.

Hungarians experienced a very short period when they considered street demonstrations both possible and necessary. By the fall of 1989, and particularly by October, when the conversion and transformation of the MSZMP took place, the game was over and nobody really felt the need to flood the streets to support political demands. The conversion of the ruling party was most apparent in ideology, where liberal concepts like "civil society" could bridge the gaps between various trends of the new Hungarian pluralism. Suddenly, everyone was talking about civil society, though without specifying whether the concept came from Locke, Hobbes, Gramsci or Arendt. Sometimes it was explained how the "totalitarian" states of Eastern Europe completely destroyed civil society. Others argued that it was the strong civil society that managed to destroy the rule of the communists. The terms and phraseology of Western political thought were suddenly taken over, though without producing any lasting value in political or social theory. The fact that the East European "revolutions" did not create any new ideas was immediately noticed by Western philosophers like Jürgen Habermas and François Furet. The newly reborn "civil society" was autonomous only in importing institutions and policies from the capitalist world.

Institutions of Liberal Democracy

The National Round Table negotiations determined the new constitutional framework of postcommunist Hungary. The discourse at the table, however, was somewhat different from the discourse before the eyes of the public. Publicly, there was not much discussion about varieties of democracy. Whenever a new arrangement needed legitimacy, it was declared that "in a democracy, this is so and so." Behind the curtains, however, varieties of democracy clashed and eventually resulted in certain compromises.

For some, it was an open question whether Hungary should become a kingdom or a republic. It was not only tradition, however, that made some people think about the need for royalty, but also the experience of some democratic traditions of previous decades. The democratic transformation of post-Franco Spain, for example, suggested that it might be useful to have a personality at the top of the state hierarchy who would not necessarily be the most powerful politician but whose authority could not be challenged. It was believed that this could provide guarantees for a democratic constitution.

Since 1949, when the first written constitution of Hungary was adopted, the country had been called a people's republic. This name was no communist invention. The phrase had been in use in 1918, when a broad progressive coalition under the leadership of Count Mihály Károlyi declared the end of the Habsburg monarchy in Hungary. However, because of its association with the forty years of state socialism, the phrase "people's republic" had to go.

Before the people's republic, Hungary had been a republic for three years. Before that, Hungary had been a kingdom for nearly a thousand years. Had tradition been the only guide for framing the new constitution, Hungary could easily have become a kingdom once again. There was a strong candidate for the throne, who had dropped his claim to it previously but could not have resisted popular demand in this case. Dr. Otto von Habsburg, the son of the last king of Hungary, was alive and well when the disintegration of state socialism became apparent and actively campaigned in the country for Hungary's democratic transition and "return to Europe."

Liberalism, however, had a much stronger hold on the imagination of Hungarians in 1989 than did tradition. Apart from implicit comments, there was no open suggestion made to restore the Hungarian kingdom, and the crown jewelry rested safely in the National Museum, where it had been returned in 1978 by U.S. Secretary of State Cyrus Vance. At the National Round Table, both populism and republicanism were much stronger ideologies than monarchism, and the EKA concluded that the first president of the new republic should be elected directly by the people before the end of the year.

For the election of the parliament, EKA created a most complicated electoral system that barely resembles any other European system. This special Hungarian mechanism combines proportional representation with the plurality principle. Some 40% of the members of parliament are elected in individual constituencies, and slightly more gain their mandates through party lists organized on a county basis. The rest of the seats are distributed from the national party lists according to the residual votes transferred from the constituencies and the county lists. To give another twist to the mechanism, the general election was divided into two rounds: The first round requires 50% participation for validity and the second round allows 75% to abstain. Winning the first round in the individual constituencies requires more than 50% of the actual votes cast, while the second round can be won with a relative majority by one of the best three candidates from the first round.

Mixing the two electoral principles was a logical conclusion of the debate in which one side—namely the ruling MSZMP—was interested in the maintenance of the individual constituencies, while the newly formed small parties were interested in the introduction of proportional representation. Leaving half of the mandates up to PR did favor the small opposition parties, even if an agreement emerged that parties below a 4% threshold should be excluded from the parliament, and their votes should be distributed among the larger ones. The large parties could take advantage of the fact that, as a result of reducing the number of individual constituencies by half, the size of these districts increased from about 20,000–25,000 to about 40,000–50,000 citizens.

Comparing the new Hungarian polity to existing European political systems, it is Germany where the most relevant resemblance can be found. Following a debate about the desirable strength of the head of state, EKA concluded that, similarly to the German president, his Hungarian colleague should possess fairly limited authority, this being concentrated mainly in the approval of new laws and the representation of the country abroad. Such a restricted political role would allow the Hungarian prime minister to act as the German chancellor, whose replacement is only possible through a constructive vote of no confidence. The German example was followed, and even overstated, by the establishment of a most powerful Constitutional Court as well.

Surprisingly for many, the new system was immediately more restrictive in certain aspects than the communist political system had been. Under state socialism, a surviving Leninist principle allowed the recall of elected officials, which applied among others to members of parliament. Of course, during the longest periods of state socialism this right was hardly ever used. When the MSZMP was losing its legitimacy and public acceptance, the opposition started to take advantage of Lenin's gift, which was the first item to be eliminated from the electoral arrangement.

A further restriction on the direct authority of the people was introduced after November 1989, when a referendum changed the course determined by the National Round Table. The referendum was promoted by the Free Democrats and three other parties in order to prevent a popular election of the president of the new republic, because the only politician with a real chance of winning such an election would have been Imre Pozsgay of the MSZP.[1] The leaders of the MDF tacitly accepted the early and direct election, which symbolized a Polish-type compromise with the reformist wing of the communist bureaucracy. When, however, all other Communist parties of East-Central Europe were collapsing, the opposition did not need to insist on this compromise. With just a slight majority, the initiative of the SZDSZ won the referendum, and the election of the president was postponed beyond the parliamentary elections, when the new parliament was able to draw this right into its own authority.

By the summer of 1990, a liberal democratic political system had been established in Hungary. However, it was not yet a capitalist society, since the enormous mass of state property still existed. UCLA professor Iván Szelényi even used the phrase "democratic socialism" to describe the sociopolitical system of Hungary after the first postcommunist multiparty elections.

The task of accomplishing the construction of capitalism in Hungary was executed by two alleged enemies of the new liberal democracy—conservative nationalism and postcommunist socialism. They both had developed their own respective critiques of the state socialist regime as well as of the neoliberal project. However, even if they occasionally wanted to do so, they were unable to break with the key ingredient of the transition—neoliberal economics.

The Extremes of Neoliberal Economics

Until 1989, discourse in Hungarian economics concentrated on the perfection of socialist economic reform—that is, a search for a mixed economy or a Third Way. The cult figure of the reform economists was Tibor Liska, an extravagant personality with an anarchist attitude toward politics and economics alike. What István Bibó represented in politics and sociology, Liska represented in economics. He was against state socialist central planning, but his proposed model was based upon self-management and a combination of free enterprise with public ownership. In the early 1960s, he had been silenced for his pamphlet on price reform, but the "Liska debates" became popular events for discussing economic reform ideas in the subsequent decades. A learned young financial economist, Lajos Bokros, likened Liska's thoughts to those of Hayek. Most of the Hungarian reform economists had made the journey from one to the other by the end of the 1980s. In February 1989, when the old and apparently sick Liska was chairing one of the last Liska debates, he understood that events were going in a completely different direction from that which he and his movement had worked for for four decades, but his outcry against the rule of banks was blown away by the winds of neoliberalism.

The strong influence of Hayekian thought has been observed and analyzed by sociologists of various schools, from Ralf Dahrendorf (1990) to Hilary Wainwright (1993). Friedrich Hayek's and Milton Friedman's classic works were published in Hungarian in 1991 and 1992. The neo-Keynesian Samuelson–Nordhaus textbook, the publication of which had started a few years before, was nearly outdated by the time the third volume came out. The neoliberal tendency became dominant in Eastern Europe not because it had won the intellectual debate, but rather because it represented a moral crusade of market fundamentalism in a battle against all different forms of socialism. Most followers of the neoliberal trend became admirers of Hayek and Friedman before actually reading their works.

Nevertheless, dozens of Hungarian academics already had a good knowledge of right-wing economics as early as the beginning of the 1980s. It might be a puzzle for some students of the East European transition as to how the intelligentsia of the state socialist societies could learn about the neoliberal thought of the contemporary West "in total isolation." Of course, the isolation of Hungary as a socialist country was never total, and, particularly after the beginning of the New Economic Mechanism, the elite of the economists had access to international sources. At the University of Economics, the history of non-Marxist economics had been taught since the late 1950s, keeping the students up-to-date on the developments in neoclassical, Keynesian and monetarist thought. From the early 1970s on, dozens of young scholars studied in the United States with the help of Ford, IREX and other scholarships.

From the mid-1980s on, the Soros Foundation played a crucial role in educating the neoliberal intelligentsia, providing scholarships to study in Western universities or to work at home and provide intellectual ammunition for the radical reforms and the envisioned systemic change. The beneficiaries of Soros scholarships represented all different currents in economic and political thought, however, with a strong bias for neoliberalism—an economic theory that was, as it became apparent in the mid-1990s, in contradiction with Soros's own views on economic and political issues.

After the policy shifts of 1987, Károly Grósz's and Miklós Németh's governments were already advised by economists who were relatively young experts or even new graduates during the implementation of NEM in the late 1960s, and who had become true believers in the free market by the end of the 1980s. Németh ended bookkeeping tricks that hid the enormous deficits of the state budget and promised full compliance with the rules and policies of the IMF. At the end of 1989, he submitted a virtually balanced budget for 1990.

The Németh government was forced to adopt the policies of the opposition in all the different policy areas. In economics, it shifted toward an extreme neoliberal position, as represented by the Free Democrats. The continuity between MSZMP, MSZP and SZDSZ economic policies was made apparent in the related expert committee of the National Round Table. Once the general NKA agreement had been signed in September 1989, the work continued in expert committees on various policy areas. The economic policy committee discussed the most important questions of the day: foreign debts, privatization, liberalization. One side of the debate was represented by the neoliberal economists of the MSZP and the SZDSZ, the other by the rest of the parties and NGOs. The shape of the debates helped to make the political economy of the transition understandable, though it did not have a direct impact on anything because, as the elections were approaching, the expert committees left behind by the NKA slid into insignificance.

At a time of liberal euphoria, a first-class international conference of progressive economists went down largely unnoticed and unreported.[2] Leading postKeynesian and Marxist economists from Western Europe and North America, like John Kenneth Galbraith, Ajit Singh, Edward Nell and Geoff Harcourt, gathered in Budapest in September 1989 to celebrate the life and works of the late Lord (Nicholas) Kaldor, the Hungarian-born economic advisor of Labour Prime Minister Harold Wilson. Their powerful arguments fell on deaf ears when most of the Hungarian public did not want to hear any warnings about the dangers of free-market policies.

Without considering a social-democratic, or any other compromise between socialism and capitalism, the dominant stream of Hungarian economic thought imported a full-blooded Thatcherite ideology of economic policy. Hungarians, however, were not unique in that choice. The whole of Eastern Europe seemed to choose a brand of capitalism that was strongly biased toward small firms and weak states (Amsden et al. 1994: 5). The idea of a "big bang" also appealed to many, once the state socialist system was declared "not viable." This "Walrasian endeavor" resulted in a mix of contractionary macroeconomic policies and do-nothing microeconomic policies (Amsden et al. 1994: 6–7). These choices were dictated by political or even cultural considerations instead of studying the real economic and social consequences of neoliberalism in the advanced and peripheral capitalist countries. Leading transition economists either ignored the pain shock therapy would inflict upon society or claimed that there was no alternative to this way, even if the costs were barely tolerable for some.

János Kornai—a leading Hungarian economist at Harvard University—is often seen as the father of these ideas, though originally he proposed a different script for economic transition. Kornai wrote his famous pamphlet (later published in English as *The Road to a Free Economy*, 1990) against the neoliberal shock therapy, a belief shared by the SZDSZ and the reform wing of the MSZMP. He advocated gradualism, heavy regulation of state industry, a slow development of a new middle class, and thus an organic transformation into capitalism. He was viciously attacked by SZDSZ politicians, and under this threat of political marginalization he had changed his views by the time his book was published in foreign languages.

In the early 1990s, Kornai propagated the property rights theory of business organization and economic development—one of the major neoliberal ideologies—until he was frightened by the consequent rise of the far right in former socialist countries. Thus by 1993 he had become a Keynesian and promoted "progrowth" policies. Once Kornai saw that it was not the fascists but the ex-communists who had come to power, he returned to neoliberalism and announced the need for structural adjustment by slaughtering what he called "a premature welfare state." When, however, the government finally accepted his advice under the unrelenting pressure of the IMF, he appealed to the U.S. ambassador for generosity after a public lecture at Collegium Budapest. During the transition decade, Kornai embodied the Keynesian economist who not only understands how the models of economics work but who also knows which one to chose in a certain situation. His frequent change of opinion explains why he has been a typical gradualist for some and a big-bang theorist for others.

On the other hand, there have been other economists who have never changed their minds, even after acknowledging the failure of their work. In a radio interview in 1996 László Antal, a leading "reform economist" of the 1980s—and an advisor of MSZP finance ministers in the 1990s—admitted that illusions had been entertained about the outcomes of their reform project. "We were wrongly dreaming," Antal said, a notion that he would have rejected firmly five or ten years earlier. The reason the reformers were fatally wrong is now known—and was known to many at that time. They ignored the international context of the reforms, and the tendency of the world markets to polarize national economies into central and peripheral positions.

Despite the fact that Eastern Europe was hit by the same global debt crisis that made the 1980s the "lost decade" for Latin America, even among economists there was very little awareness of the origins and the nature of international indebtedness. Events related to the debt crisis and the IMF-type stabilization and structural adjustment policies were not part of the public debate. In 1989, the demonstrations at Beijing's Tiananmen Square were frequently shown on television, while the food riots in Venezuela remained largely unreported.

The ignorance about the long-term consequences of the debt crisis was also displayed in the debate on the renegotiation or even repudiation of foreign debts. It was a dispute comparable to the debate on war debts after the war of independence in the United States two hundred years earlier. Equipped with scores of true free-market economists with the highest possible level of loyalty to the IMF and the World Bank, the SZDSZ represented a Hamiltonian view of Cold War debts, while it was the MDF that entertained Jeffersonian ideas about many issues, including the cancelation of debts and the need for a fresh start with a clean sheet. Since leading SZDSZ economists were experts who had been working for the MSZMP on economic reforms since the early 1980s—a few of them as MSZMP members, of course—they lacked the legitimate basis to reject the love child of their decade-long work on market reforms: the towering foreign debts of the country.

Interestingly enough, the Hungarian Democrats found an unlikely ally in this debate—namely, George Soros. Soros, who has been an active participant of the policy debate and a sponsor of economic research and education, was the one who tried to convince the MDF leader, József Antall, about the need for, and the advantage of a substantial debt relief. His counterpart, György Surányi, the newly appointed head of the National Bank of Hungary, with all the intellectual power of the Free Democrats behind him, represented the view of no retreat and the servicing of debts, whatever the circumstances.

The mainstream of Hungarian economists rejected the idea of debt reduction even when half of the Polish foreign debt was canceled in 1991. The attitude of the new liberals toward foreign creditors and investors became a major reason for their decline and for the rise of a conservative–nationalist right—it was the latter who were to be chosen first by the people.

CONSERVATISM:
THE RISE AND FALL OF RIGHT-WING NATIONALISM

In the first half of 1990, political sentiment in Hungary shifted toward conservatism and nationalism. This was the first response to, and replacement of the liberal breakthrough that had destroyed state socialist rule in Hungary. The right-wing coalition that came into office after the general elections of 1990 faced hard choices amidst a transitional economic crisis and the disintegration of the East European cooperation networks of the country. Although the new conservatism had a chance to consolidate itself in power, this opportunity was destroyed by the endeavor to link the ruling parties to the prewar tradition of Hungarian conservatism instead of its modern versions, which can be found in Western Europe. In four years it became apparent that the first postcommunist right-wing elite of Hungary had tried to base itself on a nonexisting social foundation and had failed to rebuild this foundation within the time span provided by the parliamentary cycle. Their sudden rise terminated in an equally sudden fall.

Forward into the Past

In April 1990, the Hungarian Democratic Forum (MDF) won the general elections (see Appendix 2, Table 10). The leader of the party, József Antall, was invited by acting President of the Republic Mátyás Szűrös to form a government. The government was formed in May 1990 by three parties sharing 60% of the parliamentary mandates. The three parties were the MDF, the Independent Smallholders' Party (FKGP), and the Christian Democratic Peoples' Party (KDNP). On certain constitutional issues, the MDF still needed the consent of the opposition SZDSZ in order to acquire a two-thirds majority in parliament. The pact that worked out this agreement was accomplished soon after the elections. In exchange for their cooperation, the SZDSZ was given the right to nominate the president of the republic. Thus the parliament elected Árpád Göncz, a liberal writer and translator, to be head of state of postcommunist Hungary.

The government was first led by József Antall, an expert on medical history, who died in December 1993. He was succeeded by Péter Boross, who was invited into the cabinet in 1990 from retirement after a successful career in the catering industry. Double "l" and double "s" at the end of these surnames indicate the legacy of nobility, which became a prime factor in the politics of the government. From a populist movement of writers and other intellectuals, Antall turned the MDF into a party of the historic Christian–Nationalist middle class, with roots in the nineteenth-century liberal nobility.

Without changing the official rules of governance, Antall adjusted the mechanism of decision-making so that persons of similar social background had an increased influence, while elected politicians had to follow the course set by the first group. He surrounded himself with formal and informal advisors like Gyula Kodolányi and Pál Tar, and he used the cabinet meetings to lecture his ministers like a schoolmaster.

Antall's rhetoric suggested that there was a way "back to normalcy" for Hungary, and that normalcy could be found in precommunist social and political institutions. In the international dimension "return to Europe" became the major slogan, which again suggested that Hungary had had some normal and natural place in a peaceful community of European nations that could be restored after the end of the Cold War.

The cultural conservatism of the new Hungary soon received symbolic framing. August 20, the day of St. Stephen—the first king of Hungary—became an official national holiday by beating March 15, the day of the 1848 revolution, in the parliamentary vote. After endless and resultless votes, and after the conversion of one Socialist MP, the old royal coat-of-arms was selected to be the new national emblem of Hungary, though the opposition movement of the 1980s had held up Kossuth's coat-of-arms—that is, the one without St. Stephen's crown on the top.

At the elections, many of the voters favored the MDF over the SZDSZ because of the relative tenderness of the first, but the victory made Antall's party rather arrogant. They immediately presented themselves as the natural ruling elite of the country and reduced the sphere of social and political dialogue. The new foreign minister Géza Jeszenszky claimed in a parliamentary speech that the coalition parties were representing "Hungarianness" with a greater credibility than the parties in opposition. Not surprisingly, the latter left the assembly room before Jeszenszky could finish his speech.

Antall and other MDF leaders did not appreciate in time that their party had received a relative majority of the popular vote and secured dominance of Hungarian politics in the second round of the general elections because they had not pursued such a harsh anticommunist campaign as had the Free Democrats. The first and most moving recognition of the gap between popular sentiment and initial government attitudes was the so-called "pyjama interview" by Antall, taken in a hospital after the gas riots of October 1990. This was the fist major domestic political crisis of the government, which also resulted in a reshuffle and a change in the course of economic policy.

When the government was formed, Antall appointed Professor Ferenc Rabár, an advocate of shock therapy, to be finance minister. Rabár could have worked well with central bank governor Surányi; however, he had an antagonistic relationship with György Matolcsy, head of Antall's economic policy unit—Matolcsy being more of a Keynesian. First, Matolcsy had to go as a result of the conflict, but Rabár also submitted his resignation because he saw that the situation was more complicated than he had thought. What convinced the prime minister to accept Rabár's resignation was the so-called "gas riots" at the end of October 1990. The events represented a three-day national crisis, which demonstrated the unity of various social classes against shock-type policy changes (in this case, a 60% rise in the gas price). The riots, which had begun as a spontaneous demonstration by taxi drivers, turned out to be the greatest popular demonstration in the country since 1956, blocking the road for Polish-type shock therapy in Hungary.

The retreat of the government was shown in two respects. First, they started to engage in a form of social dialogue by recognizing the legitimacy and importance of the tripartite interest reconciliation council. Second, as a replacement for Rabár, Antall found Mihály Kupa, who came from the same Financial Research Institute as Surányi but represented a somewhat different view.[3] He was able to come to a compromise with gradualism and thus developed a four-year program of transition, which was backed by two World Bank structural adjustment programs. Unlike Surányi, Kupa made his political commitment open when later he ran in a by-election and became a member of parliament for the MDF and thus "became a real politician," in Antall's words. Since then, he has preserved his economic nationalism and progrowth attitudes, and this has made him a leading economic spokesman of the moderate right-wing parties.

Kupa's emergence, however, did not abolish the government's internal divisions over economic policy. Presenting structural adjustment as his own policy, Kupa became an advocate of neoliberal reform, however gradually and cautiously that reform was tailored. Interventionism and nationalism was, on the other hand, represented by the Ministry of International Economic Relations (NGKM), led by the distinguished economics professor, Béla Kádár. When Kupa's program really started to have an effect, privatization minister Tamás Szabó formed an economic policy working group (GAM) to push government policies toward economic populism and nationalism.

In order to reconstruct precommunist socioeconomic relations, Antall pursued a specific compensation policy. His coalition partner, the FKGP, demanded full restitution of the owners in accordance with to the conditions of 1947. Antall, however, had to please another part of his constituency, which was the new entrepreneurial layer that would have been sidelined by a full restitution plan. The management of public enterprises would have been alienated too. Therefore, he attempted to find a middle way between total restitution—which would have restored the rights of precommunist owners of firms, land and real estate—and the selling-off of state assets. The latter appeared as a method with the least threat to the continuous operation of the economy and even promised some revenue for the budget. This compromise resulted in four consecutive Compensation Acts, which gave so-called compensation vouchers to expropriated owners in proportion to the value of their lost assets. These vouchers were used to buy assets as well as certain consumption goods, and were also traded on the stock exchange. Because of imperfect information about the precommunist relations, close to a million people were eventually involved in the compensation exercise, which the government expected to create some loyalty to the coalition.

Religion also played an important role in the restoration policy of the government. Though the visits of Pope John Paul II to Poland and Cuba attracted much greater attention, he also visited Hungary twice in the 1990s. The first time, he came in August 1991; on his second visit he came to be a highlight of the Millecentenarium celebrations in 1996. The invitation for the first visit was issued by the Németh government, but the Pope's arrival took place when József Antall was prime minister. Interestingly enough, on the second occasion it was the right-wing government that invited the Holy Father, and the Socialists were in office at the time of his appearance.

The Pope's 1991 visit was just one of the widely televised events that tried to spread and solidify conservative values among the population. Funerals, again, became demonstrations of great political importance. The hero of the religious right, Cardinal József Mindszenty, was brought home from a cemetery in Austria, to be buried in Esztergom. In September 1993, Admiral Miklós Horthy, who had vanquished the 1919 Soviet Republic of Hungary and was Regent between 1920 and 1944, was also reburied in his homeland. Given the controversial role Horthy had played in the interwar years and during the war, his state-sponsored funeral already triggered off great resentment, particularly because half of the government attended the event in Kenderes.

Antall himself was unable to attend Horthy's funeral because of his own deteriorating health, but his wife and family did pay tribute to the late Regent. The next televised funeral, this time a real one, was Antall's, who had fought cancer publicly ever since October 1990. The directors of his funeral took their pattern from those of fascist Prime Minister Gyula Gömbös (1932–36), who had established Hungary's alliance with Mussolini and Hitler, and of Count Pál Teleki, who was PM when various anti-Jewish laws were enacted. This symbolic event was a peak of a process by which the ruling parties pursued a slow revaluation of interwar Hungarian politics and promoted some authoritarian leaders of those times as outstanding heroes of democracy.

The Racist Card

However strongly Antall's government wanted to pursue a nationalist economic strategy to help domestic business and capital accumulation, they could not escape the deepest economic depression since the 1930s. Due to the U.S.$20 billion foreign debt inherited from the communist period, they had no choice but to obey IMF conditionality and World Bank structural adjustment, the policies of which were incorporated into the four-year transformation program advertised under the name of Antall's second finance minister, Mihály Kupa. Another effect that pushed the economy further into depression was the collapse of the East European trading system (CMEA) and of the Soviet Union. In the meantime, however, West European economies were hit by recession as well, which made recovery practically impossible.

The depth of this crisis, however, should not simply be blamed on transformation and external difficulties. Despite the presence of experts like Péter Ákos Bod and Béla Kádár in the cabinet, industrial policy remained a secondary issue behind transforming ownership and replacing personnel in well-paid jobs in ministries and state companies. Thus, in the light of external shocks and internal mismanagement and ignorance, it is not a surprise that aggregate figures show a dramatic decline for the Antall years (see Appendix 2, Table 1). Taking the figures of 1989 as 100%, GDP in 1993 was at 70–75%, industrial production at about 65%, and agriculture at 60–65%. Inflation stood at 30% (between 23% and 35% annually). The rate of unemployment rose from 1% to some 13–15% within the same period.

It was already understood in the half-time of the parliamentary cycle that the economic record of the government was dismal. Both inflation and unemployment were exceeding all expectations and forecasts; GDP was still in decline. The coalition was shaken by a split of the Smallholders, and the ruling parties were rapidly losing popular support. The prime minister's illness was widely publicized.

István Csurka, a vice-president of the MDF, offered an explanation and solution. In the summer of 1992, in a lengthy article published in his *Magyar Fórum*, he blamed the world-wide Jewish–Bolshevik conspiracy for the failure of the systemic change. He compared the IMF to the postwar Allied Control Commission. He accused President Árpád Göncz of being an agent of New York, Paris and Tel Aviv. He also called for the replacement of the ailing prime minister. The article was published on August 20, the national holiday, just when the World Association of Hungarians was holding its congress in Budapest.

The reaction of the prime minister was calm. When asked about the issue in Parliament, he claimed all that was part of Csurka's literary works and not the politics of the MDF, which sounded ironic since Csurka was not just a deputy leader of the party but editor-in-chief of the weekly paper associated with the MDF. Despite increasing domestic and international pressure, Antall rejected the idea of Csurka's expulsion, because he was afraid of "salami tactics"—the game Rákosi played in the postwar coalition period to slice up the then dominant Smallholder's Party. The situation became extremely inconvenient when József Debreczeni, an MP on the left of the MDF, claimed in an article that Csurka's views were not unrelated to Nazi philosophy. Democratic Congressman Tom Lantos also came to Hungary to convince Antall that Csurka's behavior could ruin the international acceptance of the MDF. Despite the disgrace, however, Antall was still afraid of losing the populists of his party and, with them, much of the popular support.

Indeed, Csurka was not alone in presenting conspiracy theories about alleged anti-Hungarian activities. Another MDF MP, Gyula Zacsek, published a similarly lengthy article in the same magazine about the Soros Foundation, claiming that the networks sponsored by George Soros were undermining Hungarian society and culture like termites. Not many politicians came out to support actively what Csurka and Zacsek were saying, but the members of the ruling parties feared disunity more than possible repercussions from the international community and the domestic opposition.

The importance of the racist outburst from the ruling parties was usually played down or covered up by government officials. Similarly, an official cover-up protected the skinheads who caused a political scandal on October 23 by whistling and booing President Göncz when he was about to start his speech outside Parliament. The television news program that reported the cause of the abandonment of the speech was suppressed.

Nearly complete control of television and radio was possible because presidents Elemér Hankiss and Csaba Gombár had been forced to resign, and the MDF-appointed vice-presidents Gábor Nahlik and László Csúcs were reigning over the national electronic media. Nahlik and Csúcs had been selected by Csurka, who was responsible for cultural and ideological affairs in the MDF. They reshaped the structure of television and radio broadcasts so that only a few programs remained where nonconservative opinions could be aired. Liberal-minded presenters were forced to leave if they refused to compromise with the new course. The enfolding media war appeared to be the crucial battle of Hungarian politics. Cultural pluralism—and, through that, political pluralism—were at stake.

Csurka's open supporters were not many but very loud, and the weak government felt the need to compromise with them. Beyond the populist tendency in the MDF, Csurka was popular with skinhead and other far-right groupings mushrooming in Budapest and also in some other cities, like Eger and Miskolc. One of these groups was led by Albert Szabó, who had lived in Australia and organized the World National Party of Popular Rule (a close translation of *Világnemzeti Népuralmista Párt*), which claimed the legacy of the Arrow-Cross Party of Ferenc Szálasi, the Hungarian Nazi leader of the 1930s and the war years, who became dictator after Horthy's resignation, was responsible for much of the Hungarian Holocaust, and was sentenced to death by a popular court after the war. With Csurka in parliament and Szabó on the streets, the rise of racism had an intimidating impact.

The main counteroffensive against the authoritarian and racist tendencies of the right-wing government came from an organization called Democratic Charter. This loose formation was established in September 1991 by leading liberal and Socialist intellectuals, with a demonstrative absence of Fidesz, who called the Charter a Trojan Horse of a social–liberal coalition. George Konrád, one of the founders of the Charter, characterized the organization as an umbrella that can be opened and used whenever the institutions of democracy are in danger. The largest demonstration of the Charter was organized in September 1992 in response to Csurka's racist manifesto.

Csurka's movement combined all three forms of traditional Hungarian racism—anti-Semitic prejudice, anti-Romanian and anti-Slav chauvinism, and anti-Gypsy hatred. However, none of the right-wing parties of Hungary was entirely free of these racist tendencies. The further to the right we looked, the greater level of these racist attitudes we found in political opinion and party policies. Though Csurka's party did not enter parliament in 1994, views close to his surfaced among the politicians in the more mainstream parties, especially the Smallholders, led by József Torgyán (Tismaneanu 1998: 84). Instead of throwing it into the rubbish dump of history, the establishment and consolidation of the new democracy revived racist politics, and its immediate threat was over only after the demise of the parliamentary right in 1994.

Meltdown

Despite Antall's efforts to keep his party and the coalition around it together, the Csurka affair signaled the beginning of a social, political and moral breakdown of the right-wing government. It was not the beginning of the breaks and splits, but it indicated that the hope to restore a wide social and political basis for the MDF and other right-wing parties was fading away.

Well before Csurka's recklessness caused a scandal, some democratic—or left—nationalists split from the MDF, to join forces with ex-communist ex-minister Imre Pozsgay, who had left the MSZP in November 1990. Together, they formed the National Democratic Alliance (NDSZ), which was to occupy a "middle ground" in politics. Then it was the FKGP that split over the issue of compensation or restitution. Later, several individual members of parliament left the MDF, including the leader of the Entrepreneurs' League, who later formed the small but rich Republican Party (KP). This latter was a clear sign of the disaffection of domestic entrepreneurs with the policies of the right-wing government.

After more than half a year of internal fighting, Antall resolved the Csurka question by expelling both the reckless racists and some liberal nationalists from his party. As a result, two MDF MPs joined the small opposition faction of Fidesz. When Csurka was forced to leave, a dozen members of parliament left with him and formed small far-right parties, such as the Party of Hungarian Justice and Life (MIÉP, led by István Csurka himself), the Party of Hungarian Interest, the Party of Hungarian Justice, and the Hungarian Market Party (Gyula Zacsek being one of the founders).

Having seen this spectacular fragmentation, it became urgent for the government to modify the Election Law in December 1993, by increasing the entry threshold from 4 to 5%. This change was also a message to the Kádárist MSZMP, which came close to 4% in 1990 and changed its name to Workers' Party in January 1993. The increase of the threshold was supported by all parties in parliament, since all of them expected themselves to get more than 5% and all of them considered stability and governability an important factor of democracy.

The permanent crisis of the ruling coalition encouraged four liberal parties to form an alliance to campaign jointly at the 1994 election and to form a government afterwards. This unofficial shadow coalition was formed by the SZDSZ, Fidesz and two extraparliamentary parties: the Agrarian Union, which turned themselves from defenders of collective farms into a modern bourgeois agrarian party, and the Entrepreneurs' Party, led by the liquor producer industrialist Péter Zwack, who had surrendered his U.S. citizenship to become Antall's first ambassador in Washington, D.C. (He was fired after six months.)

Although this liberal shadow coalition was highly publicized, events between its creation and the elections made it impossible for them to fulfil their mission together. First of all, it was less and less likely for the two small parties to jump over the 5% threshold. Although Zwack is a popular person due to his famous Unicum liqueur, and the Agrarian Union has won one by-election in coalition with the Republican Party, their voters had to stand behind the two major liberal parties in the second round of the constituency elections.

Secondly, the Free Democrats did not have an easy time in opposition, despite winning the municipal elections in the autumn of 1990 and one by-election in 1992. They consumed three presidents and four faction leaders in four years. They had to find a new economic identity when shock therapy became unpopular and compromised in the whole region. However progressive they could be on cultural policies, they were nevertheless criticizing the government from the platform of even faster privatization and liberalization, and their election manifesto included further privatization in public services as well. They also had to combat dirty tricks attacking the Jewish origins of some of their politicians, and the communist police career of the parents of some, including president Iván Pető and leading economist Tamás Bauer. "Hungarians must have Hungarian opposition" was an infamous slogan of the far right against leading SZDSZ politicians, including ex-Marxist philosopher János Kis. Eventually, they managed to find a perfect candidate for premiership, Gábor Kuncze MP, a former company manager with an old-fashioned moustache and impressive rhetorical skills, who even happened to be one of the alumni of the same Catholic high school as József Antall.

While the SZDSZ was struggling with all these problems and the government was becoming increasingly unpopular, the Young Democrats had an extremely hopeful year in 1992, when they were polling above 30%. They started as a liberal political youth movement in 1988, with strong links in environmentalist and other postmodernist circles. However, they slowly eliminated these grassroot connections, which could have disturbed the pursuit of power by the party leaders, and especially by president Viktor Orbán.[4] In their image, Fidesz placed a strong emphasis on expertise. Their economic policy was a supply-side plus monetarist voodoo, and, accordingly, they took on a pure yuppie character, or, as András Bródy, a distinguished ex-Marxist—now left–liberal—economist claimed, "took on the image of a leasing company." In the Hungarian context, this was equivalent to swindle and fraud. Indeed, one of the major issues causing severe damage to their popularity was a secret deal, when they acquired a huge sum of money by selling real estate received from the government for the purpose of establishing headquarters.

This case, as well as other gestures of Fidesz toward the right, slowly made it apparent that they were playing a double game, in readiness to join either a liberal or a nationalist coalition. This made their most popular politician, Gábor Fodor MP, leave Fidesz in November 1993 and run as No. 2. on the party list of the

SZDSZ. After all, the Fidesz dream was over, and the party received exactly the same number of votes in 1994 as in 1990. This outcome justifies previous analyses that doubted the realism of a liberal alternative, based on the fact that nowhere in postwar European history has the liberal pole alone made up a government, let alone in Central-Eastern Europe, amidst economic depression and nationalist cleavages. The liberals either have to join forces with conservatives against the left or undertake social reform. In Hungary, the developments of 1993 clarified the profiles and placed Fidesz into the first role and the SZDSZ into the second one.

While the chances of a liberal alternative seemed real, the government believed that its most important task is to undermine the credibility of the liberals, and particularly to cut off their strong media channels. Perhaps the most shameful maneuver of the government was the one against the electronic media. In 1990, with an agreement of the six parties in parliament, two famous social scientists were appointed to govern the national radio and the television. However, it soon turned out that the government had very little intellectual influence on the population and was prone to permanent communication disturbances. The daily and weekly papers they founded or gained control over remained at very low levels of circulation. They felt the need to seize the electronic media. After a one-year pitched battle, they forced the two presidents to resign, and the two vice-presidents, right-wing MDF–loyalist bureaucrats, started to close down sections and programs that had allowed alternative voices on the air. Finally— allegedly for financial reasons, but with an apparent political objective—they fired 129 journalists and other employees in March 1994, just when the election campaign began.

Silencing alternative voices was just one of the preelection policies of the ruling parties. They also launched a campaign to provide economic benefits to their potential constituencies, primarily small investors. They offered the shares of a few large state companies for cheap sale to regenerate enthusiasm and trust among the segments of society with ambitions to become part of the new capitalist class. They raised the salaries of state employees, and industrial wages also increased somewhat in real terms.

While public finances and foreign accounts were deeply in the red, the coalition timed quite a few pay increases and other achievements into the campaign period. They raised the annual hard currency package that private persons could buy from U.S.$300 to U.S.$800 from April 1. They launched the issue of the fourth round of compensation vouchers in March, and public sector employees were also receiving pay increases. Pensioners had good news as well, which was delivered by the post office together with MDF advertising in some districts. Of course, it is a pleasure for Hungarians, as for anyone else, to get more money rather than less, especially if that money is convertible. However, the government was doing this at the expense of runaway foreign indebtedness. Furthermore, all this was too little and too late to have a significant impact on the outcome of the elections.

Just when these heavy attacks might have improved the fortunes of the MDF, the leading party of the right lost its semicharismatic leader. Two weeks before Christmas, the death of Prime Minister József Antall ended a long struggle against cancer, as well as a period of uncertainty for the political life of the country. The MDF lost its leader, who had shaped it into a competitive and capable ruling party in 1990 but who had definitely become a vote loser, given the public awareness of his illness. The person who took over the premiership was Péter Boross, whose career was somewhat similar to Antall's, while displaying some differences in style of speech and leadership.

Boross also played some minor role in the 1956 uprising, for which he suffered some retaliation. But, as politics changed in the Kádár regime, he could receive substantial compensation for his losses, and he worked as a managing director of a large catering company in Budapest for nearly 20 years. He retired in 1989, but a year later his friend, Antall, invited him as a nonpartisan politician to be a minister without portfolio responsible for the secret services. And, in December 1990, at the first government reshuffle, he became minister of interior affairs (Secretary of the Interior). So, even though he was not a member of the victorious MDF or an elected member of parliament, he had now become the most powerful politician in the country.

However, the Boross government was widely understood as a transitional one, functioning only until the general elections. (Boross did not even move to the official residence of the Prime Minister.) The most apparent sign of the critical state of the government was that even the KDNP, the party that has been the most loyal to the coalition, also started to release critical comments about some controversies regarding privatization and economic policy just before the elections.

When the chances for the survival of the right-wing government looked minimal, it was not a liberal but a left-wing victory that became more and more realistic. A left victory at the general elections became believable when the left-wing trade unions won the elections for the control over the two social security boards in May 1993. Sándor Nagy, leader of MSZOSZ—the largest trade union federation—became head of the National Pension Fund as well, while his deputy became the head of the National Health Fund. Their alliance with the MSZP dated back to summer 1991, when two antiunion laws were passed by parliament, with protest displayed only by the Socialists. On the election list of the MSZP, Nagy ran as number two, after party president Gyula Horn, while former finance minister László Békesi came third.

The MSZP managed to settle internal disputes quietly, won two by-elections, and climbed to around 25% in the polls in 1993. This was partly due to the fact that the extraparliamentary Social-Democratic Party (MSZDP) committed numerous mistakes, to remain unserious and unpopular in the eyes of the voters. So while both liberal and conservative votes were split, on the left, Kádárist and Social-Democratic competition to the MSZP remained weak, and both tendencies were expected to support the Socialist candidates in the second round unconditionally.

While focusing on the elections and the media war, less attention was paid to the appalling economic results of 1993. Although the decline in GDP appeared to be less than before (some 2–3%) and the rate of inflation was kept at the previous level (some 24–25% per year), in the meantime the trade deficit increased to a dramatic U.S.$3 billion, and the budget for 1994 ran to an unprecedented 340 billion forint deficit. The National Bank of Hungary continued to be one of the most successful borrowers in Western financial markets, but the above figures implied that the national finances of Hungary came close to collapse.

Thus, there was not much room for maneuver waiting for the new government after the 1994 elections. Nevertheless, there was still an important stake of the elections, which was about the style and social linkages of the government. What could be ended by the rise of a social–liberal coalition was the ultimate arrogance of a nationalist and conservative elite, which took all their patterns from the prewar times, which were, with some understatement, not the heyday of Hungarian democracy. Without a complete change in government, there was no chance for building links between certain social groups and the circles of government, which under Antall and Boross neglected communication with society and had to rely even more upon their memories and readings of precommunist times.

However important such gains were, they appear to be minor and marginal if we compare them to the expectations entertained by the liberal press in relation to the elections. The irony of the situation was that without raising high expectations, one could not mobilize popular support even for smaller changes. Once the room for actual improvements seems to be small indeed, popular disappointment turns either into apathy or against those who had promised more than what was possible in order to achieve at least something. The Socialist Party drew some conclusions from these paradoxes, inasmuch as they were the ones in 1994 who promised virtually nothing in relation to incomes and living standards. At the elections, however, they gained an overall majority in parliament.

According to the doyen of political transitology, Guillermo O'Donnell, the acid test of a new democracy is to replace the government peacefully at the second general elections. In Hungary, the new democracy was thus tested and found adequate.

SOCIALISM: THE LIMITS OF BUREAUCRATIC MODERNIZATION

Following a trend that began in Lithuania in 1992 and continued in Poland in 1993, Hungary in 1994 was the third FSC where ex-communist politicians won parliamentary elections and formed a government. This increased popularity was fed by a significant amount of nostalgia toward the past state socialist regime, though the transformation of the postcommunist parties excluded a return to pre-1989 times in any serious sense of the word. The Hungarian Socialist Party was eager to present itself as a mainstream social-democratic party, and its leaders did not hesitate to implement harsh austerity measures when no other solution to the economic problems was in sight. The MSZP preserved its integrity despite major corruption charges too, and remained without rival on the political left. Due to the reconstruction of the political right, however, the MSZP did not manage to repeat the electoral success of 1994.

Economic and Political Credentials

In postcommunist Eastern Europe, liberal democracies could be created by liberals, but they could not be run by them. It was either the conservative right or the socialist left that could come to government. Shortly after the liberal euphoria of 1989, both tendencies were considered to be a threat to the new institutions of liberal democracy. On the one hand, it was feared that right-wing conservatism could go to extremes by admitting racism into government offices, threatening a scenario of Weimarization; on the other, the revival and in certain cases the return of postcommunist parties represented a threat of restoration.

For such reasons, the MSZP had to display certain credentials to prove that a return to state socialism was ruled out even if the party did form a government after winning the elections in 1994. Electoral support was surely not enough for the international community. In the case of the MSZP, a prominent role of right-wing politicians, a coalition with a liberal party, and gaining membership in the Socialist International were the most important factors to prove that Hungarian Socialists are no longer what they used to be.

Some analysts argued that the MSZP and other postcommunist parties cannot be successful until they "really become social democratic," meaning that they had to adopt procapitalist policies without the least intention of reform or compromise. At least in 1990, however, the source of possible electoral success lay elsewhere. According to Gowan,

the poor performance of the Polish and Hungarian parties had little to do with freedom versus totalitarianism, but was linked to another feature that distinguished these two parties from the Czechoslovak and East German parties: the fact that their party leadership had for some years been vigorously promoting policies of increasing marketization and social differentiation, with increasingly negative effects on those sections of the population in whose name they ruled; policies which were not being promoted by the Czechoslovak and East German parties whose economies under centralized planning were more successful than those of either Poland or Hungary. [Gowan 1997b: 150]

After the 1990 elections, most analysts believed that the MSZP could not become a leading party again before 1998 or even 2002. In 1994 May, however, the MSZP won the elections, obtaining 33% of the popular vote. One month later, under the premiership of party leader Gyula Horn, they formed a coalition with the liberal SZDSZ. Half a year later they also formed a coalition to run the capital city Budapest, although there the SZDSZ maintained the relative majority gained in 1990.

Ironically enough, the MSZP was the youngest party of the 1994 parliament. It was born in 1989 October as a postcommunist reform party and developed itself into a Western type social-democratic party in the subsequent years. In September 1996, the MSZP became a full member of the Socialist International, although the Social–Liberal platform of the SZDSZ had also been an associated member ("observer") in the Socialist Internationale (SI) since the transition began.

Originally it was the Social Democratic Party of Hungary (MSZDP) that represented Hungarian social democracy in SI. The party was revived by those who had been active in the party as young people in the late 1940s. Despite the immense material support they received from their Western comrades, they failed to enter parliament either in 1990 or in 1994. Following the second failure, their congress elected a new leader, László Kapolyi—a minister of industry in the 1980s, and a major sponsor of the party. His election confirmed the stand of the MSZDP between the MSZP and the Workers' Party taken under the previous leader, Zoltán Király. As a result of internal scandals, the position of the MSZDP was weakened in SI too. The Workers' Party shared one feature with MSZDP: it did not manage to stop being the party of the left-wing elderly. Particularly after the electoral victory of the MSZP, it had very few ideas about the direction of progressive left-wing politics until the issue of NATO enlargement came on the agenda.

The major domestic credential for the MSZP was the experience of the population with the Németh government. After resigning from membership in parliament in 1990, Miklós Németh distanced himself from everyday Hungarian politics and left for London, to work as vice-president of the newly established European Bank for Reconstruction and Development (EBRD). Although he had had to govern in extremely difficult conditions and to implement a series of unpopular measures, he left a largely positive memory in the population.

Leading politicians of the MSZP wedded themselves with neoliberal economics as early as the time of the Németh government, and that became the cement of the coalition they made with the SZDSZ in 1994. This coalition was formed even though the MSZP gained an absolute majority—54% of the mandates—in parliament (see Appendix 2, Table 10). The reasons for that are several. First, international credibility required the postcommunist MSZP to ally itself with someone immaculate in the eyes of Western capital and governments. The SZDSZ, which could with very little exaggeration be called the political wing of the IMF in Hungary, was an obvious choice to fulfill this job. Second, the responsibility for the proposed macroeconomic austerity had to be shared with another party, especially when the given policy belonged much more organically to that party than to the socialists. Third, the SZDSZ was ready to accept the coalition because it could show the voters that it was worth while to vote for it, and the party did represent power. Fourth, negotiations between the two parties about coalition had started months earlier, although with no clear figures about the majority they would get together, let alone thinking about an absolute majority for the MSZP.

The allocation of portfolios as a result of three weeks of negotiations mirrored the power relations between and within the two parties. For joining the coalition, the 69-MP-strong SZDSZ was invited to nominate three ministers: Gábor Kuncze (Interior Affairs), Károly Lotz (Transport and Communication), and Gábor Fodor (Culture and Education). Kuncze and Lotz used to be company managers and belonged among the least known members of parliament until early 1993, when the SZDSZ moguls found Kuncze the only appropriate person for premiership. He could not achieve this, after all, but apart from being a minister he was also a deputy for Prime Minister Gyula Horn. Fodor, once one of the most popular politicians in the country, was not mainstream SZDSZ either, inasmuch as he joined the SZDSZ only before the elections, following his forced departure from Fidesz in November 1993.

The rest of the ministers in the first Horn government were Socialists and represented different wings of the party. The most right-wing of all, and undoubtedly to the right of many free democrats as well, was László Békesi (Finance). He had held the same post in the government of Miklós Németh as well, in 1989–90. Békesi represented the commitment of the MSZP to austerity, and that was why his ministership, and the unchallenged acceptance of the so-called Békesi program, was an elementary precondition for the SZDSZ to form a coalition with the MSZP.

László Békesi was the archetype of the Socialist politician who was never seen releasing a positive comment on socialism in recent times. He would easily have found a job on the right wing of the British Conservative Party or the American Republican Party. In an interview published in 1997, he mentioned that a conversation with Milton Friedman was influential in confirming his commitment to the "right" economic principles. When master and acolyte met at the Hoover Institute in 1988, Friedman lectured Békesi on political economy, and agreement emerged on various issues, including property relations (Fáy 1997: 14).

The readiness of the SZDSZ to ally itself with the Socialists became more and more apparent when they joined forces against authoritarian tendencies in government circles under the auspices of the Democratic Charter. However, the openness of the SZDSZ toward the left was not unconditional; they demanded Békesi's neoliberal economic program to be unchallenged in the MSZP. Békesi rejected suggestions about unemployment below 10% and promised an acceleration of privatization, while initiating the rebuilding of Eastern markets as well as collective bargaining at the national level.

The emergence of the Békesi program dates back to August 1993, when the MSZP came out with a political advertisement about the bright future to come if people vote Socialist. As it turned out later, the advertisement was a creation of the party apparatus and lacked any kind of analysis of the economic conditions of the country. Following a period of open dispute, Békesi, the strongest critic of the advertisment, came out with his proposals based on what he thought feasible. This looked rather grim. He acknowledged GDP growth and low unemployment as ultimate objectives of a social-democratic party, but he made it clear that due to the twin deficits of record scale, the new government must start with a period of austerity, when both inflation and unemployment would increase.

Békesi also approved neoliberal economics as the prime economic philosophy of the MSZP. Budgets must be balanced, public expenditures must be cut, trade must be totally liberalized, taxes on capital should be decreased, and the sale-off of state firms, especially that of commercial banks, must be accelerated. On privatization, for instance, the Békesi program wrote the following:

We consider the introduction of fresh capital, technological modernization and both the protection and creation of jobs as the principal aims of privatization. Consequently, we wish to create equal conditions for foreign and domestic professional investors through clear competition rules. We would decrease the red tape surrounding privatization by organising state property holding and privatization preparation mainly on a commercial basis. We would give more significant roles to company management and independent consulting firms in the preparation of privatization. While we would carry through the restitution process through effective laws, we are not planning to satisfy newer demands. We do not support free property distribution of any kind during the privatization process. [Békesi, 1994: 4]

Békesi seemed to be completely ignorant of the social context of his economics. His view on the trade unions was very similar to Stalin's. He believed and said on many occasions to journalists that the advantage of the MSZP, and the reason for him to be a socialist politician, was that the Socialist party had good connections with the trade unions and could make the society accept the right economic policy more easily than could other parties. In this "transmission-belt" approach trade unions have a role in social dialogue up to the point when they do not just listen to the experts but start suggesting alternative policies as well.

The liberal wing of the MSZP had been strongly embedded in the political interests of international capital ever since the party was formed in 1989. Gyula Horn was proud of his special relationship with Chancelor Helmut Kohl—a privilege he had earned as foreign minister in 1989 when the Hungarian border was opened up for East German tourists heading toward Austria without a passport. As prime minister elect, he was invited to an extraordinary multilateral summit meeting in Innsbruck, Austria, before he announced the composition and policies of his government in the summer of 1994. Despite all that, however, the Socialist-led government was not fully accepted by the international community until the Horn government did not implement the program of macroeconomic stabilization in the mood of financial conservatism.

The Dirty Job of Stabilization

The Horn government started its operation with a dual strategy. On the one hand, it said it needed time to learn the real situation of the country, since it had been prevented from doing that in opposition. On the other hand, it immediately announced some austerity measures, since it anticipated the results of the above mentioned investigation to be rather grim. The experts of the IMF had also been very active in convincing Békesi to be determined to do what he would have done anyway. Soon after the government was formed, it devalued the forint by 8% and announced tax increases, cuts in public expenditure and other austerity measures. On 27 September, Horn made a widely broadcast speech in Parliament about the critical economic situation and the requirements of the IMF and the World Bank. This "Churchill speech" of the prime minister was presented just when the Bretton Woods Institutions (BWIs) held their annual meeting in Madrid. A month later the annual budget law was modified to reduce the PSBR, just a few days before Michel Camdessus, head of the IMF, arrived in the country.

While hesitant on economic decisions (privatization slow-down, compromise on expenditure cuts in the budget amendment etc.), the main offensive of the government was launched in foreign affairs. With the credentials of Horn, the MSZP wanted to present itself as a party of European integration. The government wanted to use the time when Germany functioned as chair of the European Union to gain a significant advantage in the integration process, by acquiring a concessional 2 billion ECU loan for structural adjustment and by forcing the European Union to outline a schedule for integration. By linking Hungary to the European Union, Horn and his foreign minister, László Kovács, not only pursued long-term visions, but also sought a very definite short-term refuge to escape the mounting pressure from the BWIs to implement further austerity measures and public sector mutilation. However, the special relationship between Horn and Kohl did not work as the Hungarians had conceived, and the enormous efforts invested by the Hungarian diplomacy were lost. Concessional structural adjustment loans and schedules for integration remained as remote as before, and even a dinner invitation for Horn and Kovács was not easy to obtain at the Essen summit of the European Union in December.

Thus, the MSZP was unable to present the success of foreign policy for the electorate at the municipal elections, just a day after Essen. However, the support for the MSZP did not seem to fade by that time. What appeared was a balance between the Socialists, the Free Democrats, and the fragmented right-wing forces. The leadership of Budapest—one fifth of the population—was kept by the Free Democrat mayor Gábor Demszky, who then created a coalition with the MSZP to govern the capital city. The Budapest coalition of the two government parties took shape fairly smoothly, regardless of simultaneous disputes between the two parties at the national level.

The disputes culminated in the resignation of Békesi in January. The immediate cause for his resignation was a disagreement on how privatization should be handled, as well as the dismissal of the privatization commissioner, Ferenc Bartha. The MSZP had promised to accelerate privatization, while it virtually stopped in the second half of 1994. Privatization revenues would have been vital for the 1995 budget, Békesi's main concern. Over the sale of HungarHotels (a chain with 13 hotels), which was vetoed by Horn, and a few other issues, there were some bitter debates between the two coalition parties. SZDSZ heavy-weights strongly criticized Horn for being "irresponsible" on various economic issues, doubting that he would really go along with neoliberalism, wholesale privatization and austerity. In December and January, the liberal media gave Horn a very hard time both abroad and at home. However, the reason for Horn to get rid of Békesi was not simply disagreement on policies, but much more the political ambitions and disloyal behavior of the finance minister. The left of the party celebrated Horn, but it was too early.

By the first anniversary of its inauguration, the government had five new members. On 1 March, Horn appointed Lajos Bokros, President of Budapest Bank and of the Stock Exchange Council, to be minister of finance, György Surányi, Managing Director of the off-shore Central-European Investment Bank (CIB), to be governor of the National Bank, and Tamás Suchman, a MSZP MP, to be minister of privatization. The first two are archetypes of the so-called "Chicago boys," while the third is a self-made businessman, well known for his loyalty to Horn. (The Governor of the Bank is not a member of the cabinet but is, in case of vacancy, nominated by the Prime Minister. Horn had forced Péter Ákos Bod to resign in order to create a vacancy for Surányi, who had held the post in 1990–91 and was hinted as a potential finance minister of the Young Democrats or the Free Democrats before the elections of 1994.)

With a small group of experts, Bokros put together an austerity package that would end the universal welfare state as it had existed for the last thirty years (family allowances, child-care benefits, free higher education etc.). Horn, Bokros and Surányi presented the measures for the public, together with a 9% devalua-tion of the forint, on Sunday, 12 March. The package was justified by the historically outstanding deficit of U.S.$4 billion in the current account in 1994 and the fact that the government had reached half of the planned annual budget deficit by March. There could have been, they explained, an immediate bank-ruptcy of the government if they did not make this move. No matter how dire the overall economic situation was, this latter argument was obviously untrue. When the foreign exchange reserves of the National Bank are so high (U.S.$8 billion, i.e. more than 50% of the annual import bill), the liquidity of the government is up to the policy of the Bank. And that was, for the moment, also in the hands of the Prime Minister, given his power to appoint as governor the person he wanted.

Two ministers, Pál Kovács (welfare) and Béla Katona (secret service), re-signed immediately. According to opinion polls, 66% of the population was outraged by the measures and the way they were done. (Just two weeks earlier the government had promised not to devalue, and not to introduce tuition fees in 1995. This latter was brought forward by Bokros to September 1995. On the morning of "Bloody Sunday," Imre Szekeres, vice-president of the MSZP, said on the radio that the government did not plan any measures to decrease living standards. He, as leader of the parliamentary faction, apparently had no information about what had been prepared.)

The IMF played a significant role in pushing the Hungarian government onto the austerity track, though it did not stretch out a helping hand when the government eventually decided to implement the stabilization package. When the Mexican financial markets collapsed at the end of 1994, IMF officials did not hesitate to hint in the international press that Hungary was one of the few countries threatened by a similar accident. Despite a completely different structure of the balance of payments, the economic credentials of Hungary were destroyed, and the situation required urgent action. In such cases the IMF had been eager to sign standby agreements, which it did not favor this time, leaving the Hungarian government to cope with the stabilization package. It even lobbied against a syndicated credit that was to be organized under German initiative.

Even though two thirds of the population was outraged by the Bokros package, however, no significant resistance was organized, apart from a few student demonstrations. The MSZP was losing its popularity, but Horn's position was strengthened by his readiness to take the initiative and appoint loyal bureaucrats in the place of the two ministers who had resigned. The MSZP faction also found an appropriate ideology to avoid shame for this heartless austerity. It took pride in achieving something "unpopular but inherently good" for the economy, which was to bring fruit a year or two later. Many of them proudly announced: this is the real end of Kádárism (most welfare measures now abolished had been introduced under Kádár 25–30 years ago) and a test for the MSZP not being a Kádárist party any more.

Along with the austerity package, an agreement on friendship and nonaggression with Slovakia, signed in March in Paris by Horn, was to prove that Hungarians are prepared to match Western standards and requirements. In the meantime, however, Socialist leaders became more and more occupied by the question of whether or not the MSZP faction would be able to remain in one piece for four years. Analysts called attention to the fact that the gigantic MSZP faction contained some "subfactions," like their youth, trade union or agricultural factions, which were larger than some opposition parties in parliament. It was feared that, as austerity hit, these factions would attempt to come forward with their own demands and stretch the faction to its limits. Hence Szekeres's job appeared rather difficult.

It was apparently the relationship between the trade unions and the MSZP that was tested first by the March austerity package. Sándor Nagy, the leader of MSZOSZ, had already been frustrated by his failure to become minister of finance after Békesi and by his failure to acquire some positions in the governing body of the newly established privatization agencies. However reluctantly, he then had to come out protesting against the Bokros plan and supporting the railway workers when they went on a two-day strike at the end of April. After all, the alliance between Nagy and Horn was confirmed by a joint Mayday rally, in response to a surprise attack by the sidelined Békesi, who had claimed to the press a few days earlier that the alliance of the MSZP and the unions before the elections was a historic mistake.

In June, Nagy was quoted as saying that he was fed up with supporting a government policy with which he disagreed. He and others had to put up with the eventual passing of a World-Bank-tuned Privatization Act in May, as well as a decision to continue the compensation of precommunist owners by a scheme to compensate the Jewish community for property expropriated before and during World War II—another U-turn in government policy. Finally, almost all conditions were met to design and sign a new contract with the IMF. The only task left to Horn was to fire his minister for industry and trade, László Pál, who had openly opposed the privatization of the national electricity company. (Preparations to sell the majority of shares to foreign companies were under way.) While the IMF delegation visited Budapest, the Prime Minister delivered them this favor: that of nominating another technocrat, Imre Dunai, as a new member of the cabinet.

Opinion polls did not leave doubt about the reception of government performance. Bokros entered the club of the best-known 20 politicians at the lowest popularity rate and remained there firmly without a hope of improvement. Bokros also had to face opposition to his policies within the party. These groups mobilized heavyweight intellectual support for their complaints. This movement resulted in a public appearance by Iván Szelényi at a policy debate at the headquarters of the MSZP. In the view of Iván Szelényi, the 1994 elections showed that class continued to be a dominant factor in politics.[5] He attributed the revival of the left to the increasing political consciousness of the Hungarian working class, and particularly the mobilization of educated workers. He also claimed that the Socialist–Liberal coalition opened up the way toward a "postcommunist New Deal," or a social-democratic alternative to the ruthless neoliberal transition project. This alternative strategy—presented in a Reichian spirit—put forward the vision of an activist state that would have been able to promote national competitiveness through investing in education and maintaining social peace.

Szelényi's analyses always attracted attention in Hungary, but his was not the only possible interpretation of social democracy. One can argue that the framework of the Bokros package was itself a contemporary version of social democratic economic policy. Social democracy in Western Europe, similarly to the New Deal in the United States, was a framework of a class compromise between big business and big labor, at the expense of small business. The first transition period in Hungary was strongly antilabor, creating mass unemployment and diminishing labor's influence on economic policies. Antall's coalition, however, was not always friendly to big business either, which happened to be foreign. The meltdown of the political representation of Hungarian small business created a ground for a new political formation after the 1994 elections. It was true that

Hungarian wage earners and pensioners lost 10% of their real incomes during the Bokros year, but the MSZP managed to implement the austerity package by maintaining the existing level of workers' rights and union influence.

It had to be understood that the country left behind by the right-wing government was in a financial crisis, and stabilization was not possible without an immense sacrifice by the working class. And, after the year of pain, the austerity policy paid off. The first major harvest after the stabilization efforts came one year after the Bokros package was introduced, when Hungary signed an agreement with the IMF and, as a result, was adopted by the OECD. By this time, it was clear that the one-year austerity had worked, and the foreign balances of the country were coming back toward equilibrium. The commitment to the means and ends of stability restored the credentials of the government and opened the doors of the IMF and the OECD. Ironically, by then Hungary did not need the money of the IMF, though its seal of approval was important to help reach lower interest rates with private creditors and eliminate doubts in the offices of the OECD.

Foreign acceptance was the most important asset that MSZP leaders thought would be enough to win the 1998 elections, despite the loss of popularity in 1995 and 1996. In early 1997, there was still widespread speculation about the possible and perhaps necessary replacement of Gyula Horn as prime minister before the elections in order to restore the chances of the party. One year later there was no doubt. In February the party announced that Horn would be nominated prime minister again if they win the elections. Some opposition politicians and political analysts even started to talk about the threat of the revival of the one-party system, or at least of a dominant party system, and that the latter was alien to European norms.

Until just a few weeks before the elections, the MSZP seemed to be a likely winner of the race; this made many observers blame the weak campaign for the defeat the party suffered "unexpectedly." Most Socialists were confident or even complacent during the campaign because of the improving macroeconomic figures of the country and the substantial lead of the MSZP in the opinion polls. The actual unity of the right-wing parties became apparent only in the last weeks or even days of the race, which also showed that the recovery of the popularity of the MSZP in 1997 and early 1998 was only temporary.

The recovery of the Socialists, similarly to that of the macroeconomy, was indeed remarkable, but it did not completely eliminate the impact of two major blows the popularity of the ruling coalition suffered between 1994 and 1998. These blows were inflicted by the stabilization measures of 1995 and the corruption scandal of 1996. The MSZP lost and the FKGP gained popularity in the first case, while Fidesz–MPP picked up what was lost by the MSZP in the second case. The SZDSZ was hit by both factors, which accelerated the continuous decline of the party that did not stop even temporarily.

Although he was a minister only for a year and left the country soon afterwards, Lajos Bokros and his package were the basis on which the evaluation of the Socialist–Liberal government was possible in 1998. The Socialists claimed that the Bokros package was the only way to sort out the financial problems of the country in a hostile international environment. The implementation of the harsh austerity measures restored the international respectability of Hungary and the Hungarian government, which accelerated the inflow of foreign capital and lowered the interest rates on the foreign debts of the country. In the second half of the four-year governmental period, economic growth was significant again. Though unemployment remained at 10% and inflation close to 20%, wage earners also experienced an improvement in their incomes.

The Right has opposed the Bokros package ferociously, claiming that restriction was unnecessary and that the crawling devaluation of the forint—which was also implemented in March 1995—caused more harm than good by boosting inflation. Bokros also wanted to cut many of the social benefits inherited from the Kádár era, which was—though temporarily—obstructed by the Constitutional Court and declared inhuman by the Right.[6] On a number of issues, the moderate Right and the radical Left shared their criticism of the neoliberal economic and social policies of the government.

The Bokros package was controversial enough, but the popularity of the ruling parties was even more damaged in the autumn of 1996, when a major corruption scandal surfaced. The affair was related to the privatization revenue owed by the national privatization agency (ÁPV Rt.) to the local governments. The leaders of ÁPV Rt. hired a private lawyer to broker deals between the agency and the municipalities, and its oversized "success fee" was tapped by financial agents close to the two ruling parties. Horn fired his privatization minister, Tamás Suchman, and the entire board of directors of ÁPV Rt., but belief in the morality and expertise of the MSZP and the SZDSZ had nevertheless evaporated.

Despite these two blows and the impact of the crisis of the Socialists in Yugoslavia and Bulgaria in early 1997, the popularity of the MSZP started to recover, and the party was expected to win the elections again. Indeed, it won the most popular votes in the first round of the 1998 elections and managed to increase the number of its voters to nearly two million by the second round. This relative success, however, could not compensate for the losses suffered by its coalition partner, the Free Democrats.

The campaign slogan of the SZDSZ claimed that we just need "to continue in the right direction." This phrase was nothing but a failure when the majority of the population believed that, with corruption in the government offices and increasing social differences, the country was not going in the right direction in the first place. The credibility of the SZDSZ was also damaged by the rapidly deteriorating public security in Budapest and other major cities under a Free Democrat interior minister.

The two ruling parties believed that it was enough to present the improving international acceptance of the country (NATO and EU integration) and the favorable macroeconomic figures of 1997 and 1998. They failed to understand that the electorate needed something more—a vision about a different society that provided hope for those hit by the repeated austerity packages. The pragmatic attitude of the MSZP ceased to be a virtue, and the lack of vision became apparent when the Socialists were facing the ambitious Young Democrats at the election campaign.

The Reconstruction of the Right

The parliamentary elections of 1998 resulted in two major changes in the power structure of political parties. First, the elections were won by a new right-wing coalition that emerged from the reconstruction of previous ruling parties of the early 1990s. In this sense, the Hungarian results followed the Polish example of 1997, when the ruling postcommunist Social Democratic party was replaced by a revitalized Solidarity coalition. Second, first time in the postcommunist era, an explicitly far Right party entered parliament, similarly to the East German state elections of the Magdeburg region just a month before the Hungarian elections.

The Hungarian elections were won by the Right despite the fact that the party that won the most votes was the MSZP—the only parliamentary force of the Left. Just like in 1994, the MSZP won 33% of the popular vote. Due to the highly disproportional electoral system, however, this 33% was enough for 54% of the parliamentary mandate in 1994, but only for 35% of the seats in 1998. Due to the fragmentation of the Right in 1994, the MSZP then won nearly all individual constituencies. By 1998, the unity of the Right prevented them from winning any seats in seven counties (Győr–Moson–Sopron, Vas, Veszprém, Zala, Csongrád, Bács–Kiskun and Pest).

The MSZP remained dominant in the traditional industrial districts of the north, mid-west and southwest, and also in the poorer agricultural zones to the east of the river Tisza (Wiener 1998: 12). The FKGP became a leading force in the regions formerly dominated by the rich peasantry, and the Fidesz–MPP carried the conservative West, mainly by attracting former KDNP and SZDSZ voters. Due to fatal infighting lasting several years, the KDNP as a party did not qualify at all for the new parliament, while the SZDSZ was diminished into a small party.

In the first round, just slightly more than half of the electorate participated in the elections. This ratio was much lower than the roughly two-thirds participation of 1990 at the first postcommunist "free" elections and of 1994, when participation was stimulated by the need to oust a demoralized cabinet. In 1998, political scientists suggested that a low turnout would benefit the Socialists, who possess the most disciplined membership and constituency. Inasmuch as the MSZP repeated the 1994 result, the forecast was right. However, the low turnout did not prevent the entry into parliament of the MIÉP and the emergence of a right-wing coalition supported by a disciplined constituency ready to vote for other parties in case their leaders asked for that.

The entry of the MIÉP was not forecast by political analysts, and, according to the rules of the house, they were not meant to form a parliamentary faction with only 14 representatives. When István Csurka was expelled from the MDF, some new rules were adopted to prevent them from forming a faction and re-entering parliament in 1994. These new rules required at least 15 deputies to form a faction and at least 5% of the popular vote to be able to enter parliament.[7] In 1998, however, the MIÉP passed the 5% limit with ease, and the Constitutional Court decided that despite having only 14 deputies in parliament, it must be allowed to form a faction. Thus, for the first time in the history of the new parliamentary pluralism in Hungary, the final result of the elections was determined not exclusively by the electorate but also by the Constitutional Court.

The first time the Hungarian Right believed they could oust the ruling MSZP was early in 1997, when MDF leader Sándor Lezsák announced "the second Velvet Revolution." His optimism was based on the events in the Balkans—the fall of the Socialist Party in Bulgaria, the electoral defeat of the social democrats in Romania, and the permanent anti-Socialist demonstrations in Belgrade. The opposition became so enthusiastic that the weekly paper most intimately associated with the opposition (*Demokrata*) published a photo-illustrated list and introduction of their suggested shadow cabinet—the government of national unity. Major right-wing parliamentary party leaders were given heavy portfolios, but extraparliamentary politicians and experts were also recommended. István Csurka was nominated as minister of privatization and Imre Pozsgay as minister of culture. György Matolcsy, head of the Privatization Research Institute, was recommended to be minister of finance, and the well-known populist economist Erzsébet Gidai, president of the futures studies committee of the Hungarian Academy of Sciences, to be prime minister.

Domestically, the coalition was challenged by a series of demonstrations on the part of rural entrepreneurs. Then, however, neither the strength nor the unity of the Right was enough for a change. The government fought back against the demonstrating smallholders by tighter supervision of wine-producing methods and a closer look at the tax-paying attitudes of the producers. After a couple of weeks, popular opinion changed, and the government was able to resist, and later even ignore, the recurring noise coming from the farmers.

The right-wing unity was made possible by a few issues they could campaign on jointly. Such an issue was, first of all, the question of the Gabcikovo–Nagymaros dam, which, after a less than favorable decision of the International Court at the Hague, was again on the agenda of the government with the explicit aim of relaunching the construction. Another major issue was the increasing crime rate in the country, with rampant gang violence on the streets of Budapest and other cities. Campaigning for law and order was a key to mobilizing potential right-wing voters. Having collected all possible issues and social linkages, the young and ambitious Viktor Orbán carried out a most successful vote maximization project that Anthony Downs would have been very pleased to see.

The profile of Fidesz had to change enormously until the party became the main ruling political force in Hungary. Out of the many changes of the recent years, most foreign observers highlighted the long journey Viktor Orbán—the leader of Fidesz–MPP since its foundation—had already made in his political convictions since 1988. In the 1989–90 period, Fidesz was presented as a liberal party whose main concerns were human rights and environmentalism. Orbán, just like his friends in the Fidesz faction of the first postcommunist parliament, walked to the meetings of the parliament in jeans.

Yet he turned Fidesz into a party with mass appeal by sounding anything but liberal. His economic pronouncements are tinged with demagoguery: taxes and inflation will be lower, he promises; growth faster; welfare more generous. He also champions the ethnic Hungarians living outside Hungary in ways that unnerve Romania and Slovakia, where most of them live. And he has rattled the EU: for the sake of those Hungarian cousins, he has said, Hungary should not join the EU's borderless Schengen area until they are in it too. And all good Hungarians should, like him, have three children. [*The Economist*, 30 May 1998: 25]

Orbán's party started to move to the Right from the liberal center as early as 1993, well before the 1994 elections, when Viktor Orbán got rid of the other popular leader of the party, Gábor Fodor. By that time, it became clear that Hungary would never have a purely liberal government. For Orbán's team the only way to government office was to become part—and, if possible, a leading force—of a broad Right. "Budapest is worth a mass" could have been Orbán's philosophy that guided him in building a conservative Hungarian Civic Party on the ruins of the liberal Fidesz. Fodor was followed by other liberal—or left liberal—politicians as Orbán invited more and more ex-MDF and ex-KDNP politicians into the party. The age limit of the party was abolished, and the name was amended to be acceptable for a broader right-wing constituency.

The strengthening of the social basis of the new right-wing coalition was due to the awakening of the new entrepreneur class. Back in 1990, the MDF had been the party of domestic entrepreneurs. The meltdown of the MDF by 1994 was a political expression of the critical condition of this small business class. The MSZP–SZDSZ coalition pursued the policies of an alliance between the multinational business sector and domestic organized labor. The campaign of Fidesz–MPP promised compensation for the domestic middle class by restoring their benefits, which had been abolished by the Horn government, diminishing the influence of labor in national politics and restricting the positions of foreign capital in the Hungarian economy.[8]

At the 1998 elections, Fidesz–MPP was campaigning on the basis of civic values, which were also expressed in the popularization of the new and full name of the party: Fidesz–Hungarian Civic Party (Fidesz–MPP). The Hungarian equivalent of "civic" [*polgári*] incorporates the meaning of *citoyen* and bourgeois, and also that of civilian. Thus, though the widespread use of this word left a good deal of doubt about the proper meaning of the intentions of Fidesz–MPP, nevertheless it was good enough to crystallize the strengthening class consciousness of the new entrepreneurs and the conservative-minded civil servants.

The most frustrated layers that supported Fidesz–MPP and the Smallholders were indeed the domestic entrepreneurs, who saw the Socialist–Liberal coalition favoring foreign investors in privatization and maintaining a restrictive monetary policy that prevented the strengthening of the Hungarian-owned enterprise sector. These layers believed that a looser monetary policy with lower tax rates would be possible, and at the same time the devaluation of the forint could also be slowed down. From such a policy mix, they expected an annual GDP growth of 7% for about ten years.

Orbán also managed to increase his popularity among students and other young people by promising greater material security and better life prospects for them. Since Horn pursued a neoliberal economic policy, for Fidesz–MPP it was easy to expropriate traditional socialist demands and turn them against the Socialist–Liberal coalition, claiming that a civic government would achieve what the left-of-center parties had promised (Bayer 1998: 23)

As a clear indication of his political objectives, Orbán made an electoral alliance with the MDF more than one year before the elections. When the KDNP was splitting, the Fidesz–MPP faction incorporated the liberal wing of the KDNP that later formed the Hungarian Christian Democratic Alliance (MKDSZ). In addition, following the agricultural demonstrations of early 1997, and particularly the land debate of autumn 1997, a tacit cooperation emerged between Fidesz–MPP and the Smallholders too. This slow convergence turned into an open agreement a few days before the second round of the 1998 May elections and developed not just into the formation of a common government, but also into a pact on the subsequent municipal elections and the presidential election of 2000.

During the campaign, Orbán rejected any open cooperation with the tiny Hungarian Democratic People's Party (MDNP) too, but this approach changed in June when the new government was being formed.[9] He was completely surrounded by the remnants of the old Antall brigade. Though it was Fidesz–MPP that collected much of the right-wing vote, it looked as if a reunion of Antall's team had hired a new captain to restore their chances to qualify for the Premier League. And it worked. Orbán and some other Fidesz politicians provided a fresh media face for more conservative social and political groups.

The overall right-wing revival benefited not only the moderate and populist Right forces but also the neo-Nazi MIÉP. Though the activists of the MIÉP cooperated with other right-wing forces at the local level, they had no chance of becoming part of the new government. Nevertheless, they voted for the program of the Orbán government when it was put before the Parliament in early July.

Following the announcement of the election results, president Árpád Göncz invited Viktor Orbán to form a coalition government. For him it was obvious to start negotiations with the MDF and then with the FKGP, though the possible alliance with the latter was denied before the public until the last moment. The coalition agreements with the two parties were signed at Hotel Gellért—a building with a notorious right-wing political legacy.[10]

In the "Fidesz government" there was only one minister—apart from the prime minister—who had been an actual Fidesz politician since the party first entered parliament in 1990; he was László Kövér, who had been—together with Orbán—one of the founders of the party in March 1988. He had always been on the rigidly anticommunist Right of the party, and he now became Orbán's deputy in his absence. With a few exceptions (eminently Zsigmond Járai and Attila Chikán), the rest of the ministers had even less to do with liberalism than Kövér. Since in Hungary not only members of parliament can become ministers, most of the members of the Orbán cabinet were introduced weeks after the elections. To the surprise of many voters, a party that is liberal in name brought back the second line of a conservative, authoritarian and nationalist government apparatus left behind from the Antall era (Sándor Pintér, Kálmán Katona, János Martonyi, János Szabó, József Torgyán).

Finance was the area where the nomination of the minister was surrounded by the heaviest social and political bargaining. Zsigmond Járai was the third person named as finance minister within just a few weeks following the elections. First, before and after the polling days, György Matolcsy had been said to be the candidate for finance. During the Fidesz campaign, he was the most prominent to argue for the promise of a 7% sustainable annual economic growth. He directed the work on the economic manifesto of Fidesz and published a good many articles about the harm done by the IMF, Bokros and others to the Hungarian economy.

The reason Matolcsy fell was that following the appearance of the election results the index of the Budapest Stock Exchange started to dive—a clear indication of the lack of trust in the unfounded promises of the winners and a rejection of the economic nationalism represented by Matolcsy. Fidesz responded to the crash by nominating Professor Attila Chikán as minister for the economy and László Urbán as minister of finance.[11] Neither Chikán nor Urbán had taken part in the election campaign of 1998, but they had been active economic advisors of the party before 1994, in the neoliberal period of Fidesz. The college headed by Chikán was one of the cradles of Fidesz in the 1980s, and many of his students—László Urbán among them—became prominent members or supporters of Fidesz. After two weeks of candidacy, Urbán was replaced by Járai, with no public explanation apart from the ten-year age difference and the greater experience that goes with it. Unofficial sources, however, suggested that the reason Urbán had to withdraw was that his blueprints about a tough restructuring and privatization of Postabank—the second-largest savings bank of the country—were considered unacceptable by Viktor Orbán and his advisors.

Orbán declared his cabinet to be "the government of liberty, order, families, economic growth, togetherness, and European cooperation." By calling it "value-driven" instead of pragmatic, he subscribed to continuity with the Antall government instead of the defeated Socialist–Liberal one. If ruling on the basis of values really follows Antall's example, those values simply serve as a cover for the pursuit of crude business interests. The main test of the new Orbán government is whether it will be able to reward its main supporters—small- and medium-scale entrepreneurs in industry, trade and agriculture.

NOTES

1. The partners of the Free Democrats (SZDSZ) in the referendum campaign were the Smallholders (FKGP), the Young Democrats (Fidesz) and the Social Democrats (MSZDP). Since the serious condition of the Eastern bloc was apparent as early as September 1989, the SZDSZ and Fidesz refused to sign the documents of NRT, which was a departure for the referendum campaign.

2. A conference volume was published by Michie (ed., 1992).

3. The importance of the transition from Rabár to Kupa is highlighted by Przevorski (1993: 150).

4. Orbán was characterized as "the Tiger" by the leading political commentator László Lengyel; it was an expression of fear, even if the Tiger image was taken from the tale of Winnie the Pooh.

5. Szelényi's contribution to the rehabilitation of the concept of class in social science has been remarkable, though his new theory of "manager's capitalism" was less convincing, and his apparent insistence on the class power of intellectuals can only be seen as a misplaced extrapolation of his politically important pamphlet from the mid-1970s.

6. The function of the Constitutional Court is to judge whether or not a new law is in line with the spirit of the Constitution. In its decisions, the Court has displayed a predominantly conservative attitude. It should be noted that the CC of Hungary holds much greater authority and power than any similar bodies in other countries.

7. The benefit members of parliament enjoy once they have formed a faction is that they can be represented in various committees of parliament, they are given more opportunities to speak from the floor, and they have greater room to maneuver to influence the agenda of the house.

8. Many of the entitlements to social benefits abolished by the Socialist–Liberal government (family and child care benefits, free higher education etc.) had supported the middle class primarily. The Horn government also attempted to impose stricter taxation on domestic entrepreneurs.

9. The MDNP emerged from a split in the MDF in 1995. Their prominent politicians, former minister of finance Iván Szabó, former minister of foreign affairs Géza Jeszenszky and former interior minister Imre Kónya, presented themselves as the true followers of the Antall legacy.

10. In 1919, Admiral Miklós Horthy announced the seizure of Budapest after defeating the troops of the short-lived Hungarian council republic with the support of the French and Romanian armies.

11. At the December 1999 cabinet reshuffle Chikán was replaced by Matolcsy, and this was evaluated as an attempted return to the original economic nationalism of Fidesz–MPP.

4

Transition Policies: Building the New Capitalism

In the 1990s, the Hungarian elite constructed capitalist social and economic systems in the country. The main ingredients of the respective systems were created through massive—though not always apparent—political conflicts and at a very high social cost. Despite the fact that the construction of these new systems has demanded tremendous sacrifice, their actual performances are still disappointing.

Regional comparisons put Hungary among the most successful of the new capitalist states of Eastern Europe, but this fact qualifies the state of the region rather than the country. Though the state socialist systems of Eastern Europe were in a severe economic crisis in the 1980s, the experience of the 1990s suggests that reform and not transition would have been the rational answer to that crisis.

Any reasonable assessment shows that political purposes and special interests were driving the Hungarian economy on the road toward capitalism (which by no means should be called a "free economy"). Private accumulation—the crucial mechanism of capitalist restoration—was pursued through a large-scale disinvestment from human capital and the state, which raised doubts about the stability and sustainability of the new system.

The consequences of transition policies look even more dismal if we compare them to the expectations of the time, when the small opposition forces made their bid to lead the country and to replace the old state socialist leadership. The results of capitalist restoration fall very short of the promises of 1989. Ten years after the beginning of the systemic change, it is quite apparent that the transition policies have served the interests of a minority, which explains why they had to be carried through against the interests and will of the majority, and particularly of the working majority.

CAPITAL: PRIVATIZING PROFITS

Privatization in Hungary, just like anywhere else in Eastern Europe, was by no means a rational or scientifically designable process. Privatization has been a political exercise by its essence, and the political struggles over property have left lasting marks on the face of the new system. First of all, privatization aimed at appropriating the already existing profits of the economic units rather than creating new surpluses by boosting productivity. A distinctive feature of the Hungarian return to capitalism is the outstanding role of foreign investment, which is due to the attitude of the management and the quality of the labor force.

An Irrational Choice

When the changes of 1989 took the idea of a mixed economy off the political agenda, the ideology of transition suggested that the policy of comprehensive privatization of publicly owned enterprises was supported by economic science as such. The rationale for privatization was summarized by the World Development Report of 1996 as follows:

At the heart of transition lies a change in incentives, none more important than those for managers of enterprises. Managers in centrally planned economies faced distorted incentives that sooner or later led to poor enterprise performance. Transition requires changes that introduce financial discipline and increase entry of new firms, exit of unviable firms, and competition. These spurs needed restructuring, even in state enterprises. Ownership change, preferably to private ownership, in a large share of the economy is also important. Once markets have been liberalized, governments cannot indefinitely control large parts of a dynamic, changing economy. Decentralizing ownership is the best way to increase competition and improve performance. [World Bank 1996: 44]

The argument presented by the World Bank does not simply tell us what the logic of privatization should be. It also highlights how important the policy of privatization was for the entire process of transition. Despite its importance, however, politicians never requested scientific evidence to prove why privatization was necessary. It simply derived from the perception of capitalism being more efficient than state socialism. As a Hungarian economist in a high office in the area of government finance put it: "The evidence for privatization is obvious if you compare the economic performance of East Germany to that of West Germany." Neither the social and political cost of East German privatization, nor the fact that the privatization of East Germany was a loss-making exercise disturbed this postcommunist common sense.

In 1990, the new Hungarian political elite was united in the opinion that a wholesale privatization of state industries must begin immediately. The overlapping field of their ideologies suggested that privatization is a good thing, though the rival political tendencies disagreed on every detail (e.g., what needs to be privatized and how, by whom and at what price). In reality, privatization in Hungary, as in other countries of Eastern Europe, has not been a rationally guided process and has not lead to the outcomes predicted by the World Bank study.

Had science supported the need for urgent privatization, it should also have given indications about how this policy should be implemented. Scientific debates indeed emerged on issues of privatization, but without much impact on actual government policies. Sometimes these debates lacked a theoretical background or reference to the actual circumstances.

Joseph Stiglitz writes in his book *Wither Socialism?* about the irony of the privatization debate: "There is a joke about the debate on the speed of privatization in Hungary, with those who advocate rapid privatization arguing that privatization must be achieved in five years while those who advocate slow privatization urging that matters be taken calmly—privatization should take place over five years" (Stiglitz 1994: 181).

According to Stiglitz, the only clear economic advantage that may be reached through privatization is the establishment of hard budget constraints and increased competition.[1] However, many of the arguments presented by the theory of property rights do not hold, since they were based upon the assumption of perfect information and zero transaction costs. When the reform of ownership is on the agenda, the costs and benefits of privatization must be assessed thoroughly, and there can be serious reasons to postpone the implementation of privatization policies (Stiglitz 1994: 193–194).

In Hungary, any suggestion that privatization could be delayed because of the consideration of costs and various drawbacks was seen as a heresy. The confusion in the academic and professional debate greatly assisted the emergence of a situation where special interests, through nontransparent lobbying, dominated the directions of actual ownership reform. Lobbies and interest groups channeled their endeavors through political parties. This also brought a great deal of ideology into the economic policy debate.

The political nature of Hungarian privatization can be shown by explaining how conflicting priorities appeared in the privatization debate and how various objectives or concerns were pursued or rejected by different political forces. The political history of the transition also explains the dynamic of the history of ownership reform. There was not a single moment of this process when privatization could have become a nonpolitical issue. It was always the constellation of external and internal political factors that decided what methods of privatization were to be used in certain policy periods.

Under prime ministers Grósz and Németh, the balance of payments was the main concern of the government. However cautiously, government policies were prepared to be conducive to foreign investment that was meant to assist Hungary's recovery from the foreign debt crisis. Reform policies were accelerated by the perception of Hungary being the forerunner of East European reform, and extra benefits from that position were also expected. Beyond legal preparations, under Németh, the first cases of large sales to foreign owners took place. In order to make the management interested in this project, spontaneous privatization was facilitated too.

Under Antall and Boross, an attempt was made to nationalize privatization policy—that is, to make ownership reform help to create a new Hungarian middle class. The government made its intention clear to limit the opportunities of foreign owners and also restrain the room for maneuver of the management of state companies. The political control over the privatization process secured a situation in which domestic entrepreneurs would have a good chance to acquire profit-making assets, and they would even be able to expect some assistance in competing against foreign professional investors offering large sums of cash. The party that advocated restitution became part of the ruling coalition, though its policies were modified to a politically manageable compensation scheme. Compensation vouchers issued in various rounds became the major vehicle of privatization in Hungary. Since the Christian Democrats were also part of the coalition, the share of the churches was also guaranteed. Toward the end of the first parliamentary period, the government developed schemes to benefit small investors who aspired to be at least small capitalists in the new world.

The 1994 elections brought a new attitude to privatization again. After the MSZP won the elections, finance minister Békesi announced that cash revenue was to be the main guide for privatization. Given the dire state of national finances, his new policies were understandable, though his apparent ignorance about other objectives raised serious resentment. This controversy continued under Horn's second finance minister, Lajos Bokros, who made it even more clear that the government again wanted to use privatization to get out of the trap of foreign debt through an applied version of debt–equity swap. Political aversions against privatizing public utilities were simply swept away by Horn's left-leaning privatization minister, Tamás Suchman.

Apparently, not much state property was left to the Fidesz government that came into office in 1998. They, however, quickly found a way to re-collect those parts of the national economy that continued to operate under state control or under the influence of the state. Quasi-denationalized assets, like the property of the social security funds, were again centralized within the revitalized State Privatization and Holding Company (ÁPV Rt), which, under new leadership, took control over state shares in commercial banks as well as the surviving state-owned enterprises. After the apparent end of privatization, the Orbán government opened a new round through which favored social groups could benefit through easy access to state property still available for privatization.

Apart from being a product and a matter for political struggles, another main problem of privatization is its lack of moral foundation and public support. Ironically enough, the introduction of a kind of market economy was indeed supported by the Hungarian public, but hardly any particular method or case of privatization has enjoyed overwhelming popular support during the transition period. The privatization agencies have made some attempts to improve the public relations image of privatization, with mixed results.

Objections were also made to privatization because it was seen as a process forced upon Hungary by foreign agencies and advantageous to foreign investors. Therefore, Antall's nationalist government attempted to "Hungarianize" privatization by calling the policy *magánosítás* instead of the more common *privatizáció*. Hungarian slang, however, created a new word for the process, which is *lenyúlás*. This word is an expression of the perception that, through wholesale and politically controlled privatization, the black economy virtually invaded the entire public sector; moreover, national industrial policy now became subject to means previously only known in semicriminal activities.

Regardless of ideological background, studies on privatization agreed that different privatization methods serve different objectives. Sale to outside owners leads to better corporate governance and access to capital and skills. It also raises more revenue than other forms of privatization; however, it might be slower and less fair than other methods. Equal access voucher privatization could be quick and fair, but it does not raise revenue for the government and its impact on corporate governance and access to capital and skills is uncertain. Management–employee buyout can be fast too, but it scores badly on all other criteria. Spontaneous privatization might be fast and may improve corporate governance, but it is very hard to say anything more positive about it (World Bank 1996: 52).

The alternative objectives and methods could not be measured against each other scientifically, especially not in advance. The view that "the more private the economy, the better it performs" did not help with the question concerning the way in which to start the process and the immediate aims that it should serve. Some "experts" argued that "it is worth selling the state-owned companies even if the revenue is only 1 forint," but they were never asked how to decide who should be the new owner should the privatization agency take their advice seriously. Since in the first period a naive approach dominated privatization policy, no effort was made to restructure the companies before privatization in order to increase sales revenue. Later presale restructuring became a practice, but it was carried out in a rather confused way by the Antall–Boross government.

Once it became a consensus that the required economic system was a stateless, free-market economy and that it had to be reached as soon as possible, the way was open to an uncontrollable and untransparent "give and take" game within the political and economic elite. Behind the screen of laissez-faire ideology, many invisible hands—those of politicians and their associates—distributed small and large pieces of the national economy, regardless of long-term considerations. This was the process called "pseudoprivatization" by Amsden et al.—"an attempt to create capitalism without any capital, or without the credit, skills, and expertise necessary to restructure now 'private' enterprises hindered by long-term bottlenecks" (Amsden et al. 1994: 12). However, whatever the degree of spontaneity in privatization at certain periods and in certain industries, the role of government remained extremely strong throughout the process. The very fact that the new private sector was created by a rapid top-down distribution mechanism instead of an evolutionary bottom-up accumulation meant that the new private entrepreneur class remained disorganized and fragmented in fractions of political networks and clientele (see Bruszt and Stark 1998).

Privatization operations were often guided, or just covered up, by obsolete economic ideologies. The dispute between advocates of commercial banks and of universal banks represented one example of this. Due to the influence of nineteenth-century Mancunian liberalism, most financial economists in Hungary argued for the Anglo-Saxon model, which focuses on short-term return. Financial culture, however, has long passed this primitive stage of institutional evolution and created the so-called German model, with a long-term perspective and a heavy role for development banking. In the first years of the transition, the Hungarian banking sector was directed toward the old English model, in a period when the legitimacy of that model was also under fire in England (Hutton 1995). It should not have been a surprise, therefore, that the asset-market approach, which treats stock markets as the only mechanism for allocating capital, proved to be particularly inadequate for transitional economies.

The choice of obsolete models was not the only problem of Hungarian privatization. These drawbacks were combined with the postcommunist legacy of informal coordination. Thus the elusiveness of property rights that is typical for an insider-dominated system was not avoided in Hungary. Large enterprises maintained major ownership stakes in the commercial banks, which, in principle, could have strengthened the developmental aspects of transition economics. The intertwining of banks and firms, however, prevented market competition from functioning as written in the textbooks and delayed the introduction of financial discipline to a later phase of the transition. Between 1988 and 1992, the amount of interfirm debt (or "queuing") increased to nearly unmanageable levels. Sorting out the related problems consumed hundreds of billions of forints under the ministership of Iván Szabó, and some hidden financial time bombs were left behind for the later period as well.

Some economists argued that the opportunities for abuse during large-scale restructuring could have been avoided if the new market economy could have grown out of a genuine small entrepreneurship. Advocacy of small-scale ownership, however, has always been a transitory policy or situation in history, no matter whether it arose from the ideology of people's capitalism or the principles of petit-bourgeois socialism. The common example of this is the privatization policy of the Conservative government of Britain in the 1980s (stocks and council apartments). However, Hungary had its own examples, such as the transitory creation of small-scale private enterprise, like the communist-led land reform in 1945.

During the Hungarian transition, the idea of popular shares and other forms of small-scale ownership had some appeal for the people, but it never dominated the agenda. "Finding the real owner" was a widely popularized slogan, and this real owner was personalized by respected entrepreneurs like Péter Zwack or János Palotás. The first name represented international experience and the second provided a remarkable example of the Hungarian private businessman who had cultivated his firm with success in the shadow of the giant state socialist economy.

The moral decline of the entrepreneur in the Hungarian public discourse can be charted from Palotás to Prisztás. The latter was the first major victim of gang violence in Budapest, following some disturbances in the illegal oil trade. The day after József Prisztás was executed by his rivals, the newspapers told stories about his involvement in dirty businesses and called him "the alleged mafia leader." The lawyers of the family, however, demanded corrections, saying that the person who was called "mafia leader" by the papers had never been accused of any crime by any court. As a result of the legal clarification, the papers started to write about Prisztás as "the well-known entrepreneur."

József Prisztás became a nationally known figure only after his death. What really undermined the moral standing of the entrepreneur in Hungary was the case of some individuals who had been celebrated as successful examples of a new era just a few years earlier. József Stadler, an agricultural businessman who used his profits to sponsor a soccer club and to build a stadium in the middle of the *puszta* (i.e. grassland plains region, mainly in the southeast of Hungary), was later convicted for tax fraud.[2] János Palotás himself was similarly accused for tax fraud, and the judge who dropped the issue was suspended from his job. József Lupis, the owner of a large stockbroker firm, was found guilty. In the early 1990s, he wasted a part of the funds of the defense and education ministries and of some major state-owned companies. Péter Kunos, managing director of Agrobank, was arrested in 1994 and sentenced to two years in jail in 1998. Iván Kelemen, head of the once powerful Kordax Rt, also belongs to the group that fell from grace, because of the confusion about the tax and customs practices of his oil trade firm. Finally, Gábor Princz, chairman and chief executive of Postabank—the second-largest savings bank in the country—joined the group of shame when the entire management team of the bank was suspended on accusation of illegal practices and misleading the stockholders.

Thus, by the mid-1990s, the meanings of "businessman" and "criminal" had strongly converged. For a while, it was believed that the total criminalization of the market economy experienced in the former Soviet republics could be avoided in East-Central Europe. Of course, the extent to which various mafia groups have captured the "commanding heights" of the Russian economy has no parallel in Hungary, the Czech Republic or Poland. Nevertheless, the optimism that a rapid and unfettered privatization program could bring the legal and moral status of the ECE economies closer to Western Europe has faded away.

Conventional economists would suggest that one must separate the economic and moral sides of the new system. One is not responsible for the other—the new market economy must be judged not on its morality but on its efficiency. This, however, would not result in a great improvement in the balance sheet of privatization. The most important factor of the transformational recession, as it was described by Kornai, was the dwindling propensity to invest. The new owners, partly due to the surviving uncertainties in the new system, often turned out to be very reluctant to modernize production and gained their yield purely through tax evasion and lay-offs. In terms of economic performance, the new system failed the same way as in the moral area.

Agriculture was the sector that suffered the most devastating consequences of the uncertainty created by the general transfer of ownership. In 1992, the output of Hungarian agriculture declined by a quarter, and in 1993 by a further 8%. To some extent, the collapse in demand was a reason for this decline, given the disintegration of CMEA markets for Hungarian agricultural produce and the shrinking domestic purchasing power. More importantly, however, this output decline was a consequence of the collapse of the supply side. Collective and state farms stopped investing in the land because they did not expect themselves to be owners by the middle of the decade. When small-scale private ownership emerged, however, the new private farmers lacked the know-how and information about the tendencies of production and of the markets.

While in the 1980s the total grain production of Hungary was about 13–14 million tons, in the late 1990s this figure stabilized at about 11 million tons. In recent decades, Hungarian agricultural producers have used about 2.7–2.8 million hectares to produce grain. Between 1986 and 1990, on average some 5.6 tons of grain were produced per hectare. Ten years later this specific figure was 1 ton less. In the meantime, the ton-per-hectare indicators continuously improved in the European Union. The best grain producers of Western Europe—the French and the Dutch—produced more than 7 tons per hectare. The obvious reason for the declining performance was that the distribution of landed property in the 1990s was less capable of grain production. During the ten years of transition, the fertilizer consumption of the new Hungarian agricultural sector shrank to one third of the earlier quantity (Raskó 1998: 21).

Though privatization was carried out in a most damaging way, those who doubt its historic necessity are also wrong. Privatization in Hungary, as in other FSCs, became inevitable because the systems of central planning—even its reformed versions—were incapable of responding to the world economic crisis by an appropriate restructuring of the economy. Privatization became unavoidable given that the government bureaucracies of state socialism had failed in this crucial area. Without conscious government policies, however, privatization itself cannot help in progressive economic reconstruction either. Privatization should thus not be seen as a necessary precondition of a new economic recovery, but rather as an inevitable consequence of a type of government failure.

The assumption that privatization is a good thing but was politicized and mismanaged in Hungary is wrong. The point is that privatization is by definition a political process that requires great economic and social expenses. These costs can be minimized in principle, but the postcommunist countries of Eastern Europe did not concentrate on maximizing benefits from ownership reforms and minimizing the losses it caused. The collapse of state socialism created new political elite groups that were linked to social forces concerned about their own gains instead of the pursuit of the public good.

Ironically enough, the new political parties of Hungary claimed that they were taking over power from the communists on behalf of the people, but the people were never seriously considered by them as potential owners of enterprises. The idea of workers' self-management—the most radical form of socialist ownership—never reached the level of government, though it did surface in national politics occasionally. In 1989, self-management was an explicit objective of some of the workers' councils. The latter were under the intellectual influence of some anti-Stalinist Marxist activists in the Left Alternative Association; this was also a major force behind the People's Democracy Platform of the MSZMP and later of the MSZP. Mainstream economists in East and West claimed that such initiatives were inadequate answers to the challenges of the era, though it should not necessarily been seen that way. As Elster explains,

the idea of cooperative ownership is rooted in a conception of justice that can provide the necessary motivation. The extension of equality from the political and social realms to the economic domain is bound to come up against many vested interests that will slow down the rate of progress. Owners will offer pseudosolutions and rituals of participation to buy time. Labor unions will resist this encroachment on their authority....these will be seen as rearguard actions. At the very least, it makes sense to argue for cooperative ownership. It aims at doing away with the most important remnants of authority and hierarchy in society. [Elster 1989: 216]

Moves toward cooperative or workers' ownership would have required an active labor movement aimed at taking over the decisions over its own fate. As we see later in this chapter, the labor movement in Hungary was not in any condition to have a significant impact on industrial policies. Cooperative and other forms of popular ownership did not arise to a significant extent in the economic transformation of Hungary. The most distinctive feature of Hungarian ownership reform was the outstanding proportion of foreign capital involved in the privatization process.

The Role of Foreign Investment

The outstanding weight of foreign investment has been a main distinctive feature of Hungarian privatization, as opposed to postcommunist privatization in other countries (see Appendix 2, Table 7). Selling state-owned enterprises to foreign owners became a practice under the last MSZMP government in 1989 and continued with no significant interruption throughout the 1990s. Mainstream economic thought suggested that Hungarians did the right thing by opening up to foreign capital investment, while a good many alternative thinkers claimed that it should be seen as something of a failure to hand over large segments of the national economy to foreign owners.

Were Hungarians simply more astute than others? Or were they more stupid when they forgot about the dangers of foreign ownership and gave everything away at a lower than reasonable price? Judging simply on the basis of the share of foreign investment in the national economy is not necessarily the right way to evaluate this Hungarian specialty in privatization. However, the taking into account of both quantitative and qualitative factors, and particularly the search for reasons for the special Hungarian policies, is an inevitable process if we want to develop a balanced picture.

The main reasons for Hungary jumping ahead of other East European countries in order to attract foreign capital were the heavy indebtedness of the country in the 1990s and the fact that most of the economic bureaucracy had become interested in a privatization process with foreign involvement. The country had been locked in a foreign debt trap since the end of the 1970s, but the ruling MSZMP only had a limited circle of policy instruments to tackle the crisis. They wanted to escape from the debt trap without pressing down the average living standards of the workers, and also without too heavy centralization of economic management. They launched a wave of market reforms instead; however, until the end of the 1980s, the political leadership was unprepared to sell state property to private investors—foreign or domestic. In 1988, preparations were made to launch socialist privatization; it was realized that this process could contribute to debt management if extended to foreign buyers.

For socialists other than market socialists, privatization to domestic or foreign owners was the least desirable policy, but it was made acceptable because the alternative was to cut back domestic consumption even more drastically. Privatization to foreign owners was not favored by nationalists either, because they would have preferred the cultivation of a national bourgeoisie, even if this required the political exclusion of foreign rivals. The latter, however, could have undermined the domestic legitimacy and the international acceptability of Hungarian privatization, so no drastic measures were made against the inflow of foreign capital—either under Socialists or under conservative nationalists. In East-Central Europe, Hungary proved the least reluctant to sell the so-called "crown jewels" as well.

Once it had become a strategy to import foreign capital, the government had to find out how the interest of potential investors could be increased and how the inflow could be accelerated. The question concerned not simply increasing the number of foreign firms and the total value of foreign investment, but also securing a leading role for Hungary in the capital movements of East-Central Europe. A prominent aim of the Hungarian governments and the financial elite was to make Hungary the financial center of East-Central Europe by beating Prague, Warsaw and perhaps even Vienna in this race. Government policy attempted to convince multinationals to establish their regional centers in Budapest.

Management textbooks suggested that tax breaks and provision for the infrastructure are the best means available to a government for attracting foreign capital. Infrastructure, however, often means much more than roads or communications networks. According to Péter Lőrincze, secretary general of the Hungarian Chamber of Commerce, the availability of golf courses, shopping malls and foreign language schools are usually among the most important factors that can convince foreign businessmen to bring their firms to a particular place, inasmuch as such facilities can provide occupation and entertainment for the foreign entrepreneurs, their wives and their children.

Having seen the main ends and means of Hungarian policy, it is also necessary to ask why foreign capital did not move into other FSCs. Countries with no substantial foreign debt in 1989—such as Czechoslovakia and Romania—did not feel the same need as Hungary to overcome the balance of payments crisis through capital import. Their governments had time to think about the best way to restructure nationalized industries. On the other hand, Poland, similarly to Hungary, embarked on the transition with a heavy debt burden; however, the Polish government managed to get rid of half of this debt through a politically motivated debt reduction in 1991. Furthermore, the attitude of discontent of the Polish working class, so much admired by Western sympathizers in the 1980s, became a factor that was negatively judged by foreign investors looking for a disciplined labor force. Despite the fact that the population of Poland is three times larger than that of Hungary, the amount of foreign capital inflow matched the Hungarian level only in 1997.

Thus the Hungarian share of foreign capital inflow not only looks high because of the actual scale of foreign investments in Hungary but also because the level of such flows to other FSCs, despite optimistic expectations, remained extremely low. Until the mid-1990s, half of the foreign investment going to the FSCs of Eastern Europe went to Hungary. In the second half of the decade, as privatization accelerated in other countries of the region, this ratio started to decline, though not dramatically.

The number of countries that appeared as sources of capital import to Hungary was about 33–35 in 1996. According to the number of enterprises, the order of countries was Germany, China, Austria, United States, Italy and the Commonwealth of Independent States (CIS). However, the total value of invested capital shows a different order: Germany, Austria, United States, the Netherlands, France, Belgium, Switzerland, Cyprus and the CIS (Pitti 1998: 16). These lists differ from those of the early 1990s, when the United States appeared as a leading source of capital inflow to Hungary.

Of course, foreign investors targeted particular industries where the prospects of profitability were higher than elsewhere (see Appendix 2, Table 6). Thus their representation exceeded the national average in telecommunications (62.8%), manufacturing industry (50.9%), retail trade (36.0%), financial services (43.7%) as well as real estate affairs. Their share remained low in agriculture (6.2%), transportation (4.6%) and, despite the vast sales at the end of 1995, in energy supply as well (21.4%).

With the involvement of foreign investors in privatization, Hungary also entered the era of multinational corporations (MNCs). From their point of view, market growth and low-cost production have been the major motivating factors in buying Hungarian firms or bringing new units to Hungary. Some prominent representatives of the first type have been Henkel, Unilever, Parmalat and GE. The second type of MNC motivation was displayed by Electrolux, Samsung, Audi and Ford.

As with any other country that has opened up to foreign multinational firms, a recurring debate also emerged in Hungary about the increasing role of MNCs in the national economy. Advocates of MNCs argued that they would bring civilized economic conduct and the advanced technology that the domestic agents had been unable to produce. "Catching up with the West is the easiest if the Westerners come here and tell us how to do it" was the opinion of many modernizers. Opening up to the multinationals was also seen as a policy that could accelerate our accession to various Western organizations, like the OECD, NATO and eventually the European Union.

Opponents of foreign privatization suggested that the more control foreigners had over large sections of the economy, the less room there would be for a Hungarian middle class. Nationalists argued that it would be a historic tragedy to make Hungarians the servants or wage-slaves of Western capitalists. The fear of foreigners was fueled by the experience of the recent decades, in which multinationals had established "footloose firms" in developing countries without a long-term interest in the modernization and prosperity of the entire economy and society. The debate over the legitimacy of foreign ownership became extremely sharp in the case of agriculture, since the right-wing nationalist parties from Fidesz–MPP to the MIÉP became united on the platform that no foreign person should be allowed to buy Hungarian land.[3] Moderate protectionists modified this demand by saying that no such privatization should occur until Hungary joins the European Union.

In the debate on the role of MNCs, it was often forgotten that multinationals can only use or abuse the regulations provided by the host government itself. If that government allows the MNCs to skim the yield of productive sectors, then they will do it. If the government provides benefits to foreign investors, for whatever considerations, they will take advantage of those. The unfortunate fact that the entire sugar industry, similarly to the seed oil industry, was sold as one unit in Hungary was not a nasty act of multinationals but a failure of the Antall government. Despite the nationalist rhetoric of the latter, it allowed virtual monopolies to fall into foreign private hands. The National Competition Office—a Hungarian equivalent of the British Mergers and Monopolies Commission—turned a blind eye to these cases, saying that its authority did not cover the operations of foreign investments.

Nevertheless, if the intention was there, it was possible to sell entire industries to foreign owners and maintain competition at the same time. The beer industry has been such a positive example, since the seven major Hungarian breweries were sold to seven different owners, including German, Austrian, Dutch, South African and other investors. The quality and assortment of available beer rapidly improved. The competition has helped to keep beer price increases at the rate of general inflation. Nevertheless, due to the overall decline in the purchasing power of the working population, the consumption of beer has declined among the lower- and middle-income layers. (Hungarians drank 30% less beer in 1999 than in 1989.)

All postcommunist governments have been criticized at various times for being reluctant in foreign privatization, despite the fact that foreign ownership has become a dominant part of the economy in only half a decade. Foreign investors have been successful in choosing the more successful segments and have run them efficiently; on average, foreign-owned companies have been significantly more productive and profitable than Hungarian-owned ones. In 1996, just above a quarter of Hungarian employees (26.2%) were employed by foreign-owned firms whose net receipts amounted to close to half (44.6%) of the total. These companies provided more than two thirds (68%) of the total value of exports. Their share was 45% in the total capital stock and in the total costs and expenditures, while their net profits and dividends and bonuses represented 76.6% of the total. Apart from internal factors, government assistance has played an important role in achieving this successful performance. The same circle of firms received 96.3% of the tax breaks and paid only 40.4% of the taxes on companies. Due to the strong performance and favorable regulations, the foreign-owned sector has been able to grow more rapidly than the rest of the economy. The increase in their own capital (49.6%) exceeded their share in the total capital stock (Pitti 1998: 31).

The fact that foreign firms operate successfully in the national economy does not contradict the fact that this economy is and continues to be an underdeveloped one, and thus belongs to the periphery or semiperiphery of the world system. Opening up to foreign investment and to the expansion of multinationals is not simply an economic policy of a particular country but part of the emergence of a new international division of labor (Radice 1995: 283). The latter started to take shape in the 1960s and in the subsequent decades reallocated the units of production on a global scale. The global economy has become more integrated than before, but this process has not abolished the huge developmental gaps within the world system.

In underdeveloped countries, a significantly large section of the labor force does not work on the basis of any formal contract. In former colonies, it usually implies the existence of a traditional sector, which represents a permanent pool of labor for the relatively more advanced sector that is linked to the world markets. In the Hungarian case, the duality of labor and the economy is highlighted by the so-called shadow economy. This sector has always existed to some extent, even in the period of the most centralized planned system. However, the proliferation of small and semilegal enterprises started in the early 1980s, when the increasing financial problems forced the communist leadership to make concessions that ran counter to the principles of central planning.

Economic analysts have not paid too much attention to the coincidence of the emergence of the debt crisis and that of the small enterprise sector. By not linking the two together and by connecting neither of them to the analysis of an underdeveloped status, the illusion was created that this enterprise sector could provide a strong basis for the future private economy. For instance, in his famous manifesto, János Kornai (1989) suggested that the Hungarian economy had one healthy sector and one sick sector: the first was the emerging private economy, and the second was the ailing public one.

Following Hayek's ideas, the reform economists of the 1980s suggested that the introduction of the market would automatically eliminate the corrupt tendencies in the national economy and politics and would raise the standard of morality. In reality, we have experienced the total opposite of this. Everybody knows that the privatization process has been inseparably linked to corruption, and many of the new private entrepreneurs live from tax fraud. Thousands of enterprises have been established just in order to write off living costs of families, and entrepreneurs who have officially never made any profits drive luxury cars and spend their holidays in Cyprus or Abu Dabhi.

The former state firms, now in private hands, and the newly fabricated private companies have made practically no significant contribution to the national budget. In order to tackle this problem, the nationalist government introduced a so-called "minimum tax," which was later abolished by the Socialist–Liberal government. This is not the only example of the lack of clear policies in relation to the so-called shadow economy. The latter is, on the one hand, perceived as a way to avoid due payments to the state, but, on the other hand, it is also recognized as a protective layer for that part of society which is unable to live from the official market economy, which is supposed to be protected by the law.

In our "emerging economy," as it is usually called in the neoliberal newspeak, the financial sector has practically no limits to accumulating wealth for institutions and individuals. The government cannot and does not want to control their incomes, because in such a case they would immediately be accused of obstructing the emergence of the market economy. Employees in Budapest banks, for instance, have practically "joined Europe" and may easily forget how the rest of society lives.

The new regional patterns of economic development also suggest that the national framework and integration have lost their importance. Some parts of the country are becoming integrated into the international flows, while others are left idle in the conditions of high unemployment and industrial decline. The region benefiting from the new geography is the capital city and the zones to the west of it, which means that ours may become very similar to the geographic character of Washington D.C., inasmuch as only the northwestern quarter will be considered a safe and desirable area in which to live.

All the major greenfield investments in the automotive industry, for example (General Motors, Suzuki and Audi), have been located in northwestern Hungary. Similarly to other ex-socialist countries, industrial policy has sometimes appeared on the agenda, while regional policy has not even been discussed seriously. It has appeared as insignificant compared to issues like privatization, price reform and the attraction of inward investment. "The new governments lacked the capacity and experience to attempt to guide such investment as a tool of regional policy" (Sadler and Swain 1994: 387).

In recent decades, semiperipheral countries have been more likely to go toward the extremes of neoliberalism than those at the core of the world system. An example of such extremes is the privatization of public utilities, and particularly their sale to foreign owners. Countries like Argentina pioneered this policy, and Hungary followed suit at the end of 1995 under the Socialist–Liberal government. The major purchasers were German companies, but French and Italian involvement was also significant. The government initiated the sales as a form of "debt equity swap"—the sales revenue was used to repay foreign debts and reduce the exposure of the country to foreign creditors.[4] After the decision was made, some experts raised concerns about the weakness of regulatory power and the likely repatriation of profits. However, financial interest proved to be by far the strongest argument.

Apart from asymmetrical financial linkages, various channels of external political influence have also become part of the core–periphery relationship. The most apparent institution of dominance is the group of multilateral financial agencies that control all the major decisions of the dependent governments. The hands of the IMF and the World Bank also became visible in Hungary. The Antall government was forced to sign two Structural Adjustment Programs with the Bank in 1990 and 1991. When the MSZP–SZDSZ government was inaugurated, it also had to work under heavy international surveillance. In July 1994, an IMF delegation arrived at Budapest. No substantial information was given to the press about the purpose of their visit, but during and after those days the government announced an 8% devaluation of the forint, the cancelation of the World Expo scheduled for 1996 and plans to cut government expenditures in the welfare systems.

The major speech of prime minister Horn about the need to make social sacrifices for the sake of modernization coincided with the celebration in Madrid of the 50th anniversary of the IMF and the World Bank. One month later a modification of the annual budget was passed by parliament, just a few days before the managing director of the IMF, Michel Camdessus, visited Horn in

Budapest. The March visit of the IMF delegation was preceded by the announcement of a very severe austerity package by the new finance minister, Bokros. The arrival of an IMF delegation at the end of August coincided with a coalition crisis, when the Socialists and the Free Democrats almost split over the nomination of the trade union leader Sándor Nagy for the position of deputy prime minister or minister of the economy.

In addition to the leverage exercised by the creditors and their representatives, foreign investors have also become a major political lobbying group in Hungary. In the mid-1990s, the previously independent political scientist Iván Völgyes (University of Nebraska) became an official representative of General Electric in Hungary. During the 1998 election campaign, he became a spokesperson for the ten largest foreign investors in Hungary, and he presented their view on the chances and outcome of the elections. With stable foreign exchange reserves and a decreasing foreign debt, Hungary was out of the debt trap and no longer needed either the money or the guidance of the IMF. At the same time, however, the multinationals started to act as an independent interest group and continued to be symbols of external dependency.

LABOR: HEAVY ADJUSTMENT

Working people and their unions have been at the "receiving end" of capitalist restoration in Hungary. They have faced the emerging mass unemployment at a level never seen by any active labor force in the country. The purchasing power of wages rapidly declined, and the unions were unable to do anything to save jobs or real wages. The slow and uneven recovery after 1993 resulted in an improvement in some regions and some internationally competitive industries, while leaving much of the working class in misery and with very little hope.

Employment, Wages and Living Standards

The first years of transition brought about a dramatic decline in output. Between 1989 and 1993, GDP declined by some 20% (see Appendix 2, Table 1). Within the same period, the rate of unemployment increased from 0.2% to 13% of the labor force. After 1993, the country experienced more or less steady growth in production, but the rate of unemployment only fell to about 10% and remained so in the second half of the 1990s.

All transition countries in East-Central Europe, with the exception of the Czech Republic, were faced with a double-digit unemployment rate within a very short period (1–2 years). At the end of 1994, about 2.8 million people were jobless in Poland—an unemployment rate of 16%. In Slovakia 370,000 people (14.6%) were registered as unemployed, in Bulgaria around 500,000 (13%), in Romania more than 1.2 million (10.9%), in Hungary 520,000 (10.4%), while in the Czech Republic the number of unemployed remained very low (170,000 people—3.2%) (Fassmann 1997: 170).

In Hungary, the rise in the number of unemployed from 10,000 to 600,000 in four years came as a shock—in some respects worse than the impact of the Great Depression. As compared to West European standards, 10–12% unemployment would not be seen as exceptionally high, but in former socialist countries this dramatic emergence of mass unemployment was a new experience for the working class, and it found labor market institutions totally unprepared to deal with a problem of this scale and nature.

Furthermore, the 600,000 newly unemployed were accompanied by another 700,000 who also left the labor force in the first transition years. Altogether, the Hungarian economy employed 1.5 million people fewer in the late 1990s than in the late 1980s. Patterns of leaving the labor force were distinguished by age and gender characteristics. Older workers could go into early retirement, young people could postpone their entry by extending their studies, and women could go "back to the household." For a few years, disability pensions also provided an outlet.

In Hungary, half of the jobless fell into the category of the long-term unemployed.[5] The return of the unemployed to employment remained low, and many of the long-term unemployed simply fell out of the statistics. Despite the recovery after the transition shock, there was no significant improvement in long-term unemployment, since the short-term unemployed have always had a better chance of getting new jobs.

The problem of unemployment in transition economies was as much due to institutional causes as to macroeconomic ones. In the state socialist economy, internal labor markets played a much greater role in the allocation of labor than did occupational labor markets. The transition disintegrated the first and thus caused a shift toward the second, but without the proper institutional arrangements for a rapid response to the unemployment shock.

When, under Kádár, ignorance and irresponsibility had been aspects of the official policy, it was widely believed that "some unemployment" would help to discipline the labor force. Instead of "some unemployment," however, the transition made joblessness familiar to almost every family. Nevertheless, one may say that employment and industrial relations remained within "civilized standards" despite the drama. The witholding of wages, which became common in postcommunist Russia, did not become a practice in Hungary, apart from some small examples in largely foreign-owned companies.

Unemployment showed great regional disparities. In the capital city Budapest it hardly ever grew above 3–4%, while in some villages of the northeast the rate reached 40–50%. It was particularly in these hard-hit areas that the so-called second economy took away the pressure of unemployment, though the emergence of a grey zone between the legal and illegal economies has become a nationwide phenomenon. According to widespread estimates, some 30% of the entire output was provided by the unmeasured second economy.[6]

When the first large-scale redundancies occurred in 1989, the prevailing ideology suggested that the vitality of the new market economy would rapidly eliminate the problem. Entrepreneurship would be encouraged, and, if necessary, the state would help private entrepreneurs reemploy workers who had been made redundant by bankrupt state industries. The chances of finding new employment would be increased by state-financed retraining programs, and those temporarily unemployed would be assisted by generous benefits.

Indeed, the starting level of unemployment benefits was relatively high in most East-European transition countries. After 1992, however, when conditions became tougher in these countries, the amount and duration of these benefits were reduced, and the requirements for eligibility were raised. In Hungary, the entitlement period was cut from 18 months to one year at the end of 1992, and the replacement ratio (the proportion of the unemployment benefit in relation to the last wage) also started to fall. In 1999, the Orbán government further reduced the entitlement period, to just nine months.

Those who lost their unemployment benefits were entitled to income support from the local government. In 1992, close to 500,000 Hungarians received unemployment benefits. In the middle of the 1990s, both groups (unemployment benefit and income support receivers) totaled about 200,000 persons.

A minimum wage was also introduced as another income protection policy of the new era. In Eastern Europe, 60% of the mean wage was the average level of the minimum wage in the starting period. Similarly to unemployment benefits, the minimum wage levels also declined as the transition proceeded, and due to the high rates of inflation they often fell below the subsistence level. At the end of 1999, the minimum monthly wage was less than the equivalent of U.S.$100.

Active employment policies in the first period of transition appeared more in the rhetoric than in actual measures. All the leading political parties paid lip-service to the need for active labor market policies while in reality they were waiting for the post-transition recovery to eliminate the mounting problems. Of the former socialist countries, only the Czech Republic pursued a deliberate though somewhat hazardous policy of employment maintenance, through various forms of government intervention. When Poland and Hungary started to treat employment as a more serious issue, they favored retraining and public works projects instead of tighter labor regulation.

To distinguish between active and passive labor market policies, in the first years of the transition, the Hungarian policy was to create two funds to address the problem. The Solidarity Fund was established simply to provide an income for the unemployed in the first period after they were laid off, and the Employment Fund was set up to finance direct job creation. Since, however, the remainder from one fund could not be transferred into the other, the two funds were merged in 1996 as a new Labor Fund. This was seen as providing a financial basis for a more comprehensive labor market policy.

Government policy also attempted to involve nongovernmental organizations in the process of job creation. To encourage such activities among NGOs, the Ministry of Labor set up the National Employment Foundation (OFA) in June

1992. The OFA gave financial support to foundations devoted to job creation, subsidized local initiatives and other nonprofit organizations aimed at reducing unemployment, encouraged research projects on labor-market problems, gave financial support to experimental measures not covered by the Employment Act and financed the creation of employment companies in regions where the likelihood of massive redundancies threatened. The OFA started to work in 1993, but its funding was cut in 1994 because of the increasing budget deficit. Despite the complications, it has contributed to easing the pressure on certain target groups, like the unemployed youth and the Roma (Romanies).

Public works, like other labor market policies, were widely advertised in certain periods, but they only had a marginal effect on the employment picture. In 1993, only 14% of the resources spent on active measures were used to finance public works projects. They mainly involved unskilled and young people, though it was soon realized that public works could not resolve the problems of the young unemployed; it was realized that their long-term chances could only be improved by better and more competitive training.

Training, however, was also seen as a controversial policy, given that the question of what jobs to train people for was hard to answer amidst a deep recession and economic uncertainty. When national economic policy abandoned any attempts to forecast and influence structural tendencies in the economy by leaving decisions to blind market forces, training programs were left without adequate guidelines. The very nature of the economic transition and the contemporary technological revolution, however, gave some directions to the retraining courses, by making marketing, advertising and computer programming the most popular subjects. Research showed that reemployment among labor-market trainees was relatively high, and a major problem of this policy area was that the most vulnerable and least advantaged groups of society were largely left out of the scope of retraining opportunities.

Training and retraining has been an area where public and private cooperation became possible. Due to the import of second-hand know-how from Western schools and vast subsidies from the Employment Fund, vocational training became a very profitable sector in Hungary. Due to the lack of transparency and coherence in the newly emerging sphere of vocational training, an inflation of certificates of dubious market value occurred in the 1990s, partly due to the lack of proper regulation.

Altogether, active labor market policies had only a marginal effect on employment, and governments were also unsuccessful in reducing the costs of unemployment. Unemployment, however, helped the government to reduce the costs of labor. The representation of those employed weakened significantly, and the unemployed were left without any institutionalized voice.

The emerging unemployment rapidly reached a level that also began to contribute to a sharp decline of purchasing power. When unemployment, or even the threat of lay-offs, started to function as brakes on wage increases, governments could easily abandon central wage regulation (under Antall) and make the forint convertible (under Horn) without the threat of labor causing any significant imbalance or instability. Thus, a clear macroeconomic impact of mass unemployment was that it also helped to curb the wage claims of the workers at the micro and macro levels. Though finance ministers always spoke about the threat of a wage–price spiral, such a danger did not really exist after the first years of transition. Even amidst the recovery periods of the 1990s, the threat of wage increases boosting inflation remained negligible.

The emergence of mass unemployment was thus another factor that forced the family to become the major scene of economic adjustment. In the very first years of the transition, price liberalization made families adjust to rising inflation. As home building was phased out from the public sector, families had to take over the burden of housing too. As higher and higher prices were charged for health care and education, the family budget had to be restructured again and again. And finally, if someone was laid off within the narrower or wider family, their support also became a household duty—similarly to those on a pension—since the real value of pensions was (and remains) low.

The categories of "unemployed" and "pensioners" were vague not only at the family level but also at the national level. To create an easy outlet for those facing unemployment, the policies of the early 1990s made it extremely easy to seek early retirement, or even disability retirement. The tension of the labor market eased as a result, but this policy increased the pressure on the national pension fund and thus contributed to a strengthening campaign for an overall marketization of the pension system.

The increasing adjustment burden of families manifested itself as a gender problem too. Most of the household duties fell on women, yet it was also women who were able to keep their jobs at a higher level. In Hungary, significantly more men became unemployed than women, not just because women were more likely to leave the labor force and withdraw to the household but also because among those remaining on the job market women had received more competitive training—an atavism of Kádárist education patterns.

Under the increasing burden of multiple adjustment, the Hungarian household was heading toward complete bankruptcy in the second half of the 1990s. Some of the burdens had a delayed or creeping effect on household resources, and the recovery of 1997 saved the financial survival of many who had been threatened by a financial collapse. In the very same period, however, the increasing energy prices started to bite, and the government also cracked down on arrears on home loans. The fairness of the extraordinary austerity measures was widely discussed in parliament, without reaching a proper conclusion before the 1998 elections.

A great majority of Roma families fell into the group that quickly reached the limits of financial adjustability. Far beyond being a labor problem, the conditions of the Roma population of Hungary became perhaps the most complicated social problem in the postcommunist period. The Roma population combined all different features that has made them the greatest single loser group of the transition. Unskilled workers were first and foremost hit by unemployment, and the latter had particularly devastating effects on the northeastern region. Low-income workers and large families were overexposed to the impact of inflation and the erosion of state subsidies. Roma people, the largest single ethnic minority in Hungary, were largely unskilled, employed for a low wage, overrepresented in the northeastern counties, and they have relatively large families. They were thus caught in the cross-fire of postcommunist economic adjustment. As victims of the transition, they had to rely increasingly on state subsidies, for which they were portrayed—by outspoken political commentators—as parasites on the decent working Hungarian nation. It was not difficult to blame the largest victim group for the overall economic hardships, and this provided fuel for a new round of Hungarian racism.

The Roma population of East-Central Europe was the only social group that made the news in relation to mass migration toward the West in the postcommunist era. Indeed, contrary to widespread expectations, a large-scale migration of redundant East European labor did not begin after the collapse of state socialist employment. Expectations based on neoclassical economic considerations suggested that once the barriers to the movement of people fell between areas of highly different income levels, a flow of labor would begin, and it would continue until the reaching of an equilibrium had been reached. There are, however, a number of factors in operation that prevent the materialization of such a neoclassical scenario (Fassman 1997: 178).

Local unemployment was seen as temporary in the early transition years. Even if expectations were more pessimistic, the lack of information and particularly the lack of well-established ethnic networks made migration more risky and less attractive. The lack of an effective housing market is also a significant material constraint on the movement of people in Central Europe. Furthermore, large-scale and long-term unemployment itself is not enough to make people migrate; employed people are more likely to move than unemployed, simply because they tend to be more employable, and they also move if there are particular jobs available. In the 1990s, however, Western Europe has also been struggling with exceptionally high rates of unemployment, and this seriously discouraged East European workers from leaving their own countries. Finally, administrative and political factors have also indicated that East European migrants would not necessarily be welcome in Austria, Germany and other Western countries.

The rise of mass unemployment itself was a dramatic shock to Hungarian society. The impact of this shock was, however, largely aggravated by the circumstance that many state socialist welfare policies were attached to jobs. Such policies included the access to medical and dental treatment, subsidized food, kindergarten, and various recreation facilities. When workers lost their jobs by the thousand during the postcommunist transition, they and their families also lost such entitlements, without the possibility of compensation. Thus, the changing pattern of employment resulted not just in increased industrial conflict, but also in a widening debate about the system of social policy, and about the role of the state in general.

Price increases and job losses have been interpreted in the past six years as a price well worth paying for future membership in the European Union. While the rate of unemployment has become stagnant at a level that is considered to be normal in Western Europe (just above 10% in official statistics), the rate of inflation has remained above 20% in Hungary for seven years, and even higher in most of the "transition" countries. The runaway inflation has largely been driven by governments, with the deliberate objective to redistribute incomes and wealth along capitalist principles.

The requirements of capitalist accumulation have made governments wage a war on the living standards of the working population. Deliberate choices and the general institutional anarchy of the transition period have made the pressure on real wages permanent and inevitable. A typical example of the "new thinking" occurred, when, half a year after a very severe austerity program had been introduced in Hungary in March 1995, the finance minister claimed that since real wages had been pushed down by 10%, the competitiveness of the national economy was being restored. This is, again, a typical peripheral way of thinking, inasmuch as no other instrument for increasing international economic competitiveness is taken into account other than the reduction of labor costs. The temporary character of such revivals also remains hidden most of the time.

László Békesi, one of the finance ministers of the Socialist–Liberal government, echoing World Bank rhetoric, often claimed that "the Hungarian people have been living well beyond their means." He was mocked even by managers of some multinationals for his attempts to impose wage restraint on private foreign companies. Simultaneously, World Bank documents took over a phrase coined by János Kornai declaring that the Hungarian social security system was a "premature welfare state." This qualification was identical with a death sentence being placed upon this premature being (notwithstanding the fact that Napoleon and other geniuses were also born premature).

While both private and social consumption have dropped dramatically over the past six years, official economic slogans justified the permanent austerity by the alleged "overconsumption" of the population. Regardless of their colors, no government has been able to stop the meltdown of the vast middle class created and maintained by the regulatory and redistributive policies of state socialism. Both the number and the proportion of the population living below the poverty line have increased rapidly. According to Professor Peter Townsend (1995), the dramatic rise of poverty in Eastern Europe is the latest manifestation of global polarization.

No matter how unattractive were the political systems that operated under state socialism in various countries of Eastern Europe, it seems now certain that the system did provide a certain level of social stability, and the sudden loss of social security has already resulted in a demographic breakdown. According to UNICEF figures, in Russia, Ukraine, Bulgaria, Hungary and Poland the excess mortality caused by the "systemic change" has reached a shocking total of 800,000 between the years 1989 and 1993 (Petras and Vieux 1995: 1). The rise in heart and circulatory diseases has accounted for a proportion of the increases in deaths, ranging from 32% to 80%, respectively. As in all ex-socialist countries, life expectancy for Hungarian males has fallen to 64 years (see Appendix 2, Table 9), one of the lowest in Europe; however, it is, ironically, just above the level at which the retirement age was set for the second half of the 1990s.

While the working classes of Eastern Europe have been suffering severe attacks on their living standards, antisocial demagoguery accused them of excessive demands and of threatening the glorious transition to the modern and democratic world. State bureaucrats and the new economic aristocrats did not hesitate to blame inflation on wage pressure, while proudly talking about the swimming pools they have just built in the gardens of their new country houses. The main reason these people have not been aware of the consequences of their conduct is the weakness of labor representation.

Trade Unions in Decline

The world of labor representation has gone through a fundamental transformation over the last decade in Hungary. Basically, three major periods can be distinguished, in terms of political developments in the world of trade unions. These periods do not entirely follow the political cycle defined by parliamentary elections—rather, they are separated by major clashes on the trade union front. Therefore, a quick look back on the years of transformation is important in order to understand the current situation of the Hungarian trade union movement.

The first period (1988–91) can be called the period of emerging competition. Together with Fidesz, the first independent trade union was the organization that broke the monolithic structure of the state socialist polity in Hungary. When the wind of change from Moscow encouraged reforms in the satellite countries, the small opposition circles started to develop a strategy toward political pluralism. The MDF was formed by populist intellectuals in September 1987 but did not declare open disloyalty to the regime, and did not even call itself a political party, for two years. When Fidesz and the TDDSZ (Democratic Trade Union of Scientific Workers) were formed, on the other hand, they immediately proclaimed their commitment to promote a different political structure.

It was the so-called Democratic Opposition—that is, a few dozen liberal academics—who stood behind both organizations (and later created the SZDSZ). They were, of course, cautious enough not to start with a political party immediately; this would have triggered off serious repercussions, possibly retaliation, at a time when Kádár was still secretary general of the ruling Communist party (MSZMP). Launching a trade union seemed to be a practical idea. The official trade union federation, the National Council of Trade Unions (SZOT), was very unpopular for having thousands of yes-men in leading positions, and these toadies never ever attempted to play any role more significant than organizing summer vacations and Santa Claus evenings. The memory of the emergence of Solidarity in Poland was still alive, and this fueled expectations that a "trade union" could grow large enough to challenge the power of the ruling communists.

Following the emergence of a few more liberal-minded unions, the Democratic League of Independent Trade Unions (FSZDL or Liga) was created. The guidance and financial support they received from the American trade unions AFL–CIO and various other foreign sources was indeed substantial. They were not welcomed by official circles, although, with a few exceptions, they were allowed to operate without being obstructed. Since, however, public attention soon turned toward party politics, the appearance of the Liga as an alternative did not provoke a massive restructuring of the union membership.

In the year 1989, however, another significant movement emerged to encourage labor activity—this was the movement of workers' councils. It was supposed that workers' councils would appeal to the workers because of the memory of such councils from the events of 1956. Sándor Rácz, who was imprisoned for leading the 1956 workers' councils of Greater Budapest on a stubbornly anti-Soviet platform, returned to politics and even presented himself as a potential presidential candidate. (For this role, however, he would have been just too right-wing, much more so than the other potential candidate of those times, Otto von Habsburg.)

Two major tendencies fought for hegemony within the workers' council movement. One of them suggested that the councils should become organs of workers' ownership. This blueprint obviously disagreed with the mainstream of privatization schemes and suggested a reform of state ownership through democratization and decentralization. This idea was promoted by representatives of the Left Alternative Association, an independent movement of left activists, then actively working with the workers' council movement. The other tendency did not have such a position on ownership reform and, rather, proposed that the councils should simply become another branch of trade unions. They thought the "communist" unions should be replaced by workers' councils that would represent the workers themselves instead of a ruling party and the *nomenklatura*.

The debate came to a conclusion in the summer of 1990, following the election victory of the three conservative and nationalist parties. Imre Palkovics, who became a member of parliament in the MDF faction, was elected president of the National Federation of Workers' Councils. Thus the majority decided to take advantage of being linked to the major ruling party and buried the idea of workers' self-management. A small faction split from the National Federation but remained insignificant for the rest of the time.

There was a third movement among the new unions, called Solidarity. Its leader, Sándor Bátonyi, was well known for his militancy for a while. In 1991, he even took part in a hunger strike against permanent price increases and impoverishment. However, since this militant behavior was not attractive enough for most workers, Bátonyi and Solidarity were unable to gather significant support. Nevertheless, for a few years, they maintained a sporadic influence in certain mining areas and meat-processing factories.

The SZOT was perhaps the last organization of the old political structure that attempted to renew itself. It happened in March 1990, when a new name was given to the federation (National Federation of Hungarian Trade Unions— MSZOSZ). Sándor Nagy, a former lecturer in labor economics, who had been one of the chief leaders of the SZOT in the second half of the 1980s, holding various positions (and who had been, for a short while, a member of the Central Committee of the MSZMP), became president of the MSZOSZ.

During the same congress, three smaller factions split from the MSZOSZ. These were the Autonomous Trade Unions (mainly the chemical industry), the Cooperation Forum of Trade Unions (SZEF, mainly teachers), and the Trade Union Alliance of Academics (ÉSZT). The separation of these federations from the MSZOSZ was an attempt to escape from the political legacy of the old times, though such a strategy could only have limited success. For similar reasons, however, official links were not established between the MSZP and the MSZOSZ in this first period. The MSZP wanted to escape the image of being an old-fashioned labor party linked to trade union influence (well-known behavior in some Western left-of-center parties too), while the MSZOSZ did not want to ally itself with the political successor of the old Communist party (which in that period was treated as a party *non grata*).

The coalition government led by József Antall between May 1990 and December 1993 had an ambiguous attitude toward the trade unions. In accordance with their conservative political philosophy, they did not want to make the unions important players in national politics, and they did not believe that labor should have a say in the management of either economic or political issues. On the other hand, however, they were aware of their own weak popular support and feared that the unions could mount political pressure against their policies.

Ironically, the first major appearance of trade unions did not arise due to an industrial conflict. The three-day gasoline riot, triggered off by a sudden gasoline price increase in October 1990, was eventually handled by a tripartite conference of government, trade unions and employers. This was apparently inadequate, since the representatives of the taxi drivers, who initiated the blockade, were left out of the televised negotiation. The government had to improvise, but this improvisation implied a longer-term decision—namely, that if they had to talk to representatives of society between two general elections, they should talk to a structured representative organ, that is, unions, instead of troublemakers who make riots and paralyze traffic.

Since, at the moment, the liberal parties represented the main opposition to the right-of-center government, the main hero on the union side was Pál Forgács, the veteran president of the Liga. Forgács had been a foreign affairs chief of the SZOT. He retired and was invited to head the Liga by the liberal academics who initiated the foundation of that federation. Despite representing a much larger organization, Sándor Nagy had to follow the debate from the second line.

However, the MSZOSZ came out with a massive strike initiative in May 1991. It was, in fact, the only threat of a general strike during the transition years, when anger could have brought the masses onto the streets to force the government to abandon the price increases they planned (i.e. in electricity, transportation etc.). Facing the readiness of the people to strike, the government decided to compromise and withdrew some of the measures they wanted to introduce.

The compromise was very shortly followed by a powerful attack against the MSZOSZ. Following a three-party initiative (Fidesz, SZDSZ, MDF), the parliament passed two bills, one requiring all trade unions to reregister their membership, and a second requiring them to redistribute trade union assets according to their influence. Obviously, the implication was that the property of the MSZOSZ could be seized by the Workers' Councils and the Liga, supported by a heavy media campaign against Nagy and other leaders. A period of heavy fighting began.

The subsequent years (1991–93) became a period of heavy struggle for influence and survival. In the new situation, the MSZOSZ found it very important to strengthen their links with the Socialist Party. There had already been trade union forums organized in the headquarters of the MSZP in order to bring together Socialist politicians with union leaders and activists. The Left Alternative—still a small movement of radical socialists—played a crucial role in organizing those forums. Following the two trade union laws, the MSZP president, Gyula Horn, appeared on a forum together with Sándor Nagy. A formal cooperation agreement between the party and the federation was accomplished.

The survival strategy of the MSZOSZ involved a good deal of streamlining. The central bureaucracy of the federation shrank. The research institute of the unions, which could have been developed into a competitive social science and economic research center, was reduced to the level of just a handful of researchers and staff and moved to the headquarters of the MSZOSZ. External links were also important for demonstrating the legitimacy of the renewed federation. The MSZOSZ strengthened cooperation with the international trade union center in Brussels and built close connections with the Austrian and German federations.

The unions linked to the liberal and the conservative parties, however, were much better endowed for their campaign. In this period, it was not only the Liga that received substantial financial support from AFL–CIO, but also the Workers' Councils as well. The delegations of the two federations were invited to Washington, D.C., where they negotiated with Treasury as well as World Bank officials about the possibilities of cooperation.

Despite the ongoing struggle between the federations, they could still cooperate within the tripartite bargaining system. Altogether, seven federations took part in the process, which became somewhat more important for the public acceptance of government policy. Later, however, the Solidarity union showed a lack of discipline and was expelled from the roundtable.

Having triggered the two-year struggle for redistributing trade union property and influence, the government was comfortable and did not have to face major industrial unrest. In fact, this was the period of structural adjustment, when the most significant contraction of the Hungarian economy took place. Fighting for reregistration and organizing a national campaign, the unions did not do too much against plant closures and massive lay-offs. The number of unemployed passed half a million in spring 1992, and it has remained stagnant at about 12–13% ever since. The unions did not have much influence on the three new labor laws that came into force on 1 July 1992 (one general labor act dealt in detail with the competitive sector, and there were two acts for public sector employment).

Throughout the transition years, trade union activity has been much more significant at the national than at the local level. Local organizations have been weak, and they have not found the resources and strategies needed for the struggle for better conditions. Examples of successful union activity can be found in cases in which certain unions have been able to lobby together with the management, and have influenced government policy toward the companies of particular industries. Such cases have been, for instance, coal mining, and also the steel industry to some extent (both MSZOSZ affiliates).

The final battle between the competing federations took place in May 1993, with the general elections for the social security boards (i.e. pension fund and health insurance fund). This was one of the most amusing elections of all times, since nobody knew precisely why the entire adult population had the right to vote for trade unions they were not members of, and for boards that did not necessarily handle their money. Nevertheless, some 40% of the electorate participated, which was generally reckoned to be a fairly high figure.

The election results showed that, despite four years of permanent and heavy anticommunist propaganda, the representation of the new unions remained far below the expected level. In both boards the representatives of the MSZOSZ took majority control. Sándor Nagy became chairman of the pension fund and László Sándor chairman of the health insurance fund. A year later Nagy ceded his chairmanship to his friend Professor Tamás Mészáros of the Budapest University of Economic Sciences. The election results provided a basis for representation in works councils and also for settlement of the dispute over trade union property.

The years following 1993 can be called the period of noncompetitive decline. With hindsight the 1993 election success of the MSZOSZ was a kind of signal for the general elections of the following year. It indicated that popular opinion among the working class had shifted toward the left; this shift was eventually the basis for the MSZP winning 33% of the vote and 54% of the mandate in the 1994 parliament.

In the 1990 general elections, trade unions played virtually no role at all. Broader issues—the rejection of one-party rule and Soviet orientation—were on the agenda. The situation was very different in 1994, when the Socialist Party made strong efforts to nurture the alliance with the MSZOSZ. From 1992 on, MSZP leader Gyula Horn appeared on the same stage as union leader Sándor Nagy at May Day celebrations. Nagy was second on the party list of the MSZP at the elections, although the final decision about this positioning was preceded by an internal battle with the supporters of László Békesi; Békesi represented financial interests in the party and later became finance minister for about nine months. Apart from Nagy, five trade union leaders (namely, András Bársony, Pál Papp, László Paszternák, Antal Schalkhammer and Mrs. István Szöllősi) acquired mandates in the giant faction of the Socialist Party (209 MPs).

Contrary to subsequent allegations from the right, the Socialists did not promise a financial bonanza for wage-earners. They made it clear during the campaign that the government would have to face the historically outstanding twin deficits (budget and current account), which had run out of control during the last two years of the cycle of the previous government. The novelty the Socialists wanted to introduce was a strengthened version of the tripartite bargaining process, and eventually a quick accomplishment of a so-called "social and economic agreement" between the government, the unions and the employers. They called it the Hungarian Moncloa pact, on the pattern of a Spanish equivalent from the late 1970s. This attempt, however, collapsed in January 1995, when it became clear that the economic and political conditions were too severe for this arrangement to be acceptable to the unions. Indeed, the austerity program brought about by the newly appointed finance minister, Lajos Bokros, reduced real wages by 10% for the year 1995.

Understandably, the March 1995 austerity package of the government provided another blow to union support for the MSZP as well as to the popular support for the unions. When the government announced its stabilization policy together with some fragments of the marketization of public services, opinion polls showed that some two-thirds of the population received the news with outrage. The union leaders, however, did not rush to ride the waves of popular sentiment, and most of them remained loyal to the government line. Slowly, the representatives of the public sector started to mobilize resistance, particularly when it was announced that the government wanted to consolidate the results of stabilization through a fundamental reform of the public sector (following the guidance of World Bank policy recommendations).

Consequently, a new division emerged within the union movement. Since industrial recovery had definitely begun in 1993, and perhaps even in 1992, unions in the competitive sector turned their backs fairly visibly on any form of militancy. The public sector, on the other hand, was heading toward a decimation of its labor force, and this made the union leaders take a stronger stand against the government blueprints.

Despite open cleavages over policy, the leadership of the MSZP never contemplated any break with the union leaders. Contact was maintained with even the most militant ones, like Mrs. István Szöllősi (popularly called Ica), the vociferous president of the teachers' union. The union leaders, and particularly Mrs.

Szöllősi, became regular targets for the Free Democrats, the coalition partner of the MSZP. They considered the unions to be major obstacles to further market- ization and austerity, and not without reason. Sándor Nagy clearly represented an economic policy paradigm based more on state intervention and *dirigisme*. Thus, whenever the prime minister wanted to bring Nagy into some ministerial posi- tion, the Free Democrats took it as a potential *casus belli* and forced Horn to abandon Nagy's promotion. Nevertheless, in late 1995 Nagy resigned from the leadership of the MSZOSZ and began to prepare himself for some position in the party; however, he failed to achieve this aim by the March 1996 congress of the Socialist party, and this was the last appropriate occasion before the 1998 general elections.

In place of Nagy, László Sándor became president of the MSZOSZ. Despite being a less colorful person and having a weaker membership behind him, Sándor managed to maintain the bargaining position of the MSZOSZ at the national level. In fact, the immediate cause of the resignation of finance minister Lajos Bokros in February 1996 was a vitriolic dispute between Sándor and himself over the management of the health insurance fund. They reached the level of personal insults during a government meeting, and, even though the Prime Minister apologized for the situation rather than the two "combatants," Bokros decided to leave immediately after the cabinet meeting (when some other ministers had already gone to a soccer match between ministers and journalists). At the end of 1996, however, Sándor also resigned from the chairmanship of the health fund, which was partly due to some inadequacies in the management of the fund discovered by the State Audit Office.

Although such conflicts could occur, the unions did not declare any opposition to privatization, liberalization or other transformation policies. This situation remained stable even though in some cases the unions had some reasons for worry—for instance, some multinational companies did not want to allow trade unions within their factories. One of the infamous cases of such character was the dispute with the management of Suzuki. In Szekszárd, a trade union leader of a German-owned meat processing factory was beaten up by the security guard of the firm for leading a determined campaign for wage increases. The case caused some outrage in the country, although without significantly affecting the funda- mentally respectful attitude toward foreign capital. On the other hand, there have been some cases when the management has searched for the "missing" unions to negotiate with. There have also been cases when collective labor contracts, required by law, were not drawn up simply because of the absence of appropriate workers' representation.

Two German researchers, Rainer Deppe and Melanie Tatur, suggest in an article for *Eszmélet* (No. 28, winter 1995) that Hungary seemed to be headed toward a type of unstable corporatism. One of the main sources of instability was the declining membership and material background of the unions. None of the unions releases actual figures about membership, although it is widely believed that numbers have fallen below 50% of the total workforce. The Liga and the

Workers' Councils are both in crisis because they have failed to build themselves up into hegemonic federations and their external support has dried up. The majority of the organized workers seem to favor unions with leaderships orientated toward the left.

Since 1993, competition between various trade union federations has been at a low ebb, but even the stronger ones face objective constraints on their activities. Industrial recovery might help, but not even that would necessarily mean that the power of the trade unions would be restored and the workers would have more opportunity to say how the economy should be managed. Recovery in the Hungarian case has meant that the hope of increasing incomes, after the 1995–96 stabilization period, has tended to weaken trade union militancy. This can be seen in the case of railway workers, who accomplished their 1997 wage demands without a strike threat (unlike in the previous five years). Having suffered so much since 1989 due to high inflation, falls in real wages and consumption, the emergence of mass unemployment, as well as the collapse of public services, Hungarian workers seem to be grateful for even the slightest improvement in their living and working conditions.

Taking everything into consideration, the weakness of trade union activity can be seen to have several points of origin. According to a widely held assumption, Hungarian trade unions have been strong at the top, weak in the middle, and nonexistent at the bottom. This description applies to the major conventional unions, like the MSZOSZ or the SZEF. The so-called new trade union federations, on the other hand, had only one source of power in the early 1990s—anticommunism. After anticommunism ceased to be an effective political fuel, the Liga and the Workers' Councils fell into insignificance. Some of their leaders, however, remained committed to carrying on the battle against the established federation. A former leader of the Liga, Csaba Őry, came back to the political arena in 1998 as deputy secretary of state at the ministry of social and family affairs. Thus he is working for a government that has degraded collective bargaining, ignored the institutions of tripartite interest reconciliation, stopped the trade unions from running the national health and pension funds and refused to implement pension increases according to the effective law.

THE STATE: REFORM OF THE PUBLIC SECTOR

Slogans concerning reform of the public sector started to circulate in the late 1980s and came to the forefront of political discourse with ever greater intensity. In a narrow sense, public sector reform meant the privatization of health care and pensions, and perhaps other fields of public services and personal entitlements. In a broad sense, however, the transformation of the public sector means the adjustment of the state to the new social system, through the very policies that transformed society in the era of capitalist restoration. Accordingly, the organization of the Hungarian state has gone through a wave of privatization, and the emergence of a hierarchical society has manifested itself with the recentralizing tendencies within the state.

Marketization and Centralization

East European privatization was outstanding not just because the majority of the productive sectors fell into private hands very rapidly, but also because that privatization was not limited to the competitive sectors. Under the intellectual influence of libertarianism and the theory of property rights, the ideas and practices of privatization penetrated the sectors of productive infrastructure, public utilities, housing, human services, as well as the government itself. It seems that once the process had been started, it was impossible to stop it spreading to all different areas of life.

The structure and the functions of the new state organization were shaped by the conceptions and misconceptions of the transition governments, the heavy legacy of the bankrupt state socialist system and the often unfriendly external environment. Bruszt and Stark describe the ensuing changes in the following way: "With its policy swing from unintended market shock to interventionist state bailouts, the Antall government turned Hungary into what we might call the antidevelopmental state. In contrast to the developmental state, which mobilizes and channels resources to high-growth sectors and firms, the antidevelopmental state siphons resources out of the economy" (Bruszt and Stark 1998: 152).

Whereas in the state socialist economy paternalism was based on the state's attempt to manage assets centrally, in the first years of the postsocialist economy paternalism was based on the state's attempt to manage liabilities centrally (Bruszt and Stark 1998: 152). In the first years of the transition, this change was not seen as a problem; the prevailing ideology suggested that the state should forget about developmental functions and should not have anything to do with asset management, with the exception of the area of privatization. The success stories of East Asia were interpreted without emphasizing the role of a strong state in promoting industrial development—a way of story-telling that would leave the Danish prince out of Hamlet. The warnings from Western economists like Fishlow (1986) and Amsden et al. (1993) were largely ignored, although they all highlighted that the lesson for East Europeans from East Asia should not be looked for in the operation of free markets but in a reasonable application of state intervention.[7]

Even if one does not accept a Korean or Japanese developmentalist approach, it must be understood that a new social system needs a new state structure to function, and the transition period requires a particular type of institutional arrangement. "The construction of newly market-oriented economies requires a secure state to initiate and regulate the reform process and to undertake a variety of costly functions ranging from political administration and state cohesion to social welfare provision and direct investment" (Harris 1995: 198).

Most theorists and practitioners of transition played down the problem of state-crafting in the early 1990s. Since so much energy was devoted to finding out how to demolish the leviathan government of state socialism, the efforts at new state building were preceded by a period of institutional anarchy. It was only the technocrats who insisted that the security of the state and its ability to carry out the functions involved in socioeconomic transformation depended on its ability to finance itself without destabilizing the economy. Consequently, financing the state became a key financial problem for economies in transition, including Hungary. This applies both to the narrow public finance sense of tax design and to a broader sense of mobilizing savings through the financial system to finance state spending.

"The new state does not appear from the imaginations of the dissident intellectuals, but from the social articulation of private interest" (Radice: 1995: 303)—a British economist warned in his study on foreign investment in transition countries. However, the lack of consensus between the major economic and social interest groups prevented the emergence of an agreement on the nature and structure of the new state. As a result of such disagreements, the attempt to create a new Constitution for the new Hungarian Republic failed badly. In 1989 and 1990, the old Constitution was modified many times in order to facilitate the launch of pluralist democracy. It was in 1994 when the newly formed Socialist–Liberal government announced that they would produce a new Constitution within the next four years, and, despite their more than two-thirds majority in parliament, they claimed that they would create it with a six-party consensus. Eventually, the passing of a new framework for the Constitution was blocked by some Socialist representatives, apparently because they recognized that the incorporation of social rights was missing from the basic law of the nation.

The source of confusion around the creation of the new Constitution was that hitherto issues concerning human rights and social rights were not part of the political discourse. This occurred even though Ralf Dahrendorf, for instance, warned the ECE transformers: "The entitlements associated with membership in society—a national society until there is a world society—are a matter of legislation and supporting policies. Civil, political and social rights must become a part of the fabric of the social and political community" (Dahrendorf 1990: 103).

In Hungary, the only effective debate about social rights focused on the question of how to cut back these rights. The slogan of "public sector reform" became a code name for abolishing all different entitlements left behind by the Kádárist regime. Ironically enough, it was during the period of the Socialist–Liberal coalition that public sector reform became one of the central issues of government policy. For finance ministers Békesi and Bokros, the key issue was financial stabilization. Their short-term policies included up-front assaults on welfare entitlements.[8] Once they had managed to sort out the major problems of the macroeconomy, the structural reform of public institutions and redistributive systems shifted to an even higher level on the government's agenda. Education, health care and pension reforms represented the key areas of this policy, and privatization and cutbacks in government responsibilities for provision made up the core of the programs.

However, it should not be assumed that these government sectors needed cuts and privatization because they devoured such high portions of the national income. The real value of total expenditure on the sick and the elderly has declined almost constantly in the transition years. Until 1998, it was only during election years that the real value of pensions was allowed to increase by a substantial margin.

The main problem with the redistributive systems was not that they spent too much but that, after years of almost constant reforms, they had become too confused—institutionally as well as financially. For sorting out the financial and management problems in health care and social security, the financial government repeatedly suggested renationalization after the establishment of the self-governments in 1993. Renationalization was also seen as a way of actually privatizing health care and pensions, as well as the assets of these funds. This endeavor finally materialized when right-of-center parties formed a government again in 1998.

It was, of course, not only the welfare state that underwent a massive transformation in the early 1990s, but the security services of the state as well. In the armed services, the introduction of civilian control was a key stage in the reforms of the 1990s. The size of the Hungarian army was significantly reduced by cutting the number of professional officers and shortening the length of the mandatory military service for young men. As soon as the possibility of membership in NATO was taken seriously, "NATO-compatibility" became the supreme slogan and objective of reform within the military. Again, the government could produce compatibility in an organizational and institutional sense, but the lack of resources prevented the Hungarian army from approaching NATO standards in actual performance.

With no substantial military industry, the technical capacities of the Hungarian army remained dependent on the import of modern weapons. The hard foreign exchange constraint thus played a key role in the diminishing power of the Hungarian military. The government could have responded by buying military equipment from Russia, or simply accepting the Russian weapons as mortgaging the Soviet-Russian debt inherited from the late 1980s. That was, however, usually seen as unacceptable for NATO compatibility, and the general trend was to turn toward the West instead of the East. The decline in the fighting capacity of the Hungarian army was accompanied by a continuous decline in the real incomes of officers, and this resulted in serious demoralization by the late 1990s.

Similarly to the army, the Hungarian police also fell into a critical condition. However, unlike the former, the state of the police had an immediate impact on people's lives and the conditions in the cities. Crime in Hungary rose rapidly after 1989, but, as a result of the general financial crisis, the government had less and less money to spend on the police. In the mid-1990s, the consequences of organized crime became highly visible—and audible—to society. It was also revealed in several cases that police officers were involved in certain gangs and helped to cover up illegal activities. Of course, the strong units of the private sphere—wealthy entrepreneurs and prosperous companies—compensated themselves for the declining efficiency of the system of public security by building up private security firms to accompany and protect those who could afford it.

While much was written about the poverty of the Hungarian police, in 1996 it was revealed that the police department had erected a new and luxurious headquarters in Budapest. The fact that the finances of this giant investment were not found to be in line with sound public spending contributed to the replacement of the entire leadership of the national and the Budapest police. This was carried out by the Socialist–Liberal government. Of course, the other reason was the inaction of the police against organized crime. The irony of the story is that Sándor Pintér, the police chief replaced by the Free Democrat minister of interior affairs, was brought back as minister of interior affairs in 1998, following the victory of Fidesz–MPP at the parliamentary elections.

The general trend to subordinate all segments of state and society to market forces did not miss any corners of the system. Government action to implement public sector reform reached the area of sports in the run-up to the 1998 elections. Up to that point, sports clubs had tried to muddle through the transition period amidst diminishing revenues and state subsidies. In the first half of the 1990s all major clubs had to abolish at least a few of their sports sections because of the collapse of their funding.

The intervention of the Socialist–Liberal government into the affairs of soccer—the most important sport in Hungary—was sparked by a disastrous defeat—or, as one might say, a Waterloo—of Hungarian soccer in November 1997. The national team had just about made it to the threshold of the 1998 World Cup, but there were still two postqualifying matches to be played against Yugoslavia. The first match in Budapest was lost 7:1 and the second in Belgrade 5:0. Just a few days later the government launched a campaign to replace the leadership of the Hungarian Soccer Association (MLSZ) and to force it to implement rapid changes in the management of the game. The essence of the required changes was privatization, which was seen as a key to success in sport.

While in the economy marketization and privatization had already displayed their controversial nature, in sports they were still seen as a means to Western quality. György Bodnár, the entrepreneur whose firm already owned much of the broadcasting rights to ball sports, was quoted as saying that "people should forget that soccer is a sport. Soccer is business." The promoters of privatization used foreign as well as domestic examples to support their case. References to marketized Western clubs like Manchester United were self-evident. The domestic examples included those of Gázszer and Tiszakécske, where sponsorship from local entrepreneurs had brought minor soccer clubs into the first league within a short period of time.

In 1998, as a result of the penetration of entrepreneurial spirit, a Professional National Championship replaced the first class of the National Championship.

The change of name and other trappings gave an impression that soccer was moving toward the principle of business. In reality, however, this was a period when certain branches of the government regained control over the clubs, making ministers the heads of soccer clubs again (this used to be the system under state socialism). The promotion of the ministers under the Fidesz–Smallholder administration also put an end to a period when the most popular soccer club of Hungary, Ferencváros (FTC), had been negotiating with foreign investors. The rejection of foreign ownership was one of the major reasons for going ahead with a pseudoprivatization under the control of government agencies.

Outside Budapest, sports clubs have functioned either under the control of city or county governments, or under the auspices of major industrial firms. The decline and agony of Hungarian soccer was thus intertwined with the crisis in Hungarian industry and the problems of local governments. The latter gained formal independence from the national government after the changes of 1989, but financial dependency on the national budget preserved the possibility of central control and intervention. Fiscal subsidies to local governments were substantially cut in the early 1990s. Since, however, municipalities were interested in privatization—by selling assets like state-owned apartments and receiving a portion of privatization revenue—they were for a while able to fill the holes in their budgets. Only the most lucky—those with major prosperous industrial units on their territories—managed to recover from this hangover and create policies of long-term development.

One step toward development policy orientation was made during the preparations for EU accession. The possibility of West European subsidies gave rise to a blueprint for reforming regional government in Hungary; this was to replace twenty units (19 counties plus the capital city) with only six. The blueprint that was put forward by the Socialist–Liberal coalition was strongly opposed by the nationalist opposition, which referred primarily to national tradition and attempted to represent the interests of the incumbent bureaucrats in regional administration. Eventually, even the most conservative Smallholders recognized that the transition to regional administration from county administration had become inevitable.

Replacing twenty units of regional administration with only six can be understood as another form of centralization (which should not, however, be a surprise, given the detected general trends of the transition). While the promise of 1989 was to make giant steps toward the decentralization and democratization of an overcentralized and authoritarian system, the reforms of the 1990s usually drove the Hungarian state toward more centralization and the detachment of the citizens from decision-making circles. With their first measures, the 1998 Fidesz government continued the centralization trend in the Hungarian state. It extended the power of the executive to the control of the social security boards as well as the attorney's office. Together with the property of the social security funds, it centralized several other forms of remaining state property—state shares in commercial banks, utilities, newspapers etc.—and made the State Privatization and Holding Company a giant organization (even though it had been preparing for abolition just a few months before, under the Socialists).

Viktor Orbán also started to inflate the prime ministerial office. The office was now led by a minister, and a number of junior ministers were also appointed. The leader of the office—István Stumpf—was given authorities like the supervision, management and privatization of state property. The creators (and analysts) of the new governmental structure have usually compared it to the German chancellorship, though in most aspects the new Hungarian model represents an even greater concentration of power.

The most apparent feature of the administration that emerged in 1998 is that the structure of government institutions and the distribution of portfolios was dominated by party-political horse trading. In "human areas," a fragmented structure of ministries emerged, while in the areas of the economy some highly concentrated, strong offices were constructed. (The ministry of the economy was created on the basis of the former ministry of industry and trade by adding certain authorities from the previous ministries of finance and labor. Agriculture, previously a single portfolio, now captured regional development too.) From this distribution of forces we can expect that the ministries of culture, education, health etc. will be fighting individually for more resources against the strong economic ministries, but they will have less success than before.

In certain cases, the reorganization was justified under the title of "following a Western pattern." Thus Orbán established a ministry of national cultural heritage explicitly on the pattern of the short-lived ministry established by British Prime Minister John Major in 1992. Also similarly to John Major, Orbán abolished the ministry of labor and distributed its authorities to the ministries of economy, education, and social and family affairs, respectively.

One of the first measures of the new government was the abolition of the self-government of social security boards that had been established in the Antall era. The alleged reason for abolishing the self-governments for health and pensions was that these funds operated under a board of laymen and a corrupt management, and that their control had become illegitimate after their respective leaderships were renewed on the basis of delegation instead of a general election in 1997. Though many of the corruption accusations were true in the case of the health fund, this move was, rather, a declaration of war on the trade unions and collective-tripartite bargaining and a preparation for the privatization of the health sector. Another centralization measure is the subordination of the attorney authority to the government instead of the parliament (the latter having been the case since the democratic transition began in 1989).

Thus, the second major tendency in the new structure of governance is the strengthening of the executive power at the expense of the legislation. Apart from increasing the number of ministries, now a cabinet minister has become head of the prime minister's office, and his work is assisted by no fewer than five junior ministers. At the same time, Fidesz–MPP confirmed their previous proposal about decreasing substantially the number of members of parliament. Such a move, however, would require a two-thirds majority in parliament and thus cannot be carried through without the consent of the Socialists. Nevertheless, if this step takes place, a much smaller legislation would be supposed to supervise a much lager executive, which would provide greater room for maneuver for the latter.

Education

The revival of the Gramscian tradition in European and American political science is a most helpful development in explaining the essence of the transformation of state and society in Eastern Europe. In this perspective, the main function of the state is to enforce property rights. The means of this enforcement are various: coercive, utilitarian, normative and hegemonic. In order to naturalize power and political obedience, the ruling class needs to become hegemonic. Finally, in order to build instruments of normative and hegemonic enforcement, the system of state education must be transformed.

Though the reforms in the Hungarian educational system have largely been justified on the basis of technical arguments, the process has been politically determined and became a main vehicle for social restructuring. Just like the entire transition, the educational reforms have had a general tendency toward privatization and marketization, and thus there has been a consolidation of a class society through providing better conditions for the children of the elites in the school system. On the other hand, the first two governments of the transition had a different impact on the content of change in education. While Antall's government pursued the transformation of the educational system in a traditionalist framework, Horn's government has framed it in a modernist program.

In order to consolidate the overall political and ideological change for the next generations, the content of education had to be changed. The Németh government had already abolished compulsory Russian language courses from primary schools to universities as well as so-called ideological subjects in higher education.[9] This policy was continued by the Antall government, which initiated the creation of a National Core Curriculum that was eventually adopted under the Horn government. The restructuring of subjects and course materials took place without a general replacement of teaching staff, as was the case in the former GDR—though the wave of early retirement affected school directors and professors as well.

Also as a measure of general liberalization, the uniformity of eight-year primary schools was broken, and six-year high schools were launched for pupils who finished the sixth year of primary school successfully. The eight-year primary school had been an achievement of state socialism and was a key instrument for educating the working class and abolishing the underclass inherited from the semifeudalist Horthy regime. To the extent that it was a vehicle for elevating the poor and previously uneducated layers, however, it was a restraint on the elites, who could have financed a more intensive primary and secondary education for their children. This restraint was broken by the transition, and social polarization started to manifest itself in the differentiation within the school system.

The control of primary and secondary schools was transferred from the national ministry to local governments. In order to put parents in charge of long-term policies of primary and secondary schools, school boards were established with much greater power than the previous parents' meetings. The control of local governments, however, was limited by their financial difficulties, and thus some sort of leverage was preserved for the national government. For the same reason, schools became increasingly dependent on the financial contributions of various foundations; this strengthened the influence of alumni, parents' and other civic organizations.

Among other nongovernmental organizations, the major churches made substantial gains in extending their influence on the educational system. The Németh government had already stretched out a friendly hand toward the churches, and the Antall government made it the cornerstone of their alliance policy to restore the role the churches had played in education before the state socialist era. Reclaiming all institutions of the churches was not realistic, but the leaders of the churches really pushed their demands to the politically reasonable limits. A handful of religious high schools had continued to operate during the state socialist era, and now the way was open for establishing many more.

An act passed by the conservative-dominated parliament forced state schools to evacuate former church school buildings, even if the religious communities did not have the financial and organizational power to launch their own schools immediately after the acquisition of their real estates. This situation gave rise to a most heated debate about such a policy of cultural restoration. The restitution campaign caused difficulties and sometimes emergency situations for schools that were suffering from a shortage of classrooms, even without the demands of particular churches. The Socialist–Liberal government, however, did not reverse this policy, and the churches consolidated their role in education. Within a few years a Catholic university had also been established just outside Budapest.

A major contribution of the Antall government to the restructuring of education was the severe cutback in the child-care and kindergarten network. In their ideology, this was simply a restoration of the natural role of women in society, which is to deal with children. These facilities were built under state socialism to make employment possible for women. Now they were seen as a distortion in society, and their abolition eased the retirement of women who left the labor force. Much of the babysitting had been done by grandmothers, but they were now joined by a number of mothers who could spend their days running the household.

Another major development of the early transition years was the reduction in or elimination of certain subsidies. In the early 1990s, the financial crisis of the state manifested itself also in the still free education sphere. Antall's government was not brave enough to introduce tuition fees—nevertheless, the costs of higher education increased for the students. This had to happen once the real value of state finance for education declined sharply in the first half of the 1990s.

Among the conditions of what had formally been free higher education, students had to spend on food, accommodation and textbooks. State socialism had subsidized all of these, and students only had to pay nominal amounts for such items. Once the financial crisis forced the state to cut public spending, the real value of education subsidies eroded, and student cafeterias and textbooks became less and less affordable.

Tuition fees in higher education were introduced in 1995 as a part of the Bokros package of macroeconomic stabilization. Though the amount of actual saving by introducing tuition fees was almost negligible, it had a symbolic effect in indicating that the market and capitalism had arrived in the field of higher education in Hungary. The designers of the Bokros package expected resistance and set the first compulsory rate at a very low level—2,000 forints—which, according to Bokros, was the amount a student would spend on smoking in one month. Soon afterward, institutions were allowed to raise fees according to their needs. Often they had no real choice, since government austerity forced them to raise their own revenues.

The Socialist–Liberal government created an appearance that the introduction of a tuition fee was not a matter of financial necessity but a step toward greater justice. Finance minister Bokros explained that higher education with a tuition fee is fairer than a free university since it is mainly the middle-class and the higher layers of society who can afford to send their children to universities, and they do not need subsidies from the state. Those should go to the children of the poor through means-tested scholarships. Notwithstanding the opportunity of subsidies, however, the emergence of the tuition fee and the increasing additional cost of higher education itself discouraged less wealthy families from thinking about sending their children to universities. The social composition of students has changed to such an extent that working-class youth are almost excluded from certain institutions.

Despite increasing real costs, a constant trend during the transition decade was the increasing participation of youth in higher education. Under the Kádár regime, despite fact that primary and secondary levels of education were remarkably strong in Hungary, a relatively low proportion—some 11% of the age group—participated in higher education. This rate was the second-lowest in Europe. By the end of the 1990s, the rate grew close to 20%, which was a remarkable step forward, even if the Hungarian figures still lag behind the West-European average. The increase in the participation rate was partly due to the increasing size and number of higher education institutions and partly to a shrinkage in the age group reaching university level.

In the 1990s, a proliferation of universities took place in the country. Cities where universities had specialized in a particular subject—like Veszprém with the University of the Chemical Industry or Miskolc with the University of Heavy Industry—now saw their chance to establish real multidisciplinary universities.

Most of these institutions, however, employ part-time lecturers from Budapest universities. Thus the concentration of higher education in Budapest was mitigated, but the hierarchy of universities remained in place.

Hungarian education became more diverse not just in a territorial sense but also in terms of ownership. Although on a much smaller scale than in industry or trade, a new private sector emerged in the school system in the 1990s. A number of small colleges were established in association with Western universities by using distance-learning methods for a diploma. The most remarkable novelty in the private sector of higher education is the Central European University, which provides postgraduate courses only for youth collected from all around Eastern Europe. Despite operating as an enclave in the educational system of Hungary, the CEU has had some impact on the rest of higher education and the research community. It brought, for instance, a world-class library and a similarly outstanding bookshop into the heart of Budapest, to the benefit and the frustration of those working in state-financed universities. The CEU was established by the financial entrepreneur George Soros and became a regional amplifier of liberal arts and ideology. Most of the newly established private higher education institutions have not matched the standards of the CEU. They provide courses for children of wealthy families so that they can become businessmen with an Oxford or Cambridge diploma (at least in name).

As a final phase of restructuring in higher education, a merger of universities and polytechnics was put forward by the Socialist–Liberal government. In March 1998, education minister Bálint Magyar signed a U.S.$150 million loan with the World Bank for the reform of Hungarian higher education. The creation of multidisciplinary universities was the greatest policy item in the reform package. In principle, the merger of similar institutions should bring significant changes simply through the economies of scale. If there are not so many universities, not so many university rectors and deans (and their chauffeurs) need to be paid. Libraries can be merged, and fewer librarians are needed; departments of mathematics or those of sociology can be merged, and there is not such a need for mathematics and sociology professors. In reality, the program did not take into account many local traditions and specificities and consumed the energies and resources of the academic staff, who now had to engage in everlasting bargaining instead of concentrating on teaching and research.

Nevertheless, Bálint Magyar was a proud modernizer of the education system, and not without reason. His campaign resulted in the introduction of the internet into all the secondary schools of Hungary, which was an exceptional achievement not only among former socialist countries but even in the European context. It needs mentioning, however, that while Hungary achieved a high ratio of internet availability in state schools, in private homes Hungarians had fallen far behind the West European standards. Magyar's other achievement was to introduce the so-called Széchenyi scholarship, which was aimed at stopping the outflow of the best and brightest minds from the country by providing them with a scholarship eight times higher than the minimum wage for four years, in addition to their basic salary (which would otherwise have been humiliatingly low). The education policy of the Fidesz government that came into office in 1998 initiated several changes. Education minister Zoltán Pokorni announced that the Széchenyi scholarship would be phased out, while teachers would receive a dynamic pay rise that would bring their real incomes closer to West European standards. Tuition fees in higher education were quickly abolished for those studying for the first diploma. The government also started to subsidize religious instruction. These measures were elements of a policy aimed at the strengthening of a broader middle class while leaving the poor opportunities of the working class and the underclasses unimproved. To maintain the sympathy of the World Bank, the government carried on with the merger policy in higher education. Their slowly constructed fiscal policy, however, practically ruled out any substantial pay rise for teachers (whose support in the general and municipal elections of 1998 had nevertheless been won through these).

The Fidesz government, as all other administrations of the transition, understood well that the long-term significance of education might in some respects be greater than that of certain industries, the reason being that it is the educational system that maintains the ideology of the state, and this is vital for preserving the existing social order. Changes in particular industries may have a short- or medium-term impact on those working there, but the educational system provides a framework for the entire society for generations ahead. Though the rhetoric of the government usually emphasized increasing social mobility and creating equal opportunities, the actual transformation of Hungarian education has served the consolidation of a new capitalist society.

NOTES

1. Stiglitz's book is a clear example that it would have been possible to avoid free-market extremes once state socialism had been rejected. Stiglitz, however, portrays his powerful critique of statism as a critique of socialism, which creates nearly as many problems as it resolves.

2. In Hungary, as in other countries, tax breaks have been introduced to stimulate certain types of investment. During Stadler's tax investigation, he was found to have requested a tax deduction for the purchase of the painting "The Last Supper." When he was told that the painting he produced had nothing to do with Leonardo da Vinci's fresco, he said he had been trained as a shepherd and did not have sufficient knowledge about the fine arts.

3. In the late 1990s, when this debate became one of the most important issues of national politics, land prices were depressed in Hungary. They were expected to rise with EU accession. The nationalist parties insisted that the resulting yield must not be handed over to foreigners, who could easily buy up Hungarian land at low prices.

4. The aim to reduce foreign debts through the privatization of public utilities became obvious only in early 1996, though a chief privatizer of the government emphasized that it is not the sales price that is important, but future investment in the companies by the buyers.

5. According to ILO standards, the long-term unemployed include persons who have had no work for more than a year.

6. The 30% estimate of the share of the shadow economy in the entire GDP was produced in a totally unscientific way but became a commonplace in economic and political language.

7. Fislow's observation comes from the socialist reform period; he says that those "who counsel the countries of Latin America or Eastern Europe to adopt some of the specific East Asian exchange rate or trade policies frequently pay inadequate attention to the underlying state structure and state purpose that make them so effective" (Fishlow 1986: 399).

8. Ironically enough, when finance minister Bokros announced his austerity package, which, for the first time, launched a frontal attack on welfare entitlements, it was Imre Szekeres, the vice-president and parliamentary faction leader of the MSZP, who proudly claimed that the Socialists were now putting an end to the Kádár regime (suggesting it had not even been attempted by the Antall government).

9. State socialist education policy used the common name "ideological subjects" for political economy, scientific socialism and philosophy. Together with the Russian language, they were mandatory subjects in all institutions of higher education until Ferenc Glatz, minister of education and culture in the Németh government, abolished them or made them optional.

5

Toward Western Europe: The Test of Capitalist Democracy

The beginning of accession negotiations between the European Union and six associated countries in 1998 coincided with the period when, just before the third postcommunist general elections, leading economic researchers announced that the foundations of capitalism had been laid in Hungary. That declaration was identical with the judgment according to which the Hungarian economic and political elite considered the country a capitalist democracy. Hungary had thus already reached the broad Copenhagen criteria of accession.

Since, however, it was just the starting phase of the actual European accession, it became clear that EU membership not only requires a capitalist economy and democratic politics, but it also needs further economic credentials and political consensus within the applicant countries and among the EU member states too. The accession negotiations started to test all different aspects of Hungarian economy and society, in a period when the hardships of the systemic transformation were not yet over.

The agenda of the post-1998 period is to work out and to maintain a domestic and international consensus over enlargement while adjusting the fiscal and monetary indicators of FSCs to EU norms. The difficulties of these coinciding projects are often played down by politicians. In order to match the suggested dates of integration, for FSCs, legal harmonization and economic adjustment must be accelerated, while in the West the reform of community institutions—agricultural and structural policies, as well as the systems of voting and country representation—must be taken seriously.

While the tasks and difficulties of the potential newcomers have become largely apparent, less attention has been paid to the conflicts over the issue of enlargement within the West European community. As the negotiations on accession become more and more detailed and touch a web of special interests, the consensus in the West and East on enlargement may easily collapse. No matter whether the group includes one, four or ten states, if they become members, it will be a new type of widening in the history of EEC/EC/EU. The new features of enlargement may create new types of difficulties.

With NATO accession on track and EU candidacy announced, the problems of Hungary may indeed seem to be resolved. What has been talk so far is turning into actual action. There is some reason, however, to believe that the start of the practical phase of Euro-Atlantic accession could be the beginning of political and economic difficulties with the process. In this chapter, three areas of these possible difficulties are discussed: the domestic political cleavages over international integration, the political divisions of West European actors over enlargement and the hardships of economic adjustment to the criteria of monetary union.

INTERNATIONAL POLITICS:
GLOBAL AND REGIONAL REALIGNMENT

For the emerging democracies of East-Central Europe, full participation in the European integration became an immediate demand after the disintegration of the Soviet bloc, even if it was understood that the applicants must comply with hard economic and political criteria. From the point of view of the West, two major dilemmas emerged: how to accommodate economic and security objectives in the new integration framework and how to coordinate the simultaneous processes of the creation of a federal Europe and the extension of the borders of this federalizing Europe toward the East.

New Regional Associations

Though the new democracies of East-Central Europe built their ideologies around the concept of newly gained independence, the need for new regional cooperation was recognized from the very beginning of the new era. Hungary and other FSCs declared EU and NATO accession to be the final goals of their foreign policies. However, it was recognized that intermediate stages would be inevitable on the road to these "first-class clubs." In the early 1990s, a variety of regional organizations were formed to enhance cooperation within certain circles of FSCs and between groups of FSCs and some West-European states.

In April 1990, simultaneously with the first postcommunist elections in Hungary, the so-called "Pentagonale Initiative" was launched with the participation of Italy, Austria, Yugoslavia, Hungary and Czechoslovakia. The initiative aimed at promoting projects in the fields of environmental protection, cooperation between small and medium-sized enterprises, transportation, telecommunications, tourism, culture, education and youth exchanges. The five countries also decided to coordinate their foreign policy initiatives in the UN, the Council of Europe and the CSCE. The first meeting of heads of governments took place in July 1990, where a formal declaration was adopted to set out the objectives of the Pentagonale.

The Pentagonale grew out of another multilateral cooperation called "Alpe Adria Working Community." This had been established in 1978 with the participation of certain counties and member states of northern Italy, southern and eastern Austria, northern Yugoslavia and western Hungary, all of which used to be parts of the Austro-Hungarian Empire. The main activities of the Alpe Adria members were policy coordination, external lobbying and promotion. It was a unique example of East–West convergence, and it provided a multilateral cooperation forum for semimarketized socialist economies and their Western neighbors.

Soon after Czechoslovakia, Poland also wanted to join the group, but due to the reluctance of Italy its accession was postponed until July 1991, when the Pentagonale became the Hexagonale. Hungary played an important role in the invitation of Poland as well as in certain initiatives to broaden the scope of cooperation to security affairs, but this was not welcomed by the rest of the group. The tightness of cooperation was damaged by the rise of Czech and Slovak nationalism and even more by the beginning of the civil war in Yugoslavia. In July 1992, the organization transformed itself into a "Central European Initiative" (CEI). By summer 1993, the CEI included Macedonia and the Czech and Slovak republics as independent states. Bulgaria, Romania, Belarus and Ukraine became members of a "contact group" that met at foreign-ministerial level (Hyde-Price 1996: 113).

The CEI established a small secretariat in Vienna and a project secretariat at the EBRD. Prime ministers met annually and foreign ministers biannually. Though the CEI has provided only a limited forum for multilateral cooperation, it has remained an important club for discussing and influencing government policies—from agriculture to minority rights. The advantages of such a regional formation were recognized by others too. A similar initiative in the northern section of the East–West convergence resulted in the emergence of the Council of the Baltic Sea States (1992), which embraced ten countries of capitalist and postcommunist Europe.[1]

For Hungary, the so-called "Visegrád group" represented the most significant attempt at regional cooperation in the 1990s. The establishment of this forum was initiated in January 1990 by Vaclav Havel, the new president of Czechoslovakia, who visited Poland and Hungary and called on the three countries to coordinate their "return to Europe." Three months later, the leaders of the three countries met in Bratislava to exchange views on the new European order. In this period, however, the strengthening of the ties between the three countries was not on the agenda, partly because the political transformation was just under way in Hungary and Poland, and also because each of the FSCs expected rapid progress with their integration into the West European organizations.

By the next year, two major developments changed the attitude of ECE leaders. First, the Soviet use of force in Lithuania caused concern and created a fear that without strengthening their institutionalized cooperation, the agonizing Soviet Union may threaten their security as well. Secondly, it also turned out that the Western integration of East-Central Europe was not to be as rapid as expected, and the forthcoming years would only bring limited trade concessions.

In February 1991, a summit meeting took place in Visegrád, a historic Hungarian town. Poland was represented by President Lech Walesa, Czechoslovakia by Vaclav Havel, and Hungary by Prime Minister József Antall and President Árpád Göncz. The leaders of the three countries signed a declaration of cooperation "on the Road to European Integration." Further "Visegrád" summits took place in October 1991 in Cracow and in May 1992 in Prague. For the member states and the international media, the Visegrád forum represented the group of the most advanced reform countries of the former Soviet bloc.

Soon after it had been established, the Visegrád forum faced the same challenges as the EEC/EC had before: deepening and widening. Both types of changes were implemented, and that altered the whole nature of the cooperation of ECE states.

Initiatives to deepen the Visegrád framework led to the creation of the Central European Free Trade Agreement (CEFTA) in December 1992. The agreement provided for the phased removal of trade barriers and the creation of a free trade zone in three stages. The third stage was aimed at abolishing duties on "sensitive" commodities, and it was scheduled to take place three to eight years after signing the agreement.

By the mid-90s, however, the CEFTA included Bulgaria, Romania and Slovenia in addition to the Visegrád group. The enlargement was explained by the decreasing cohesion within the Visegrád group and the growing recognition of the political and economic importance of the other three countries.

Following the breakup of Czechoslovakia, the prime minister of the Czech Republic, Vaclav Klaus, emerged as a critic of multilateral cooperation in East-Central Europe. He believed that his country had a good chance of accelerating the process of European integration without substantial coordination with the other three participants. Furthermore, the domestic political turmoil in Poland and the bilateral disputes between Hungary and Slovakia also weakened the Visegrád framework.

From the breakup of Yugoslavia, Slovenia emerged as a relatively stable democracy and a competitive market economy, with a reasonable claim to be listed among the most advanced reform economies. Economic reform in Bulgaria and Romania was not successful at all, but the importance of these two countries was recognized on a geopolitical basis, largely in relation to the military situation around the Black Sea. After the Visegrád Four, it was these two who were able to sign association agreements with the European Union, and the Essen Summit of the European Council in December 1994 made it clear that the European Union would continue regular talks with the six countries instead of "the most advanced" four. It was only a few years later, however, that Slovenia and the three Baltic states signed Europe agreements too, creating a new situation in which the Visegrád countries—and particularly the Poles, Czechs and Hungarians—had to fight for their advantages again.

In principle, the CEFTA could have been amended with a payments union, which was recommended by the British economist Stuart Holland and by the AGENDA group. George Soros had also proposed the establishment of a payments union in order to prevent the collapse of East European international trade after the disintegration of the CMEA. Since, however, these states were linked to the IMF individually, their closer monetary cooperation was ruled out by the economic and political implications of IMF control.

Deeper ties between ECE countries were also played down, on the basis of arguments about the lack of common identity and interest. Some legacies of the past have also diminished the cooperative endeavor. Hungarian foreign policy— particularly under MDF foreign minister Géza Jeszenszky—was concerned about the reemergence of a "Little Entente" between Slovakia, Romania and Yugoslavia. Those states, however, had concerns about Hungary's policy toward the three million ethnic Hungarians living on their territory as a result of the 1920 Treaty of Trianon (which had reduced Hungary's territory by 70%). To offset this problem, Hungary sought to foster good relations not just with potential West European patrons but also with Ukraine and Bulgaria.

Throughout the 1990s, the attitude of Hungarian foreign policy toward regional blocks changed several times. At the beginning, it looked as if the more seriously the EU enlargement talks dominated the agenda of particular states of East-Central Europe, the weaker the commitment of FSCs became to the development of their subregional alliances. When, however, preparations for the accession actually began, the governments in the region started to take seriously the necessity for cooperation. For the sake of more successful negotiations with Brussels, the six candidate countries started coordination talks between themselves. Out of the thirty-one areas of accession negotiations, the six countries decided to coordinate at least in seven. Hungarian political leaders also expressed their support for the Western integration of other FSCs, including those not nominated for the first round of enlargement. For instance, at the Crans Montana Forum in Switzerland in 1998 June, President Árpád Göncz confirmed that the EU accession of neighboring countries would be of vital interest to Hungary, given the three million ethnic Hungarians living in countries not selected for the first round of Eastward EU enlargement.[2]

Nevertheless, the emergence of the new subregional associations was inevitable, even if all the major political forces in the transition countries saw them as steps toward a wider framework instead of being a final destination. The wider framework, of course, was the West European economic community and the North Atlantic security community. The East Europeans expressed their wish to join both the European Union and NATO as soon as possible. Whether these accessions were to come true, and in what order, would depend not primarily on the individual performance of the applicants but on the international political developments of the continent.

Economy and Security

For the political elites of the new democracies of East-Central Europe, both EU and NATO membership constituted a first-class foreign policy objective, though until the mid-1990s it was difficult to tell which of the two would come before the other. When a decision on NATO enlargement was made by the Western powers, Hungarian politicians claimed—and perhaps believed also— that NATO and EU accessions were two sides of the same coin. Contrary to this claim, even the internet website of the European Commission made it clear that the "enlargement of the EU and of NATO are distinct processes." There is no direct link between them, the explanation at the website continued, but they both should contribute to peace and stability in Europe and pose no threat to third countries. Behind the façade of propaganda, it must therefore be discovered that economic and security integration are not unrelated processes, but the two are not so automatically linked to each other (as many ECE politicians like to claim publicly).

The general objective of EC and EU enlargement has always been the expansion of the common market and, through that, the enlargement of the zone of stability. Various earlier rounds of enlargement also had their own specific features. In the 1970s and in the 1990s, with the so-called northern enlargements, the organization had adopted countries (with the exception of Ireland) that became net payers into the budget of the Community. In the 1980s, with the southern enlargement, they adopted countries where political stabilization was required because of the Cold War, but where this was not possible without economic integration. None of those criteria apply any longer for East-Central Europe. The main hope of the applicants is to become net recipients from the EU budget, while such transfers are no longer encouraged by the threat of a rival social system or any kind of revolution. The region does need stabilizing measures, and with NATO enlargement in an advanced phase it has become apparent that Western policies seem to prefer military means of stabilization rather than economic ones.

While the discourse about EU accession is overwhelmed by hopes about economic advantages and technicalities in the East, in the West it is primarily seen as a political problem. As European Commissioner Hans van den Broek has noted, "Enlargement to the east is in the very first place a political issue relating to security and stability on our continent" (Hyde-Price 1996: 205).

In Hungary, the relationship between development and security policies has been analyzed by very few. Interestingly enough, this group includes Dr. Otto von Habsburg, a former crown prince of Hungary and a long-serving MEP for the German CSU and president of the Pan-European Movement. He declared in a recent article that "our main task is to reach full membership for Hungary within the European Union." Surprisingly for some, he added that "this is first of all a security community, and just secondly an economic order" (Habsburg 1996). Dr. Habsburg does have a point. In the postwar period the main instrument of security within Western Europe was not NATO but, indeed, economic integration. The first steps were made by establishing the Payments Union (EPU) in 1950 and the Coal and Steel Community (ECSC) in 1951. Both were created by following the initiative and guidance of the United States, and the latter was developed into the European Economic Community after the Treaty of Rome (1957).

On the other hand, NATO was not established to settle interstate disputes among the members—rather, it was to offset the external military threat for all. Nevertheless, this did not happen without an intimate connection between economy and security. In order to establish NATO in 1949, the United States had to promote economic reconstruction in Western Europe. It would be incorrect to assume that the framers of the Marshall plan had the foundation of a military bloc in mind when they were elaborating the finances of postwar reconstruction. It can be doubted, however, that without the multifunctional aid project Western Europe would have been able to create a viable military organization in the late 1940s. When, in the 1980s, NATO was enlarged toward the south, incorporation into the EC was a guarantee that the newcomers—Greece, Spain and Portugal—would bear the burden of military re-equipment. Turkey can be regarded as an eternal exception from the rule, although vast amounts of credit were provided by the IMF and the World Bank. This can be interpreted as a situation in which the United States did not want to share control over this country of great geostrategic importance, even with the West European allies.

With the invitation to join NATO issued by the Madrid Summit in July 1997, Hungary, the Czech Republic and Poland found themselves in the company of Turkey—namely, in a group of countries with membership in NATO but outside the European Union. The announcement of U.S. policy by the Secretary of State to enlarge NATO by inviting three countries nearly coincided with the rejection by President Clinton of a comprehensive aid package for the FSCs on the pattern of the Marshall Plan (the 50th anniversary of which he used to declare his principles). Whenever Western politicians have rejected the idea of a "new Marshall Plan" in recent years, they have referred to foreign investment, saying that it should (this time) be private money that must fulfill the role of reconstructing the former Eastern bloc countries that have been destroyed by economic warfare during the Cold War and the collapse of their trading bloc (CMEA).

The problem with this reference to private investment is that it strongly resembles U.S. policies after World War I, when private money also flew toward the destroyed economies of Europe, including Germany; but, due to its anarchistic character, it was unable to prevent the greatest economic and social disaster of this century. The Americans did too little and too late to remove the debt burden of Germany in the 1920s, and they supported rigid monetarist policies that exacerbated the depression for years. Private investment also started to flow to Eastern Europe after the fall of the Berlin Wall; it did not, however, turn out to be such a great engine for the recapitalized economies of the region. Hungary, the country that received half of the foreign investment of the region between 1989 and 1996, showed the slowest simultaneous economic growth as compared to Poland, the Czech Republic, Slovakia, Slovenia and Romania—countries that preferred other forms, or even a slower pace of privatization.

The failure of market principles to facilitate rapid recovery and an improvement of the living standards for a substantial majority of the population in former socialist countries generated a debate about the need for, and the possibility of, a new Marshall Plan (time after time). This very discourse has been in evidence with regard to the instability to which politicians and many public commentators have tended to call attention. This instability has a variety of components, such as personal insecurity for those affected or threatened by the loss of jobs or welfare entitlements, a criminalization of the economy from the proliferation of ordinary tax evasion to the rise of oil Mafiosi, the recurring danger of ethnic violence and racist aggression and the lack of legitimacy for the new owners of the recently privatized assets.

The progressive way to eliminate such a general state of instability would be through economic development, inasmuch as accelerated integration into the European economic framework could provide useful occupation and an increasing level of incomes for the working population of the region. That would require concerted action on behalf of the major West European governments, tied down to the project of establishing a single currency by the year 2002 and depressing their economies in order to achieve it. The only period when they paid some more attention to the East was 1993 and 1994—that is, the early years of the first Clinton administration, when the new U.S. foreign policy left the task of dealing with East-Central Europe to the European Union. This was the period when the European Union promised future membership for the associated countries, numbering ten.[3] Apart from promises, however, the European Union has done too little, too late, and in too confused a way for the stabilization and development of the region.

The Dayton agreement of late 1995—a dubious peace treaty for the Balkans—represented a robust return of the United States to ECE affairs, although only offering military stabilization, without the perspective of economic and social progress. The decision about NATO enlargement in 1997 was a continuation of this policy. The dilemma of "more jobs or more police" was answered by U.S. and West European foreign policy to the benefit of the latter at a regional level.

Though NATO enlargement seems to be the first real step toward EU membership to foreign policy–makers in Eastern Europe, there is a legitimate fear that the eastward expansion of NATO will, rather, be a substitute for that of the European Union. The West European countries have already gained what was possible from economic integration with their eastern neighbors, and the political imperatives for EU enlargement have been removed by the commitment of the United States to include a few countries of the former socialist bloc. While NATO is making practical steps toward enlargement, the European Union appears to be unprepared to do so, and it can now afford to delay such decisions for an indefinite period of time.

Following the NATO invitation to Poland, the Czech Republic and Hungary, the agreements between the representatives of the organization and the newcomer governments were signed in December 1997, and the ratification of the agreements began in national legislative bodies. The debate in the U.S. Senate was preceded by a substantial debate in the press and in the academic community about the benefits and potential dangers of NATO enlargement.

Though just a small minority of the senators opposed the enlargement at the moment of voting, they were supported by legions of historians and other intellectuals who shared their concern about the costs and the international political impact of NATO enlargement. Under the first Clinton administration, much of the military bureaucracy also opposed the White House initiative. Before 1996, national security advisor Anthony Lake appeared to be the most prominent person in the administration who actively represented the idea of NATO enlargement. His initiative was opposed by Defense Secretary Les Aspin, chairman of the Joint Chiefs of Staff John Shalikashvili and Secretary of State Warren Christopher (Goldgeier 1998: 88).

By the time the second Clinton administration entered office, NATO enlargement had become a key policy issue of foreign policy. The new Secretary of State, Madeleine Albright (who was born in Czechoslovakia) enthusiastically supported enlargement, and Assistant Secretary of State Richard Holbrooke (whose wife is Hungarian) was instrumental in bringing the military bureaucracy on board. Through generous donations and lobbying, the military industries made it clear that they demanded enlargement of NATO, and the various Czech, Hungarian and Polish lobby groups also started a vigorous campaign for inviting their homelands into the North Atlantic security community.

After the invitation was announced in Madrid, the committees of the Senate began hearings about NATO enlargement. Henry Kissinger and other authorities connected with U.S. foreign policy appeared before the senators and supported the enlargement for various reasons. The arguments for enlargement included the moral commitment to the peoples of East-Central Europe, the expected boost to East–West business and also the fear of intra-European conflicts, given that the United States might reduce its role in maintaining European security. It soon became apparent that a majority of the senators would be in favor of the initiative.[4]

The vote on enlargement was scheduled to take place in the middle of March—early enough not to be influenced by the expected debate over the role of SFOR troops in Bosnia-Herzegovina and the elections for the U.S. Congress in November 1998. Though Senate Majority Leader Trent Lott was strongly in favor of NATO enlargement, the debate over the ratification suffered a six-week delay and was started only at the very end of April. The discussion of the enlargement in the press and in the Senate raised a number of issues and concerns that had been ignored within the newly invited countries.

The New York Times became the flagship of the antienlargement camp of the U.S. intellectual and political elites, not only opposing NATO enlargement but also criticizing the way the issue was being handled by the administration and the Senate. Furthermore, the paper demanded a further postponement of the vote, saying that "the most important foreign policy decision of the post–cold-war era" would require much longer deliberation. Such demands, however, did not affect the agenda of the Senate at all. After a few days' discussion, the senators voted 80:19 in favor of the enlargement of NATO by giving membership to Poland, Hungary and the Czech Republic.

The opponents of enlargement attempted to block the road before ratification with a number of amendments to the treaty. Daniel Patrick Moynihan, for instance, suggested that NATO membership for the three countries should be delayed until these countries had joined the European Union. Though this suggestion was not realistic, it was far from being irrelevant. Despite the fact that a direct link between membership in NATO and accession to the European Union does not exist and the United States has no direct influence on the enlargement of the European Union, it is undoubtedly in the interest of the United States that the European Union should also expands eastwards to include the new NATO member states of East-Central Europe. Apart from the general concern about stability and prosperity, EU integration is expected to help the countries of East-Central Europe to consolidate their economies; the latter is a precondition for increasing East-Central Europe's military spending to the required levels—not least, to buy advanced military products from the United States (Szőnyi 1997: 132).

It was, of course, correct to expect that in order to be able to double their military expenditures, Poles, Czechs and Hungarians needed a much stronger economy than the one they had in the late 1990s. It was, however, still unknown at the time of ratification how large the actual costs of enlargement would be— especially if the "military might" of the newcomers had to be developed to approach West European standards in the first decade of the twenty-first century.

NATO enlargement was primarily a political decision, the many economic and military aspects of which were ignored. The complexity of the ECE transformation was not sufficiently appreciated before votes were cast by the legislators of various countries. Given that "many contemporary security problems in the region are internal to the states rather than external, and are economic and political rather than military, it is not clear whether NATO can effectively address them" (Hyde-Price 1996: 251). It is yet to be seen whether NATO enlargement turns out to be a stage toward EU enlargement or a diversion from that road instead.

Federalism and Enlargement

As in security affairs, it was also an economic matter whether U.S.-led or European organizations would become the most influential in determining the transformation and restructuring of FSCs. In the early period of the transition it was the IMF and the World Bank that became dominant in shaping Western policies (although West European states also reacted to the Eastern changes by creating new institutions and launching new projects). At the end of the 1990s the role of the Bretton Woods institutions diminished in East-Central Europe, while the internal affairs of the European Union prevented the acceleration of eastward EU enlargement.

The fact that it was not only the IMF and the World Bank but also the European Union that started to influence national policies in East-Central Europe did not make life easier for the leaders in the latter countries. According to Gowan (1995), a headless hegemony—in other words, a hegemonic oligopoly— has emerged in the region, running contradictory policies on micro- and macro-economic levels, in trade and finance. The Western endeavor to "help" the new democracies with ideas and recipes for success was so overwhelming that most governments in the region did not even try to form their own policies, being impressed by Western expertise (and also lacking sufficient knowledge and experience).

Following the disintegration of the Eastern Bloc and the Malta Summit (December 1989), it was a conscious decision to leave the guiding role of transition to the IMF, which had already been involved in policy formation in various countries of the region. This decision was made in a period when all countries in the region set as their goals the joining of Euro-Atlantic organizations. Few analysts concluded in that early period that the role of the Bretton Woods institutions, as defined by seemingly helpful Western governments, was totally incompatible with the attempted integration to the European Union. The last example of IMF intervention in a West European country was the case of Great Britain in 1976. Since then, with the progress of monetary integration in Western Europe, it has been inconceivable that the Washington-based institution might be able to exercise a direct influence on a West European government—even on one regularly facing financial problems (e.g. Greece, Italy etc.).

The hegemonic rivalry of the United States and the West European states became apparent as soon as the structures of the state socialist bloc started to fall apart in Poland and Hungary. Although the West European governments refused to commit themselves to a quick eastward enlargement of the European Union, they extended some programs to the democratizing FSCs in order to assist their transformation. Among the most important projects of the European Union, mention should be made of the Phare program and the creation of the European Bank for Reconstruction and Development (EBRD).

The Phare program was launched by the European Union in 1989 to assist the democratization and marketization processes in Poland and Hungary by providing expertise and financial aid. In the subsequent years the program was extended to other FSCs—and eventually to all associated countries of the region. Former Soviet republics—with the exception of the Baltic states—were given another program, called Tacis. Originally, the Phare program was meant to run for a year, but it was extended several times. The financial packages available for the transforming countries represented substantial amounts, although they also demanded that the recipient governments cofinance the projects supported by Brussels through Phare.

As with many other projects of official international aid, the operation of Phare has not been considered sufficiently transparent. An inquiry by the Brussels political analyst Jo Brew concludes that the main beneficiaries of EU "aid" to Central and Eastern Europe have been Western corporations. The lion's share of Phare contracts was received by powerful European businesses, and where "Easterners" were employed, they were paid only one-fifth the rate that "Westerners" received. There were various direct and indirect ways to support Western transnational corporations with subsidies allegedly for the aid of Eastern Europe. Some examples suggest that the abuse of Phare funds may have been dramatic.

More than forty different TNCs have been paid between 100,000 and 1 million ECU by Phare to supply pesticides for Eastern European agriculture. Beneficiaries include Monsanto Europe, Bayer, Rhone Pulenc Agrochimie, ICI, Hoechst and Shell. Some of the exported pesticides are banned in the West. Others were unsaleable and now lie in toxic stockpiles polluting land and threatening drinking water supplies. TNCs were paid to supply pesticides as "agricultural assistance," despite a 1994 European Parliament resolution that "ecologically sound and organic farming" should be a priority for EU programmes in the East. [Brew 1997: 24]

Official Phare and Tacis documents hardly ever mentioned the names of Western companies benefiting from these aid packages. Financial reports were always broken down by sector or country, obscuring the actual recipients of funding. The glossy documents given to the press and public focused heavily on projects that eventually ended up being owned locally, giving a false impression of the development of popular capitalism.

The bias towards business is further hidden behind a sophisticated veil of pretended incompetence. After several years of damning reports on the failure of Phare and Tacis to help people in the East, the EU's chief auditor for Phare concluded that there was no overall strategy behind the programmes. Rather than admit that the goal was to enrich western TNCs, the auditor decided that the bureaucrats were buffoons. [Brew 1997: 25]

Similarly to Phare, the EBRD has been unable to function according to its original objectives. Jacques Attali, an advisor of the late French President François Mitterrand, initiated the creation of this bank to serve a much broader range of purposes than conventional banks or even conventional development banks. Apart from assisting business projects, he wanted the EBRD to be instrumental in maintaining democratic values and improving social and environmental standards. In the spring of 1993, however, Attali was replaced by Jacques de Larosiére, a former managing director of the IMF and president of the French Central Bank; he abandoned Attali's socialist goals and turned the EBRD into a financially conservative development bank.

It is not only the policy of the EBRD that has changed since its start but its regional focus as well. First, the main bulk of funds was devoted to the most advanced reform countries, whose share diminished after their institutional transformation reached an advanced level. In May 1998, the board of the EBRD decided to share its resources: namely, to use 30% in the advanced reform countries of East-Central Europe, another 30% in Russia, and the remaining 40% in the rest of the former socialist block.

When particular projects like Phare and EBRD were launched, the EU Commission was still ruling out the possibility of membership for FSCs. Instead, they established association agreements—or Europe agreements—with ECE countries in order to promote free trade between East and West. It was, however, still emphasized that the Europe agreements did not guarantee full membership in any sense. The first time full membership—though without a deadline—was promised for the associated countries was at the 1993 June Copenhagen Summit. The Essen Summit 18 months later developed a strategy for eastward enlargement.

In 1994, the associated countries started to submit their applications for full membership in the European Union. Their governments filled out a vast number of questionnaires about the state of the market economy and of human rights in their countries. They had to train hundreds of new experts from the European Union whose task is to participate in the talks and to manage the Europeanization of various institutions. Adjustment to West European norms and legal harmonization became integrated parts of economic policies in the associated countries.

It was, however, not only the East but also the West that needed adjustment to make a larger union possible. Although it was not its main purpose, the Intergovernmental Conference (IGC) of 1996–97 was supposed to make preparations toward the next eastward enlargement of the European Union. These steps should have outlined the guidelines for various reforms within the European Union in order to enable it to integrate another half a dozen or more countries. The necessary reforms should touch the Common Agricultural Policy, the Structural Funds and, most of all, the system of voting and appointments in the decision-making and executive bodies of the European Union. In reality, no progress was made in these areas, and it was not even made clear when such reforms would take place.

When the accession talks began in 1998, it was already understood that the conflicts over the reform of common policies could easily decelerate the process of enlargement. According to estimates published by the staff in Brussels, after enlargement some 35–40% of the EU population would be eligible for structural funds instead of 51% in 1997. The "Objective 1" qualification would be taken away from areas like Northern Ireland, while almost the entire territory of the six newcomers would fall into this cluster. If we take into account the fact that Germany, France and the United Kingdom are not prepared to increase their contribution to the EU budget while Spain, Greece and Portugal are not prepared to give up their benefits from the Brussels budget, it is not difficult to understand why internal reforms might take years, if not decades, to implement.

According to some experts, Hungarians do not need to wait until the redistributive systems of the European Union are reformed. In a Budapest lecture in November 1995, sponsored by George Soros's Central European University, Harvard Professor Jeffrey D. Sachs suggested that Hungary could and should join the European Union and at the same time reject such "distortive policies" as CAP, Structural Funds and the "Social Charter." In his view, these policies make the national economies lose their competitive and innovative capacities by weakening their entrepreneurial spirit. He also called the attention of the audience to the fact that the proportion of the population over the age of 60 was only about 5% in the rapidly growing South East Asia, while it is about 20% in ECE. He suggested that an improvement on this front would be a major precondition for achieving sustainable convergent economic growth (6–7% a year).[5]

Due to the political conflicts arising from problems of redistribution, various countries or country groups have special reservations about admitting newcomers. Present net recipients (e.g. Greece, Spain, Portugal etc.) raise objections to the accession of new members who lack sufficient resources for development. Agricultural exporters (France, Denmark etc.) can still obstruct the accession of potential rivals like Hungary or Bulgaria. The Atlantic "great powers" of the European Union (the United Kingdom and France) may not be happy to see the strengthening of German hegemony through the incorporation of its former *Lebensraum*. Northern members could oppose the preference shown for the Visegrád Four or CEFTA, considering such favored status to be a betrayal of the Baltic states.

All these objections and reservations could be forgotten, or treated just as bargaining items when the final pact is elaborated, if the members together appreciate the two main advantages of enlargement: namely, that it could enlarge the internal markets of the union and it could help to restore the competitiveness of West European capital against Japan and the United States. An increased "social dumping" (generated by economies with one-tenth of the German wage level) could exercise a strong downward pressure on real wages in Western Europe. If, however, applicants "hand over" these advantages to Western investors and producers before membership and without guarantees for eventually gaining membership, their leverage for persuading the EU members to support enlargement will approach zero.

It is also important to analyze what the actual relationship would be (if any) between the EU agenda for the late 1990s and possible enlargement. This problem was addressed by Malcolm Rifkind, then foreign secretary of the United Kingdom, in a speech delivered in Zürich in September 1996. He expressed the old British concern over EMU, saying that it would divide the continent instead of uniting it, and thus it would be contrary to the vision of the founding fathers. He also mentioned that eastward enlargement would deepen this division, since the associated countries are still, and will remain for a long time, too immature to be fit for full membership in an economic and monetary union. Rifkind was pointing out that European integration had reached the limits of simultaneous deepening and widening. With the fall of the British Conservatives, the former foreign secretary may not be a member of parliament any longer, but the Rifkind dilemma may stay with us in the future. Therefore, we must thoroughly investigate how the former socialist countries could possibly fit into the economic framework provided by EMU.

As is known, British Conservatives supported eastward enlargement in order to obstruct further the deepening of European integration. Their support has, however, gone beyond diplomacy. Just a year before its fall, the Conservative government of the United Kingdom launched an offensive to expand trade relations with East-Central Europe. In an interview in June 1998, the new British Ambassador to Budapest, Nigel Thorpe, emphasized that British companies had long-term interests in Hungary, in particular with respect to the maintenance of the openness of the Hungarian economy. This long-term interest originates primarily from the U.S.$1.1 billion volume of British investments in Hungary, and also from the expectation that British investors will take part in future privatization in the banking and energy sectors in Hungary (Dési 1998: 3). The ambassador therefore invited the new Hungarian government to commit itself to the adoption of the *acquis communautaire* even before the country becomes a full member of the European Union.

When the accession process was officially launched, the European Union established a working group to conduct negotiations with the six applicants of the first round. The group was led by Klaus Van der Pas of Germany, who could be regarded as a general director responsible for the enlargement talks. Van der Pas used to be a close colleague of Jacques Delors and in the 1990s participated in the creation of the European Economic Area and later in the accession negotiations with Sweden. The Italian Giorgio Bonacci was named a member of the working group, with special responsibility for Hungary. Bonacci did not have much experience of Hungary, although he had been working with some other East European countries like Ukraine, Belarus and Moldavia. He had also worked at the East African desk of the European Union and had experience in financial, developmental and statistical areas.

The leading negotiators of the European Union made it clear that an acceleration of the talks was not among their most important tasks. Van der Pas recommended to the applicants that they should not even deal with the actual time of accession. EU Commissioner Hans van den Broek commented that the efforts the new applicants would need to make to adjust to the 80,000-page *acquis communautaire,* after 40 years of Communism, must not be underestimated (Kocsis 1998: 8). However, the bureaucrats of Brussels were, at least, more polite than some party politicians in Germany.

In the summer of 1998, the German election campaign witnessed some right-wing politicians making antienlargement statements, and this caused something of a scare in ECE political circles. In a press interview, Christian Schmidt, a leading figure in the Bavarian CSU, suggested that 2015 might be seen as a likely year when former socialist countries could be considered for full membership of the European Union. Politicians of Fidesz–MPP, the party that had just won power in Hungary, had to respond and called Schmidt's view an assault on the entire eastward enlargement. After a few days, the affair was explained—at least in Hungary—by claiming that Schmidt meant that 2015 would be the year when the last derogations could be phased out and thus no issues would distinguish Hungary from other EU members (Pócs and Inotai 1998: 3).

Soon after the Schmidt affair, Kult Schelter, a junior minister at the German Federal Interior Ministry, proposed that the free movement of labor should only be allowed for ECE nations around 2015. The alleged reason for this proposal was the fear of a wave of immigration from the east. Schelter's comment was clearly motivated by the circumstances of the German parliamentary elections, rather than the actual facts of East–West labor mobility. At the time, only some 5,000 Hungarians were working in Germany, mainly on building construction sites. Most of them were employed within the framework of intergovernmental contracts. It was also noticed that Hungary was usually unable to fill the quota for individuals who wanted to find employment in Germany, because the number of willing workers remained under 2,000 (Léderer 1998: 3).

The review of the assumed accession year of 2002 was, however, not just a privilege of the German Right. At the Cardiff Summit in June 1998, José Maria Gíl-Robles, the Speaker of the European Parliament, claimed that the associated countries could not become EU members before 2005. British ambassador Nigel Thorpe, on behalf of the then U.K. president of the European Union, explained this view by pointing out the complexity of the accession talks and the fact that the forthcoming screening process could discover some hitherto unforeseen difficulties (Dési 1998: 3).

Diplomats are sometimes cynically referred to as the "artists of understatement." The cited comments may just represent the tip of the iceberg—a bulk of many complex problems that, despite the political imperative for integration, may prevent the accession from taking place along the plans developed in the mid-1990s. Many of these problems can be seen to have their roots in economic considerations.

ECONOMICS:
FROM MAASTRICHT TO BUDAPEST

The economic integration of Hungary to the European Union started before the collapse of state socialism and accelerated after the association agreement of 1991. In the early 1990s, the microeconomy was the site of the main area of economic adjustment; this was a result of liberalization in trade and capital movements, and also the commitment to legal harmonization. From the mid-1990s on, macroeconomic adjustment also became increasingly important. Due to these new requirements, however, the gap between the Western and Eastern halves of the continent became even more apparent.

Fiscal Convergence and Monetary Disparities

In order to establish a monetary union, the Maastricht Treaty set out certain fiscal and monetary criteria for the member states of the European Union. Although the Treaty only applies to the actual members of the European Union, the countries that hope to be members in the future must also take into account the Maastricht criteria of economic convergence. The six countries that are anticipating accession to the European Union at the beginning of the twenty-first century are not likely to have fulfilled the criteria at the moment of accession. (See Appendix 2, Table 11.) However, if they neglect the Maastricht targets in their economic policies, they might be seen to be ignorant about the overall objectives of the Union, and this could damage the consensus of West European governments about the need for pushing ahead rapidly with enlargement. Thus, even if Hungary need not worry about the Maastricht criteria in the short run, it must assess the chances of fiscal and monetary stability in order to be able to make a better judgment with respect to medium- and long-term prospects.

In the 1990s, the fiscal indicators of the Hungarian economy have favorably changed toward full compliance with the Maastricht criteria; however, the adjustment of monetary indicators is proving more problematic. One could even talk about a trade-off between fiscal and monetary stability in the 1990s. The decade began with almost no budget deficit but with an inflation rate that occasionally ran close to 40%. At that time the government managed to bring down inflation, but it also started to borrow at record rates. After 1995 another government attempted to strike a balance between the two evils, but it found itself much more successful in fighting the budget deficit and foreign debt than in dealing with the deterioration of the value of the forint.

The reason for such a course in national finances can be found in the particular way the economic transition has been managed in former socialist countries, the neoliberal inspiration behind transition policies and the direct role the IMF has played in the design of these policies. The European Union and the Maastricht Treaty had not yet been born or even thought of when the IMF began to demand balanced budgets and a reduction of foreign debts in exchange for the seal of approval that was needed by former socialist countries if they were to become respectable members of the international financial community.

The two last communist governments of Hungary—those of Károly Grósz and Miklós Németh—implemented harsh austerity measures in exchange for stand-by agreements with the IMF. Under Grósz the runaway indebtedness that had started in 1985 stopped, and Németh submitted a balanced budget for 1990. In exchange for fiscal stabilization the country had to endure an ever-increasing inflation. The latter never approached triple digits, as it did in some other East European countries in the crisis and reform periods, but it was enough to create discontent among the people and anger toward the ruling MSZMP.

The right-wing government led by the Hungarian Democratic Forum took over the national finances with virtually no hard currency reserves in 1990; therefore, even if some forces behind the government did not like this alliance, they were forced into an agreement with the IMF and the World Bank on the principles of stabilization and structural adjustment. Once, however, the East European economic crisis and the transition policies of the respective ECE countries resulted in collapsing output, these countries decided to borrow and spend themselves out of the slump. The reconstruction of the supply-side brought down the rate of inflation as compared to the peak years of 1991 and 1992, but the lack of fiscal discipline destroyed the trust coming from the IMF. The policy (if there was a coherent policy at all) was neither politically nor economically sustainable.

In discussing the monetary policies of the early 1990s, David Bartlett suggests that Central Bank Governor Bod "followed the main policy lines set down by his predecessor" (Bartlett 1997: 187). A major difference, however, between Surányi and Bod was that, while the first championed a substantial devaluation of the forint, the policies of the second allowed a real appreciation of the national currency, with all the negative impacts on the balance of payments. Inflation went up under Surányi and down under Bod. Having been ousted by Antall, Surányi, as a chairman and CEO of the Central European Investment Bank (CIB), constantly criticized the National Bank's policy for allowing a huge deficit to emerge on the current account as well as in the national budget.

Bod, as a "leftover" from Antall's government, was seen as a major obstacle to financial consolidation by the Socialists and the Liberals, who formed a governing coalition after the 1994 elections. Even before the new government was formed, Horn started to pressurize Bod to resign, although he was protected for another three years by the National Bank Act of 1991. Eventually, in exchange for a position in the London-based EBRD, Bod resigned in December 1994; this made it possible for Surányi to return. Although Horn also considered the appointment of some other economists, the events of early 1995 secured Surányi's return to his old office and for the country to continue with the old recipes of neoliberal austerity.[6]

Between 1995 and 1998, the Hungarian economy was moving along the trajectory determined by the March 1995 U-turn in economic policy—the so-called Bokros package, named after finance minister Lajos Bokros.[7] The guidelines of this program originated in the policies of the IMF, although they were usually interpreted as preconditions for joining the European Union. It is indeed true that the relative success of the Bokros package made it possible for Hungary to sign another stand-by loan with the IMF; this was a precondition for Hungary gaining membership in the OECD in March 1996. Being a member of the OECD made the application for EU membership much more serious than it had been before.

The package consisted of two major parts. First, it implemented immediate macroeconomic measures to cut public expenditures, to devalue the forint by 9% and to impose a 10% import surcharge. Second, it launched a series of public sector reforms to abolish the universal elements in the Hungarian welfare state (e.g. introduction of fees in higher education, in health and dental care etc.). Bokros's logic suggested that a reform of welfare entitlements was inevitable because without the changes the outflow of funds from the national budget would have remained automatic, and this threatened the budget with cyclical imbalances. By reintroducing financial discipline, Bokros indeed directed the ship of the Hungarian economy toward the criteria set by EMU, although the reforms he initiated in the public sector gave the impression of a transition toward Latin American conditions instead of West European ones.

This latter charge was put forward (among others) by 17 Hungarian economists, who signed a letter to James Wolfensohn, President of the World Bank, when he visited Hungary at the end of October 1995.[8] The group of 17 asked the president not to link IBRD finance to the conditions defined by the IMF, since those were unrealistic and ill-conceived. The Budapest office of the World Bank invited the dissidents to discuss policy alternatives, which was an unprecedented event. Nevertheless, they also invited like-minded Hungarians to convince the critics about the benefits of World Bank recommendations, particularly concerning the restructuring of the state sector and the privatization of public utilities.

Notwithstanding immense public resentment, Bokros managed to bring back foreign balances and the national budget to a manageable deficit, at the cost of a slowdown in GDP growth and accelerating inflation. During his one-year ministership, the government also brought about an impressive reduction of the public debt by selling public utilities—i.e. gas and electricity suppliers—to foreign investors. Hungary's fiscal indicators thus came close to the Maastricht criteria. On the other hand, the monetary indicators remained hopelessly far from the standards of the EMU. The rate of inflation remained in the mid-20s, in contrast to the 2–3% average in Western Europe. Long-term interest rates—the fourth target of Maastricht—were still an unknown factor in Hungarian finances. The National Bank only started to experiment with 7-year bonds in the second half of the 1990s.

The controversies surrounding the Bokros package highlight the more comprehensive dilemmas of transition policies—namely, the certain trade-offs that have still not been eliminated from ECE reforms. In the early years of transition in Hungary institutional changes took place at a high speed, but the country suffered from rising inflation and falling incomes, while the government was struggling to balance foreign accounts because that was the priority of the overambitious IMF and the World Bank. When the government decided to return to economic growth, they had to abandon everything related to sound finance. The restoration of financial discipline, however, demanded an enormous social cost by increasing the gap between high- and-low income groups of society. With respect to the general elections of 1998, the Horn government was inclined to pass on benefits to wage-earners and pensioners. This again raised doubts about the sustainability of foreign and domestic equilibria.

Before the 1998 elections the government celebrated the remarkable macroeconomic results of the previous year: increased economic growth with decreasing foreign debt (see Appendix 2, Table 3) and a decreasing inflation rate, and particularly a sharp rise in export performance (which was not followed by a similar increase in imports). Economic growth in Hungary was declared sustainable, and the opposition Fidesz–MPP even promised 7% annual GDP growth for the forthcoming years if they were to form a government. Even if the poststabilization GDP growth is sustainable, it must be noted that not even the remarkable export boost of 1997 could bring the trade balance to equilibrium, and the current account also closed with a substantial deficit. That indicates that the sustainability of this growth has been primarily based upon a constant inflow of foreign investment. Preelection forecasts, and particularly expectations related to EU and NATO membership, made the business sector optimistic about the perspectives of foreign capital inflow, even if right-wing parties still saw foreign capital as an enemy that would threaten the present and future positions of a domestic middle class.

It was not only the Right that linked the issue of finance to national sovereignty. Having repaid the last cents of the last stand-by loan, Prime Minister Horn announced Hungary's independence from the IMF in February 1998 (although he also mentioned that none of the IMF policies had been harmful to the Hungarian economy). The announcement did not have much importance in financial affairs, but it appealed to a nationalist constituency that had always been critical or at least doubtful about the nature of the presence and the advice of the Fund.

The difficulties involved in joining the European Union and the EMU are very often played down by leading Hungarian politicians and their advisors. However, there are at least two warning examples that should make the political elite and the wider public think twice about the rush toward the European Union and particularly the EMU. These are the examples of the GDR and Greece. The former was a case where monetary union was enforced between two countries at different levels of economic development, and the long-term consequences have manifested themselves in high unemployment and social distress in the Eastern states of the German federation. In the case of the latter, the dominant powers of the European Union rejected the participation of a weak economy in the monetary union, setting an example of a new division between the financially mature and immature countries of Europe. Poles, Czechs and Hungarians should analyze these two scenarios in order to have a realistic picture of the possible solutions to the problems surrounding the process of accession. It is doubtful whether Hungarians and other former socialist nations are doing the right thing if they want to bluff their way into the European Union when the latter makes demands that exceed what ECE countries can do.

Neither the GDR nor Greece is discussed in Hungary as comparable cases of monetary and fiscal problems. Under the Socialist–Liberal coalition, convergence to the Maastricht criteria became part of the official rhetoric concerning European integration. During a visit to Portugal in 1995, for instance, Prime Minister Horn announced that it was now only the rate of inflation that would prevent Hungary from meeting all the criteria for joining the European Union. A year later, Finance Minister Péter Medgyessy was quoted as saying that Hungary would meet the Maastricht criteria by the turn of the century.[9]

With all due respect to the efforts of Hungary's national leaders, it must be said that their games include a good deal of hazard and bluff. Hungary has indeed been approaching the fiscal criteria of Maastricht, and those results might even look sustainable. Monetary indicators, however, are rather different. Decreasing inflation has been declared to be a prime objective of government policy, although in practice it has been a tool that has been raised or lowered depending on other goals, such as foreign balances. In October 1997, the Governor of the National Bank of Hungary, György Surányi, suggested that the Maastricht criteria should not be too strictly applied to Hungary because the rate of inflation could not be lowered as quickly as expected due to the economic measures required by the transformation process.

Nevertheless, Hungary is determined to make steps toward EU standards wherever it is possible. At the end of 1996, for example, the Central Bank Act of Hungary was modified in order to provide the National Bank with a greater and more perfect independence. The main motivation for this modification was to apply the standards of central bank independence, as found in those countries of continental Western Europe heading toward monetary union. The fact that Hungary was still far from joining the EMU did not disturb the law-makers and their advisors, although some Socialist politicians felt uneasy about giving even more power to certain financial leaders who already dictated the course of economic and social policy in general.[10]

The issue of central bank independence is a good example for illustrating that, in institutional reform, it is significantly easier to converge with European norms than with real economic indicators. Politics in Hungary is indeed determined to comply with all requirements. In reality, however, the underdeveloped nature of the economy and the tasks of transition make the necessary adjustment very difficult. There are also certain points of intersection between institutional and real economic spheres where judgment about the pace of convergence becomes extremely difficult.

It is hard to tell, for example, whether the exchange rate policy of Hungary came closer to EMU norms during the 1990s. In the first half of the 1990s, the government applied a fixed but adjustable rate, which was replaced by a crawling peg in March 1995, when György Surányi returned as Governor of the National Bank.[11] In principle, the fixed but adjustable exchange rate was comparable to that of the European Monetary System (EMS). In reality, however, downward adjustment took place so frequently and so drastically between 1989 and 1992 that it was hard to recognize that the exchange rate had ever been fixed (see Appendix 2, Table 8). After 1995, the crawling peg distanced the exchange rate regime from the opportunity to keep the same rate for longer than one month. Nevertheless, the system became more reliable, and thus in practice it did get closer to stability—which is in the center of the monetary union project. By announcing the crawling peg, the government accepted that the reduction in the rate of inflation would be slower than before, but it created a favorable environment for international investment.

The change in the foreign exchange basket—which determines the exchange rate of the Hungarian forint—has changed several times during the transition years and, similarly to foreign trade, has shown a tendency toward Europeanization. Before December 1991 the basket was designed in line with the foreign-exchange composition of foreign trade in the previous year. In this system the U.S. dollar had a much greater role than U.S. trade, since much of the trade with Third-World countries was also denominated in dollars. From December 1991 on, the forint was adjusted to a basket of 50% US dollar and 50% ECU. In August 1993 Hungarian monetary policy reacted to the increased volatility of European currencies and replaced the ECU with the Deutsche Mark (DEM). Less than a year later, in May 1994, the ECU was rehabilitated up to 70% in the basket, and the role of the—then depreciating—dollar was diminished to 30%. In January 1997, the ECU was again replaced by the DEM, and this was officially explained by the circumstance that the former was not traded in foreign exchange markets, whereas the latter was. When the Euro was launched in January 1999, the DEM was replaced by the Euro, and it was announced that a year later the U.S. dollar would be dumped and the Euro would make up 100% of the basket of the Hungarian currency.[12]

The Broad Path of Economic Adjustment

Even if an associated country meets the tough criteria of economic convergence, the government of that country cannot be sure that the country can or must join the European Union. The concept of integration includes parallel processes such as adjustment, accession and catching up. When the question is membership in the European Union, meeting the Maastricht criteria cannot be identified with either of the three processes. Maastricht only tells us about some selected macro-economic figures, while adjustment must also be applied to the realm of the microeconomy. Accession and catching up, on the other hand, must be analyzed within the broader framework of political economy.

Intensifying trade relations—which was the project between East-Central Europe and Western Europe in the first half of the 1990s—should in theory contribute to the catching-up process. However, in practice it has turned out to be a major factor in adjustment, sometimes helping FSCs to catch up, but making them fall behind in even more other cases. In principle, the logic of comparative advantages should work out an optimal division of labor between the two converging zones for the benefit of both. In reality, however, when two economic areas intensify trade relations with each other, the more productive unit tends to accumulate a trade surplus against the other. The less developed zone may concentrate on segments of production with less value added, and this halts modernization and maintains obsolete economic structures.

Hungary was forced to switch markets after 1989 and particularly after the collapse of the CMEA, in 1991 (see Appendix 2, Table 5). The country had to engage in a new division of labor with Western Europe, and for a while it was not clear what role it could take in the new era. Trade liberalization, however, was forced upon the FSCs before an internationally coordinated policy had been given a chance to lead them into a consolidated new position. Therefore, opening up the Hungarian economy to international competition resulted in the emergence of a huge deficit in the current account (see Appendix 2, Table 4). This was partly due to the substantial interest payments on the foreign debts, but also to an increasing trade deficit (see Appendix 2, Table 2).

The more Hungary turned its trade toward the European Union, the greater the deficit became. After 1992, Hungary's trade deficit with the European Union increased much faster than did the value of EU trade itself. Between 1992 and 1996, the share of the European Union in the total foreign trade of Hungary increased by 16%, while in the Hungarian trade deficit the EU share increased by 26%. This was, however, a general trend in the region. For Poland, the share of the European Union in foreign trade increased by 6%, while the EU share in the Polish trade deficit increased by 26%. In the same period, in Slovakia and Slovenia respectively, an EU surplus turned into a substantial deficit.

As FSCs hoping for quick Western integration cut their trade relations in the early 1990s, they pulled each other into a demand-driven recession. Their transformation policies undercut their supply side as well, and this ensured that the recovery from the slump would be as slow as possible. When, however, they were emerging from the long depression of the 1990s, their new role in the international division of labor was not necessarily disadvantageous. A zone of Westernizing FSCs was emerging with a solid industrial base largely dominated by multinational corporations.

Within Hungarian exports to the European Union in 1994, the share of agricultural products was 13.1%. In two years this figure fell to 9.5%. During the same two years, the share of raw materials went down from 6.5% to 4.4% and the share of chemical products from 7.7% to 6.0%. The share of semiprocessed products and consumption goods decreased from 39.6% to 33.1%. The group of machinery and vehicles, however, increased its share from 28.7% to 42.3% between 1994 and 1996 (Inotai 1997: 68). The same trends were observed in all other Visegrád countries and in Slovenia—the share of agriculture, chemical products and consumption goods decreased, while the share of machinery and vehicles increased by a remarkable margin.

In the case of Romania and Bulgaria, however, a similar restructuring of trade relations did not occur in the same period; this was a sign that these countries were not developing the same geoeconomic position as the CEFTA-5. This latter group did indeed make substantial progress toward becoming a major trading partner of the European Union. Within the decade following 1989, the four Visegrád countries quadrupled their share in the external imports of the European Union. Hungary's share in EU imports was half of Turkey's in 1989, but the country had become a comparable exporter for the European Union by the late 1990s. (On directions of foreign trade, see Appendix 2, Table 5.)

The intensity of exports and imports is only one aspect of adjustment, and it does not give a full picture about the benefits and losses of the transformation. A survey written for the German Bertelsmann Foundation in 1998 found that it was predominantly the European Union that benefited from the liberalization the markets of East-Central Europe. The freedom in the flow of goods and capital generated thousands of jobs in Austria and Germany, while, for the same reasons, jobs disappeared in East-Central Europe. In Poland alone, some 1.2–1.4 million jobs were destroyed by the export competition of the European Union. The survey expected that out of the five FSCs that became part of the first eastward enlargement round, only Poland would represent some form of threat in terms of labor migration toward the West. The other four were expected to attract capital investment instead of exporting workers.

By the late 1990s, the idea that adjustment does not necessarily lead to catching up became common sense. A conclusion was also drawn that in such a case not even accession would be able to satisfy the needs of the population of FSCs. Hence, even if the European integration of the Visegrád zone continues, measures taken by the West to insulate itself against a stream of immigrants from the East will continue to be effective. The freedom of labor mobility is expected to be restricted on both sides of the zone of enlargement. A new iron curtain may emerge to the east and south of the Visegrád countries, while the westward mobility of their population will also continue to be restricted, albeit without a hermetically sealed iron curtain.

Foreign visitors do not see why there should be a sudden mass migration. On the streets of the major cities in the FSCs one can see the signs of an emerging consumer culture. Western patterns of shopping and marketing penetrated the former socialist world in the periods of reform and transition. This process has been further championed by multinational investment groups since the early

1990s, although real purchasing power was added to the process only after 1996. After the postcommunist recovery was sensed by the large firms, giant shopping malls emerged in the cities and on the highways and started to crowd out the small- and medium-sized shops and depriving them of business, very much as in the United States and Western Europe.

As harmonization proceeded during the 1990s, all the various economic actors had to adjust their activities to the norms prevailing in the European Union. Where it was not possible immediately, calculations were carried out to estimate the future costs of adjustment. In all parts of the ECE region environmental standards were expected to represent the field where adjustment would be the most expensive during the process of convergence. Environmental adjustment, however, is not simply a matter of legislation and costs, for it deeply affects the structure of the economy and even the interests of foreign producers. According to professor Béla Darvas of the Hungarian Academy of Sciences, in 1998 there were still no barriers in Hungary against the import and sale of pesticides prohibited in the European Union and the United States. Trade in about a hundred products would have had to have been abolished immediately if the environmental norms of the European Union had been adopted in Hungary at that time.[13] Such a move would have hit not primarily Hungarians but those West European and North American corporations, and thus the latter became interested in slowing down the accession process.

Assessing the complexity of economic restructuring made some experts conclude that the main thrust toward the Europeanization of the Hungarian economy still lay ahead. Ádám Török, a leading expert on foreign trade, is one of those researchers who claim that the period of EU accession should be seen as an adjustment that requires large-scale industrial transformation comparable to the early years of postcommunist transition.

The scale of the job of restructuring was appreciated early enough by both sides, and Western Europe also committed itself to assisting adjustment in the East. In addition to the establishment of Phare and EBRD, the European Investment Bank (EIB) also became involved in assistance with the Eastern transformation. Soon after the East European transition began, the EIB was allowed to extend its investment activities to the associated countries. The loans provided by the EIB were guaranteed by the Community. In the first years of this new period—that is, by the end of 1994—the EIB had approved 57 such loans, for a total amount of ECU 2.7 billion. They were mainly directed toward infrastructural development and assistance for small- and medium-sized industrial enterprises.

In the late 1990s, students of the transition and European integration assumed that the coming round of industrial restructuring could be achieved without another recession. On the contrary, forecasts of an extraordinarily dynamic growth path were widely discussed. Following the "post-Bokros" recovery of the Hungarian economy, politicians became optimistic about the prospects for economic development. Nevertheless, even if GDP growth can be preserved at a sustainable level of 3–4% per annum, the gap between the EU average and the would-be members in terms of incomes and living standards remain enormous. In Poland and Hungary, higher than West European growth rates in the second half of the 1990s could fuel a success campaign for governments following neoliberal guidelines. One must recognize, however, that these economies had nowhere to go but up after their respective GDPs nosedived in the 1990–92 period.

Wage differences in the former Iron Curtain countries are still comparable to the U.S.–Mexico gap, while the all-European integration plans are incomparably more ambitious than the North American ones; the latter only stretch to the level of a free-trade zone. The European countries intend to establish not only free trade between the present European Union and 10 former socialist countries, but a total absorption of the emerging economies of East-Central Europe within the next 10–15 years (that is, according to political expectations).

The drive toward EU membership with full participation in the EMU raises another dilemma. This is linked to the fact that "Europeanness" has really become the only vision or motivation that can make people accept social sacrifice for economic progress. As the sacrifices become greater and greater, however, the attractiveness of this vision may fade, particularly when politicians insincerely overuse references to the European future. When living standards decline for most of the population as a result of austerity and corruption cases undermine domestic support for the ruling parties, progress reports about European integration appear as a source of legitimacy for all the different government policies. "Europe" has been elevated to a position of an ultimate authority from which the policies of reform and transition, including all austerity measures, can be derived—ranging from agriculture to banking. In 1996, the junior minister responsible for preparation for integration, Ferenc Somogyi, complained publicly that not all austerity measures should be justified simply by the requirements of European integration. It could well happen that people will eventually link the concept of Europe to meaningless social and economic sacrifices, and the whole process will thus become unpopular and could be voted against in a crucial referendum. The damage done by the heavy adjustment to IMF and NATO requirements may easily come to reflect on Europe, even though this is indeed the project with the most progressive capacities, despite its various controversies.

If Hungarians and other European nations blame the European Union and particularly the EMU for their hardships, the critique is not necessarily misplaced. The current round of deepening of European integration—that is, the establishment of monetary union—represents a challenge to the postwar welfare state in that it attacks the established institutions of redistribution. The Maastricht Treaty virtually "outlawed" Keynesianism at the level of the nation state, and it has forced governments to cut back welfare spending in a ruthless way. Enlargement, on the other hand, would be a guarantee, preventing the federal level from compensating the recipients of transfers due to the loss of national redistribution. It is simply impossible to incorporate three or four ECE countries without changing the redistribution principles (i.e. structural and agricultural policies). Without reform, the mechanism would require a substantial increase in financial contributions to the EU budget, and this would be strongly resisted by various EU members. In fact, some members, such as the United Kingdom, have supported enlargement precisely because this provides another argument for reforming CAP and regional development policies.

The Thatcherization of Europe that was launched by the Maastricht Treaty does not end at the Eastern borders of the Union. It is already under way in Eastern Europe, although there it has mainly been pursued by non-Europeans—that is, by the IMF and the World Bank. A main benefit of EU enlargement would be that it could reduce the influence of these institutions on economic policies in the associated countries. Transition under their command has taken the same path as structural adjustment in various Third-World countries in the 1980s. The latter process has been strongly criticized by a number of progressive economists, including Cornia, Stewart, and others, who have argued for structural adjustment with a human face. These institutions had become discredited by the end of the 1980s, but the postcommunist world appeared as new frontiers for them. They imported their doctrines and policies from the Third World to the former socialist countries, and this resulted in the emergence of similar forms of misery. Moreover, despite the honorable reforms initiated by the new World Bank president, James Wolfensohn, these institutions have proved to be very slow learners again. In countries with one third or more of the population below the poverty line, excessive welfare spending is still being blamed for stagnation by World Bank and IMF economists and their acolytes. The resulting policies have simply created even greater poverty and social differences. All this has been legitimized by the promise that one day all survivors will be citizens of a united Europe.

However, World Bank policies in East-Central Europe have been underwritten by the European Union on the basis that low standards in the associated countries can exercise a downward pressure on wages and overall production costs in the whole of Europe. Western European industrialists feel the need for the latter because of the sharp rivalry between European, American and Asian business. Thus, all questions about enlargement with a human face boil down to one thing: can Western Europe find a way to compete with the United States and Japan other than by pressing down wage levels and abolishing the welfare state?

Despite the remaining economic disparities, Hungary is much better prepared for joining the European Union than the European Union is prepared for its launch of the next round of enlargement toward the East. The foreign ministers of Western Europe, the Commission, and the Council have not seen a blueprint for enlargement that would be based on the necessary institutional reforms within the European Union and a broad political consensus of all the parties involved. Joining the European Union, however, should not be identified with joining the EMU. The latter seems unlikely for former socialist countries in the next decade, and it may even be seen as unnecessary altogether.

While the main obstacle to enlargement is the lack of readiness in the West, certain problems can be detected in the East too. In the second half of the 1990s, the most determined and able force promoting economic reforms in Hungary, the Hungarian Socialist Party, does not seem to be able to address publicly the real dilemmas of the international embeddedness of the new Hungarian capitalist system. In the meantime, due to the delays in enlargement and the apparent extent of the costs, the right-wing parties are developing a Euro-sceptic attitude. Extraparliamentary parties to the left of the MSZP do not excel in offering more progressive prospects of European and Atlantic affairs either. Thus it is very important to follow the debates over monetary union in Western Europe in order to gain inspiration and policy ideas for finding a more balanced and hopeful way of development.

An example of this is a movement involving progressive European economists: this movement has published a lengthy manifesto for jobs and social cohesion in Europe and has addressed the problems of associated countries (Huffschmid et al. 1997). These economists, who proposed their blueprint as an alternative to the attitude of the Intergovernmental Conference, have demanded accelerated market access for producers in East-Central Europe and the incorporation of the associated countries in a reformed EMS. They also recommend derogations from certain EU rules and special development policies for ECE countries.[14] The alternative is that the associated countries may be asked to comply with conditions they do not favor, and failure to do so would mean that accession would not take place at all, leaving the stabilization of the region to NATO alone.

Given these considerations, and while we link the issues of economy and security to each other, we also have to decompose the Euro-Atlantic package. Now that the decision has been made about the enlargement of NATO, more harm than benefit may be caused if it is not followed by the integration of the countries concerned into the European Union.

With regard to the latter, the EMU should be treated separately from the pre-Maastricht structures. If security is interpreted as a basis for economic development, it should involve not only national security but social security as well. It is not wrong at all to assume that there is an organic link between integration in the economic and security fields, but both concepts must be used in the broadest possible sense. If security structures are developed only in the military field between states, their function can only be to preserve social injustice and insecurity within those states.

The initiative of British Foreign Secretary Robin Cook with respect to the establishment of a Permanent European Conference was an example of the progressive steps being suggested toward a more inclusive European integration. This, or a similar institution, could benefit relations between the European Union and the countries to the east of it, regardless of the actual state of enlargement. For the same reasons, European politicians must pay special attention to the application of the Schengen Agreement in Eastern Europe; in the latter this policy could cut through all different cultural and family ties, unlike in Western Europe, where it is mainly applied at sea borders.

Nevertheless, eastward enlargement is a necessity for the European Union if we want Eastern Europe to be stabilized without the permanent threat of authorized violence. This would, however, require a more inclusive European integration (without the unpopular and apparently uncalculated drive toward the single currency), but with more conscious development policies, much less room for private interest in resource allocation and an association with the broadest possible security structure—namely, OSCE. This is not only in the interest of the peoples living in former socialist countries: Western Europe will also gain greater security and the benefits of economic cooperation.

DOMESTIC POLITICS:
INTERROGATING THE CONSENSUS

Despite the world-historic importance of the events of 1989 and 1990, foreign policy was not the most important policy area at the beginning of postcommunist transition. The major political forces concentrated their attention and energies on the issue of privatization, which had greater immediate importance for deciding the new positions within the new economic elite of Hungary. When, however, the major issues of domestic political economy were settled and the Western organizations started to deal with eastward expansion as a practical issue, the role of foreign policy was given more attention in Hungary, and it also became more successful under the Socialist–Liberal coalition.

Agreement on Illusions

When NATO invited Hungary to join the organization and the European Union named Hungary as being among those selected for the first round of eastward enlargement, the Hungarian political discourse was filled with the vision of rapid accession and accelerated Westernization. This period, however, was not the first time that Hungarian politicians as well as the electorate entertained high hopes about membership in the European Community or Union. In 1990, Prime Minister József Antall promised that Hungary would be a member of the EC by the year 1996. He made this statement when the international embeddedness of the new democracies was still uncertain. When the first postcommunist multiparty parliament and Antall's government were formed, both the CMEA and the WTO were in existence, and no clear plan existed about enlarging either NATO or the EC eastwards. Nevertheless, the six parliamentary parties took it for granted that there could only be one destination for the transition that began in 1989, and that was full membership in the two major organizations of the capitalist West.

Based on such expectations, a foreign-policy consensus emerged between the six parliamentary parties. Since the same six parties entered parliament after the

1990 and the 1994 elections, this "six-party agreement on foreign policy" has continued to characterize Hungarian politics throughout the 1990s. The three pillars of this consensus are (1) the so-called "Euro-Atlantic" integration; (2) "good neighbor" relations; and (3) the promotion of the interests of minority Hungarians abroad. These objectives are treated as equal and assumed to be in harmony with each other.

In everyday political discourse, European integration has been elevated to the position of a great prize awaiting the winners in the transition race. The adjective "European" replaced the earlier "socialist" or "communist" whenever social scientists, journalists and politicians wanted to express a certain quality to be reached in the future. This attitude was, of course, progressive inasmuch as there was and still is a great deal to learn from our West European neighbors. However, the belief that this learning process can be characterized as no more than copying Western institutions or simply joining certain organizations can only be regarded as naive or ill-conceived.

Some West European politicians and citizens tried to warn Easterners about the risks of EU membership soon after transition began, albeit without too much success. The subsequent EU propaganda has been so overwhelming that it has been hard for ordinary people—and even difficult for some academics—to comprehend why public opinion in countries that have joined recently (e.g. Austria and Sweden) has not shown great enthusiasm about the advantages of actual EU membership. "Let us have their problems" is a very common answer even among highly educated people, and it is not easy to explain why "their" problems would be much greater in our case.

The enthusiastic attitude toward European economic integration and its conflation with the Atlantic security community became a widespread phenomenon in all former socialist countries aspiring to EU membership. Foreign policies in ECE countries have considered EU and NATO integration as two sides of the same coin. Policy- and PR-makers in foreign affairs have popularized the phrase "Euro-Atlantic integration" as if there were a natural way of transition toward the two organizations, having left behind the dual membership in the CMEA and the WTO. It is not self-evident why there should be this consensus within polit-ical elites about the double integration, but it came into existence very early.

Furthermore, there has been unconditional support for the idea of membership in most cases. According to opinion polls, nations that had just won their independence a few years earlier would be more than happy to abandon their currencies, foreign ministries and other national institutions (see Appendix 2, Table 12). Among politicians, this "EU-phoria"—pretend or not—could be seen as an expression of loyalty to the Western powers (the lack of which would immediately shake the sympathy and assistance coming from Western governments and private sources). Among nonpoliticians, however, "EU-phoria" can be explained by the lack of information about the costs and benefits of potential membership and the long convergence process.

The infantile "Europing" that emerged from the new utopia on the ruins of common sense was tenderly described by the previously anarchist, later neoconservative, and more recently radical philosopher Gáspár Miklós Tamás. According to him, an

unchallengeable dogma of contemporary East European publicity is that the postcommunist new democracies must sign up to NATO and EU. This is not a bad dogma, especially until we get access. Till then hope restricts us from Turkish–Greek types of stupidities, which is a clear gain. Sometimes one has the impression that the Westerners had better make this procedure longer. As a professor I know how polite the students are while they look forward to exams, sometimes they even wash their hair. It is a joy to see how much the European carrot improves the manner of some of our neighbors. If it goes on like this, here and there the authorized bashing of Protestants and gays will be ended, and even the post-KGB will recess for a while. Of course, however, the East European public opinion does not have the slightest idea about what the European Union is (apart from some banal debates like agricultural subsidies), while every half-baked head preaches about the non-existing "European norms." [Tamás 1996]

Tamás and others thus suggest that European integration, even partly as a myth or utopia, can play a positive role in shaping former socialist societies. However, this is not necessarily a favorable development, particularly because of the unfair aspects of such a process. We call "unfair" all those asymmetrical economic advantages that benefit Westerners and harm Easterners and the unprecedented rivalry generated by Western policies to encourage ECE countries to get ahead in the Euro-race at each other's expense.

Hungary has a good chance of being among the winners, having jumped into the race under the first postcommunist government. The government led by the Hungarian Democratic Forum signed an association agreement with the EC in 1991 and submitted application for membership in March 1994. When the application was submitted, the early promise by the late József Antall to gain membership in the EC by 1996 was long forgotten. His successor, Péter Boross, suggested that membership in the European Union would be possible by 1998.

The motives attached to Europe started to dominate not just the political discourse but national symbolism as well. Following the 1994 general elections, a new leadership of national television changed the layout of the evening news program. The background behind the presenters became blue. The opposition parties accused the president of the television company of choosing the color of the Free Democrats to dominate the view of the daily news. Ádám Horváth, the president, replied by saying that he had not been aware that blue was the color of the Free Democrats—he said he had chosen blue because it was the color of Europe.

In accordance with the guidelines of the association agreements and of Agenda 2000, various state institutions—and particularly the foreign ministry—embarked on a propaganda campaign to maintain and strengthen the pro-European attitudes of the Hungarian people. The national television broadcast game shows on European themes, and "Europe days" were organized all around the country, with the participation of leading politicians, artists and experts. The elite groups of pro-European Hungary launched a number of magazines to analyze, discuss and popularize the goals, institutions and developments of European integration.[15]

However slowly, the awareness of the Hungarian public concerning the issues of integration did start to change. In 1998, a survey conducted by Szonda-Ipsos among the agricultural population of the country showed that two-thirds of this group believed that the media devoted sufficient time to the issues of Europe. Only 17–18% of the country's population expected more information.

The same survey distinguished between four groups concerning the people's judgment on EU accession. Some 35% were classified as "realists," whose information level on the European Union was high. These realists were aware of both the advantages and disadvantages of accession. They expected favorable developments in cultural, foreign and economic affairs and negative changes in the structure of society as well as regional disparities. These realists were mainly middle-aged employed graduates who lived in the Hungarian mid-west. Some 24% of those surveyed belonged to the group of "abandoners," whose information about the European Union was rather poor. They believed that it was largely up to the European Union to show how successful the accession would be, and Hungary would have very little say in this process. They could hardly mention any area where the accession would bring benefits to Hungary, and they feared the most dreadful outcomes with respect to the areas of social policy, social structures, regional disparities and infrastructure. This "abandoners'" group consisted of low-skilled and low-paid workers living in southwest and east Hungary. The third group was called "well-informed hopeful" and represented about 18% of the surveyed sample. They had gained a substantial amount of information on the European Union and considered Hungary to be fit and prepared for accession. They mainly focused on the advantages of integration, and they expected improvements in areas where others feared deterioration—in social and regional disparities. Most of the "well-informed hopeful" were young people with at least a secondary education who lived in the western counties. Finally, 23% of the surveyed group turned out to be "uninformed wonder-waiting." Their level of information was minimal, but their expectations toward EU accession were extraordinary. They trusted in the improvements in cultural, economic, and foreign affairs but could not tell which groups would gain and which would tend to lose with the progress of integration. Women, the elderly and uneducated youth were overrepresented within the "uninformed wonder-waiting" group. Of those who had not even finished primary school, 36% belonged to this fourth group. Geographically, this attitude can be observed mainly in the central and northeastern regions of the country (L. Z. 1998: 20).

While expert analysis has discovered more and more complications in the integration process, the political elite has not displayed the least readiness to review the project of EU accession. *Ex officio*, Hungarian politicians are optimistic and do not let themselves be disturbed by considerations like the Rifkind dilemma. It is as if, without naming the problem or talking about it, it could be assumed not to exist at all. The question as to how to reconcile the tasks of monetary union with those of enlargement does not exist for Hungarian politicians—it is presented as a dilemma for West Europeans. Hungarian foreign policy—and the entire political discourse, as a result—has tended to take Western promises at face value without paying attention to the mounting difficulties that have manifested themselves in domestic political disparities.

Disagreement on Policies

Though the rhetoric of major political parties did not differ on the need for EU accession, their actual behavior, and particularly the opinion of their supporters, started to diverge after the mid-1990s. It was the left-of-center cabinet between 1994 and 1998 that insisted on international openness and rapid integration—and even subordinated economic policies to the main foreign policy objectives. On the other hand, the right-of-center government that came into office in 1998 represents a conservative attitude that allows for slower integration in exchange for the protection of the national elites.

Under the Socialist–Liberal coalition, the Foreign Ministry was led by a Socialist cabinet minister (László Kovács) and a Free Democrat junior minister (István Szent-Iványi and, in the last year, Mátyás Eörsi). Concerning EU affairs, government policy continued the course of the previous—right-of-center—coalition—that is, preparations for full membership in the European Union. In July 1994, soon after the coalition came to office, Horn made a visit to Bonn "to secure Germany's support for Hungary's efforts to join the EU" (Hoensch 1996: 341). In December, Horn and Kovács went to Essen to attend the European Council meeting and lobby for special treatment of Hungary by the European Union.

After forming a government in 1994, the foreign policies of the MSZP were determined by the overall strategy of the government. Foreign policy, including EU accession, did not belong to those fields or topics most widely discussed within the MSZP. The left platform of the party, not represented in the cabinet, criticized the NATO policy of the government openly but lacked information and experience to form a sophisticated opinion with respect to European integration. They tended to criticize the economic policy of the government on a moral basis, but this was still very far from developing a feasible alternative.

Right-wing nationalists in Hungary also call the Alliance of Free Democrats a left-wing party. The latter are, as is the case with most liberal parties in Europe, the most Europhile party among the major political forces. Only a very few of their members—for example, Professor Tamás—can afford to voice critical statements about the Hungarian Euromania. The two internationalist parties—the MSZP and the SZDSZ—can justly be called pro-European or even Euro-enthusiasts. Consequently, it was not only the foreign, but also the domestic policies of the MSZP–SZDSZ coalition government that were focused on comprehensive adjustment to the norms and laws (and sometimes even unspoken requirements) of the European Union.

Beyond negotiations with the EU bodies, Hungarian diplomacy made great efforts to persuade West European national governments to make announcements about their support of Hungary's accession. In the first years of the parliamentary cycle, Horn and Kovács spent much of their time flying between London and Athens, Stockholm and Rome, in order to have a photo opportunity with leading EU politicians. It was hoped that this would confirm the necessity of Hungary's entry in the first round of enlargement, the negotiations for which were planned to start right after the end of the Intergovernmental Conference.

Foreign policy, and within that European affairs, were always regarded as forming the strongest aspects of coalition politics. An official party document of the MSZP produced two years after the formation of the coalition reported about the consequent results as follows:

The elements of outstanding significance of the foreign political activities of the Hungarian Socialist Party and the government led by it were and have been the development of contacts with the European Union, with NATO and its member states, further on the improvement of Hungary's relations with the neighbouring countries. Government has identified joining the European Union as the most important instrument of social and economic development. Thanks to its efforts, the most important achievement of the past two years was that Hungary has got much closer to the Euro-Atlantic organizations. The personal and organizational conditions of the domestic direction of preparations have evolved, the economy, the legal system, public administration, education and public opinion are being geared for accession. During the second half of the governmental cycle there is a realistic chance of the European Union starting negotiations about the conditions of joining with Hungary as one of the first countries. At the same time it should be made clear for the entire society that the European Union is not led by emotional but by economic considerations which means hard conditions of competition.

Hungary's relationship with its neighbours can be regarded as by and large settled. The bilateral relations have been dynamically developing during the past two years. With the exception of Yugoslavia, Treaties—Basic Treaties—have been signed with all of our neighbours. After the completion of the war waged on the territory of the former Yugoslavia, possibilities would also open up to normalize our relations with Yugoslavia too. This policy significantly contributes to the security of the region and hence to that of the entire Europe.[16]

An illustration of the Socialist attitude is that foreign minister László Kovács refused to use the phrase "disadvantages" in relation to EU accession. He said there were only advantages and commitments for would-be members, but nothing that could be called a "disadvantage". Under his ministership, the Euro-Atlantic integration made giant steps forward. In 1995, Hungary had already complied with about 50% of EU directives and reached about 90% by the end of 1997.

It was very typical of the Socialist foreign policy that, until early 1998, when the accession talks actually began, Hungarians did not discuss derogations in relation to the issues of European integration. The foreign policy elite avoided any mention of such problems, believing that this could be a sign of uncertainty and this could damage the confidence of West European politicians in Hungary and in the commitment of the Hungarian political elite to the overall project of European integration.

In the view of Socialist and Liberal strategists, there were two ways to run the accession talks with the European Union. One of them was the Finnish way—that is, with the lowest possible number of requested derogations—and the other was the Austrian, with a tough negotiating strategy. The Finnish alternative was seen as a right option that would make it easier and faster to join the European Union; such an option would be threatened by a nationalist government. Between the two rounds of the 1998 elections, MSZP politicians claimed that a right-wing government would not only spoil Hungary's relations with its neighbors but would slow down the country's integration into the European Union as well. Prime Minister Horn argued that once Hungary was in the European Union, the country could expect 2 billion forints every day from Brussels, and the best guarantee for this outcome would be to elect the MSZP again.

The period of financial stabilization, however, was a hard test of the internationalism of the MSZP. At the time of the Bokros package, the rhetoric of Smallholder leader József Torgyán was filled with nationalist and populist protest against policies dictated by the West and domestic bankers. Horn, while insisting on pursuing his original policies, started to adjust his speeches to effectively counter those of his emerging rival. He announced, for example, that the banks would not receive massive state subsidies to cover their bad loans, as had been the practice under the MDF and Békesi. Moreover, in an interview with a German Sunday paper, he accused the European Union of being inward-looking and not being prepared to understand how vast were the economic problems that the transition countries had to face.

When approaching the end of the parliamentary cycle, the optimistic tone of the half-time evaluation proved to be well based. After the end of the Intergovernmental Conference in the summer of 1997, the European Union indeed announced that negotiations would begin with five former socialist countries, Hungary included. This announcement provided a great boost to the self-esteem of Hungarian foreign policy, though predictions about the likely year of accession had to be modified again. "It is to be hoped that the talks with the Central Eastern European associate countries which meet the strict criteria of joining will be concluded by the year 2000 and that after the conclusion of the ratification processes these countries become fully fledged members of EU by 2002" (Kovács 1997: 4).

The European Commission announced the list of EU membership candidates just after the Madrid Summit of NATO had also announced that it would invite Poland, the Czech Republic and Hungary to join. By then, government propaganda pushed popular support for Hungary's membership of NATO to above 50%, a level never reached before 1997. During the four months that followed the Madrid decision, the campaign brought more than four-fifths of the active electorate on board. The referendum in November 1997 was held with 50% participation and won by the pro-NATO membership side, with 80% in favor.

The overwhelming support for government and parliamentary policy with regard to NATO might give the impression that the Hungarian people were prepared to follow their leaders unconditionally. The anti-NATO vote in the referendum (15%) was, however, much higher than the general influence of anti-NATO parties (3–4% altogether). This indicated that a substantial number of the voters in pro-NATO parties did not support the foreign policies of their preferred politicians. Public opinion is still strongly in favor of Hungary joining the European Union, although the proportion of enthusiastic supporters fell sharply, by about 10%, from 1996 to 1997, to about 60% of those asked by pollsters. If the actual policy debate reveals marked differences between different political forces, the nation may become quite divided with respect to the further course of Euro-Atlantic integration.

In the vanguard of the anti-NATO campaign could be found one of the extraparliamentary left parties, the Workers' Party, which (similarly to the MSZP) has its origins in the former Communist Party (MSZMP). This party has been an arch-opponent of NATO membership and an ardent critic of the European Union as well. It does not strictly oppose EU accession (which would be going against common sense in Hungary), but the party has suggested that it is very unlikely to happen because the European Union plays a selfish game with the former socialist countries; this is because the liberal ideology prevalent in the latter is just a cover for promoting the interests of multinational capital. Popular support for the MSZMP/Workers' Party remained between 3% and 4% in both 1990 and 1994, and declined sharply afterwards. In the meantime, the party went through various splits and was also suffering from internal cleavages at the end of 1996. Since it identifies so much with the past—that is, with the Kádárist regime of 1956–89—it can hardly remain a viable party even in the towns and constituencies where it has preserved considerable support, mainly in the north of the country and in some workers' districts of Budapest. It is very unlikely to influence the politics of EU integration and, despite an impressive campaign for petition signatures, its anti-NATO propaganda also had controversial results, actually pushing some hesitant minds into the pro-NATO camp.

The Social-Democratic Party of Hungary was the party that belonged to the SI originally, although recently it has been relegated to observer status due to internal scandals and splits. On various issues of economic and social policy it positions itself to the left of the MSZP, while on the European question it echoes the conventional slogans of West European social democracy. Similarly to the Workers' Party, the MSZDP is mainly composed of elderly people, unfortunately apparently unable to catch up with recent developments in the Western half of the continent.

We can consider the party known as the Green Alternative [*Zöld Alternatíva*] to be a left-of-center party too. It is the only political party in Hungary that says "no" to EU accession and the whole idea of federalism. Its criticism is strongly linked to and feeds on the Western environmentalist opposition to the European Union, rejecting bureaucratic centralization as well as transcontinental transportation networks and other grand projects. Despite honorable efforts, the Green Alternative has had virtually no influence on Hungarian politics. It had also campaigned against membership in NATO, but its efforts had hardly any impact.

As European integration in Hungary arrives at a more practical phase, it is the right-wing parties from which a challenge to the absolutely Europhile policies of the left-of-center government can be expected. Such a debate may develop and revolve around the six-party foreign policy consensus outlined at the beginning of this chapter. The unity of parliamentary forces around these pillars was shaken in September 1996, when opposition parties accused the government of the suppression of the third principle for the sake of the first, following the signing of the so-called "basic treaty" between Hungary and Romania by prime minister Gyula Horn. Some opposition parties have also started to criticize the EU policy of the government for its lack of selectivity and transparency, particularly concerning the questionnaire the government completed for the inquiry required by Brussels. In 1997, they also criticized government blueprints for reorganizing regional governance in Hungary aimed at harmonization with Brussels guidelines and eligibility for EU subsidies; such blueprints would apparently create a structure that is alien from the national tradition.

The opposition parties continued to challenge the European orientation of government policy in a parliamentary debate over land reform. Under a law inherited from the Antall government, companies—including transformed collective farms—were not allowed to buy land in Hungary. In 1997, the MSZP/SZDSZ coalition wanted to abolish this restriction for two reasons. It wanted, first, to invite foreign investment to agriculture, given that it was still suffering from the disinvestment resulting from the policies of the previous government, and, second, to allow collective farms to repurchase some of the land previously given to private owners (who, as amateurs, could do nothing other than mismanage it). Government policy was clearly seen as pro-European, while opposition policy was interpreted as anti-EU. The right-wing parties nearly went as far as forcing a referendum on the issue; however, this was made impossible by the unresolved dispute between government and opposition about how exactly the question should be formulated. The opposition wanted to prevent any change to the law that protected Hungarian private landowners from buy-outs by collective farms or foreign investors; the government, on the other hand, only wanted to exclude foreign private buyers until Hungary could become a member of the European Union. The referendum would have taken place simultaneously with the one on NATO membership, but, due to the sometimes comical political battles, the initiative was taken off the agenda, at least temporarily.

The Independent Smallholders' Party, the most popular party of the right between 1994 and 1996, has always been in the vanguard of the protection of Hungarian land from foreign or collective ownership. The FKGP is often characterized as a Hungarian version of Vladimir Meciar's party in Slovakia, and its temporary popularity in early 1997 was interpreted as a major threat to the process of Europeanization. Despite the apparent similarity, however, the leader of the party, József Torgyán, always tried to marginalize the most prominent irredentist and racist politicians of the party, and he kept the flag of the European Union flying outside the headquarters of the FKGP on the Belgrade Embankment in Budapest.

In the campaign on land ownership, Torgyán found an ally in Viktor Orbán, president of the Fidesz–MPP. Orbán, ironically enough, has been chairman of the parliamentary committee on European affairs since its creation after the 1994 elections. The early version of his party in the late 1980s and the very early 1990s was one of the freshest voices in the region trying to overcome the traditional cleavage of Hungarian politics between urban and populist tendencies. By the 1994 elections, however, Fidesz had clearly shifted to the right and developed old-fashioned nationalist attitudes in order to please the former supporters of the once strong Hungarian Democratic Forum. It was still a surprise to most observers when Orbán, as head of the European affairs committee, became one of the politicians most critical of the European Union, sometimes even claiming that Hungary had so far gained nothing from the European integration process. Just before the 1998 elections, Orbán's slogan was that in the accession talks the representatives of Hungary should act as businessmen rather than diplomats. Even before the actual content of the negotiations was made public, he rejected the West European attempts to include Hungary into the European Union without providing the free movement of labor and the same agricultural and structural subsidies that apply to the Mediterranean countries. He also accepted the need for derogations from environmental standards as a protective measure in favor of certain domestic producers.

János Martonyi, a top civil servant for Antall's government who later joined the Fidesz–MPP camp, rejected the idea that Europe should turn into a U.S.-like melting pot. He proposed a Europe in which nations can preserve their culture, language and identity. Martonyi wrote: "We have said it many times, that the tragedy of Trianon can only be resolved through the creation of a truly united Europe" (Martonyi 1998: 7). Europe as a compensation for Trianon may sound odd. The case, however, is comparable to the Irish question, which has also been fueling violent struggles ever since World War I. The 1998 settlement between the United Kingdom and the Irish Republic was made possible by the enormous transformation that both countries have gone through as members of the European Community and later the Union.

In 1997 it became clear that the Hungarian right was divided between a moderate and a populist wing, led by Orbán and Torgyán, respectively. A leading political scientist, Attila Ágh, distinguished between the two tendencies by calling the Fidesz–MPP a Euro-conform party and thus implicitly suggesting the Fidesz–MPP could be a possible coalition partner for the MSZP after the 1998 elections, with or without the Free Democrats. One year before the 1998 elections most analysts excluded the possibility of Orbán and Torgyán forming an electoral alliance. Given such a scenario, it was believed that the course of Europeanization could be expected to be diverted from the strongly internationalist policies of the Socialist–Liberal coalition.

Opinion polls taken in 1996 support the fact that there was indeed a significant difference between the attitudes of supporters of various parties toward the EU accession of Hungary (see Appendix 2, Table 13). While close to three-quarters of the voters of the incumbent coalition actively supported EU membership, the actual support for membership just exceeded half of the voters of the parties of the previous ruling coalition. One in five among right-wing voters actively opposed EU membership for Hungary, while only one in ten shared the opinion found among the supporters of the Socialist–Liberal coalition. Although it is possible that the approaching negotiations and accession talks would balance out these figures, thus bringing the nation toward consensus, there are more reasons to assume that the start of real negotiations and bargaining about the terms of accession will, rather, polarize domestic political opinion and thus strengthen the anti-EU attitude among the supporters, the rank and file, and the leaders of the right-wing parties.

Once it was certain that the talks on accession would actually start under the British presidency, the Hungarian newspapers were filled with predictions about the necessary amount of derogations. The more nationalist and Euro-sceptic prediction was that more derogations would and should be demanded for Hungary; pro-Europeans and internationalists wanted to minimize the number. The arguments for the latter suggested that if Hungary were to demand an excessive number of derogations, the process of enlargement would be slowed down dangerously. Of course, the definition of "excessive number of derogations" was once again very hard to define. Although a consensus was slowly emerging that the permanent guessing game about the likely time of accession was not a productive exercise, it was regarded as very important for Hungarian politicians and negotiators—as with other countries—to use at least a hypothetical year, since the set of demanded derogations would look different, according to the year of accession—demands for derogation would be different in 2000, 2002, 2005 or in an even later period.

After the new parliament of Hungary was formed, the Fidesz–MPP appointed József Szájer to head the European affairs commission of the house; his political standing was high within the party, while his awareness of West European economic and political issues appeared to be rather poor. In the executive branch, the foreign policies of the Fidesz government are managed by János Martonyi, a lawyer who served József Antall as state secretary in the ministries of foreign economic affairs and foreign affairs.[17] Due to the favorable opinion the Western governments developed about the Horn government, Martonyi promised no change in the foreign policy of Hungary—that is, to preserve the three major foreign policy objectives of the 1990s: Euro–Atlantic integration, the good neighbor policy, and the support of the Hungarian minorities abroad.

Though Martonyi and his deputy Zsolt Németh promised no change in the main objectives, they also hinted that there might be some shift in emphasis concerning the practical pursuit of these goals. They said, for instance, that EU accession would be a priority (just like before), but Hungarian interests would be represented in a more forthright way than under the premiership of Horn and the ministership of László Kovács. Despite the explicit promise of more protectionism, they also marked 2002 as the likely year of accession. Other developments in 1998 and 1999 also displayed how ambivalent the right-wing coalition was on European and international affairs (conflicts with foreign institutions, from FIFA to big corporations).

After winning the elections, Orbán carried out a massive restructuring of ministries, without paying attention to Euro compatibility. In the distribution of portfolios by the two party leaders (Orbán and Torgyán), the area of regional development was attached to the ministry of agriculture. EU experts in Brussels expressed their concern as to whether this would be an adequate arrangement for the distribution of structural aid during and after the accession. Similarly, the arrangement of Phare aid did not follow the preferences of Brussels either. A minister for the supervision of Phare funds was appointed from the Smallholders' Party, while in the view of the European Union the ministry of finance would have been the proper location for Phare management, primarily because necessary cofinancing needs to be projected into the annual budget (Kocsis 1998: 10).[18] It needs mentioning, however, that the ministry of finance had not been the center for Phare under the Horn government either, and during the period of the latter the prime minister's office controlled the distribution of EU aid for Hungary.

The new policies of the Orbán–Martonyi line demanded new personnel at the Hungarian foreign ministry. Ferenc Somogyi, the secretary of state for integration in the Horn government, had to leave. The affairs of EU integration were taken over by Endre Juhász, who was the leader of the Hungarian negotiating group for the 1991 association agreement under the Antall government. The integration cabinet—a sizeable working group that had been established by the Horn government under the leadership of András Inotai—was abolished by Orbán.[19] Along with a more forthright representation of the "Hungarian interest," Martonyi felt the need to renew the "smile offensive" of Hungarian foreign policy, since he also suspected that more than 90% of the Western press was hostile to the idea of EU enlargement.

The Berlin Summit of the European Union in March 1999 did not reject the plan for a 2002 enlargement and even set aside a certain amount of funding, however little that is, for financing the accession of new members. It was, however, also suspected that the first round determined two years earlier—the so-called five plus one—would not necessarily be able to join in 2002. Hoping to get into the first round of the first round, the Hungarian government did its best to please the Western powers with various services and favors during the spring war of NATO against Yugoslavia. The war, similarly to the Russian financial crisis of August 1998, overshadowed the entire region, but the expectation was that a general postwar settlement would include a political decision by the European Union to maintain the 2002 promise, at least for a couple of countries. Hungarian optimism was based on the level of institutional development, the interest of multinational corporations in Hungary, and a relatively friendly public opinion in the West. In the spring of 1999, Hungary was the least rejected EU applicant in the eyes of the West-European public, though it needs mentioning that among the EU nations it was Austria, Hungary's neighbor, where the people remained most doubtful about the need for further enlargement.

The impact of the Kosovo intervention did not work out, however, as the Hungarians has expected. Under the Finnish presidency, the EU decided to invite all the associate countries to negotiate about accession, and even Turkey was declared to be a candidate for membership. At the Helsinki summit it was confirmed that enlargement cannot take place until the EU institutions have been reformed and monetary union successfully implemented. Thus, at the end of 1999, the 2002 deadline was silently abandoned by the Hungarian government.

NOTES

1. The ten countries were: Poland, Denmark, Estonia, Finland, Germany, Latvia, Lithuania, Norway, Russia and Sweden.

2. The ninth Crans Montana Forum was held on 25–28 June for businessmen and other financial and economic experts on two major themes: EU enlargement and the economic development of Francophone countries in Africa.

3. The Copenhagen summit of the European Union in June 1993 was the first occasion when the European Council declared that the associated status would lead to EU membership if the necessary requirements could be fulfilled. Eighteen months later the prime ministers of the associated countries of Central and Eastern Europe attended the European Council meeting in Essen, Germany. The summit adopted the Strategy for the Integration of the Central and Eastern European Countries.

4. Simultaneously with the Hungarian referendum on NATO membership, former senator and presidential candidate Bob Dole visited Prague and Budapest and suggested that the Senate would ratify the treaty on enlargement by an 80–90% majority.

5. The lecture, which was attended by the author and another two hundred or so people, remained largely unreported in the Hungarian press. Professor Sachs did not specify the policy

implications of this comment about the aged, although other departments of the CEU became leading advocates of the legalization of euthanasia. The lecture coincided with the period when payments for dental treatment were introduced by the government and it became legal for electricity supply companies (now in foreign hands in Hungary) to turn off the electricity of those who could not pay their bills. These measures concerned mainly pensioners, whose simultaneous semiannual pension rise by the parliament was 0.5% at a time when inflation was running at more than 20% annually. It was hard to avoid the conclusion that the Socialist–Liberal coalition seemed to be searching for practical and final solutions to the problems outlined by Prof. Sachs.

6. Two of the most prominent candidates were: Imre Tarafás, a former deputy chairman of the National Bank, who was later appointed head of the Bank and Security Authority; and Ernő Kemenes, a former head of the National Planning Office, later chairman of Deloitte Touche in Hungary. Frigyes Hárshegyi and György Szapáry, vice-chairmen of the National Bank, were self-promoted candidates and not taken seriously by the broader economic and political elites.

7. Mr. Bokros was one of the few Hayekian Socialists; he resigned from the chairmanship of Budapest Bank to accept Horn's invitation to implement a heterodox stabilization program. His friend György Surányi took an active part in the design of that package. During the one year of his ministership, Bokros was the most unpopular politician in Hungary. Soon after his resignation he accepted a job at the World Bank in Washington, D.C.

8. The letter to Wolfensohn had a prehistory dating back to April 1995, when a group of almost the same individuals appealed to the government and the National Bank to follow the line of the Copenhagen summit on world development, write off the debts of some of the poorest countries owing money to Hungary, and ask for similar treatment by Hungary's Western creditors.

9. In an open policy debate of the MSZP faction in spring 1996, the author of this study was informed by the Prime Minister and faction leader Imre Szekeres that nobody expected Hungary to meet the Maastricht criteria. It is, however, clear that the associated countries must show commitment to the aims of the European Union, including monetary union.

10. Source: press coverage and oral information from Socialist Party advisors.

11. The term "crawling peg" means that the government declares that the national currency be devalued regularly—usually monthly—at a certain pace. In the Hungarian case, the government announced in March 1995 that the forint would be devalued every month by 1.9%. Later the rate of monthly devaluation was reduced, from June 1998 on, to 0.8%.

12. It was also announced that when the difference between rates of productivity increase in the European Union and Hungary would become marginal, the crawling peg would be abolished and the forint would be fixed against the Euro with the possibility of fluctuating by up to 15%. Actual dates were not set, though leading officials in the Ministry of Finance and the National Bank claimed that if Hungary joined the European Union in 2002, it could also join the ERM, and the Euro could be introduced in Hungary as early as 2004.

13. A few examples of hazardous chemicals still in use in Hungary in the late 1990s are Aldicarb, Lindan, TeraTox, Lindafor, Parathyon, Phenncap, Dantox, Parashoot, Atrazine, and Reglone. Some of these products are produced in Hungary although they are banned in EU countries like France, Denmark and Italy.

14. The idea of derogation also appears in Gowan (1997) and Inotai (1995).

15. Just a few such new periodicals are *Europa Forum, European Review, European Traveler, European Vision, European Dialogue, European Mirror.*

16. Source: *The Hungarian Socialist Party*, an official introduction issued by the MSZP International Secretariat, Budapest, 1996.

17. Under the last so-called "communist" government led by Miklós Németh, Martonyi had been chairman of the board of directors of the privatization agency.

18. The Hungarian case concerning Phare was still considered to be better than the case of Poland, where Phare aid became a victim of battles within the ruling coalition.

19. In May 1999, Inotai became chair of a newly established Foundation for European Studies, which was a nongovernmental initiative dedicated to leading representatives of the business community and the academic sphere to promote strategic thinking and influence the public debate on European issues.

6

Epilogue:
The Dependent Democracy

Hungarian society embarked on the systemic change with a number of *ad hoc* and implicit predictions. One of the most widely cited, aphoristic predictions came as a warning from the sociologist Ralf Dahrendorf. The German-born professor at Oxford University suggested during the East European political landslide that political transition required a relatively short period of time, but economic transition would take significantly more time, and cultural transition—or the creation of a self-sustaining civil society—would require an entire lifetime.

The formal process of constitutional reform takes at least six months; a general sense that things are looking up as a result of economic reform is unlikely to spread before six years have passed; the third condition of the road to freedom is to provide the social foundations which transform the constitution and the economy from fair-weather into all-weather institutions capable of withstanding the storms generated within and without, and sixty years are barely enough to lay these foundations. [Dahrendorf 1990: 99]

What forecasts were implied by Dahrendorf's idea? First, he suggested that following a relatively short period of drawing up a constitution, the political transition would end, and further changes in the quality and structural elements of the system could not be expected. Second, he also implied that, around 2020, the transformation of political and economic culture would only be half-way, and it would not be until the middle of the twenty-first century that the culture of Hungarian society could be expected to have caught up with Western Europe.

Third, he also suggested that the economic transition has its own implicit agenda, and its success and effectiveness are not related—either to the reform of the political system or to cultural transformation.

According to the Dahrendorf paradigm and its followers, the postcommunist transition process can be calculated and forecast, and its final destination can also be defined clearly. Former socialist countries will take over the social, political and cultural norms of the Western half of the continent. We cannot even assume that regional or national specificities will play a significant role in the future; these might only cause minor modifications in a fundamentally general and common scenario.

Hungarian journalism and social science adopted Dahrendorf's paradigm in this simplified form, similarly to Francis Fukuyama's theory about global perestroika as an end to history itself (discussed briefly in Chapter 3). It is worth noting that in Fukuyama's thought the East European changes assume world-historic importance, and thus our region appears as a key to world history. The question is therefore not only East European but universal: has history really ended in the countries of the former Soviet bloc? Did the political transitions really settle the social and economic conditions in those countries once and forever? Has everything been on track since 1989? Is the paradise apparently embodied by the European Union the only possible final destination of this journey?

In the countries that received an invitation to EU accession talks in the summer of 1997, there are grounds for the success propaganda of governments. To the east and south of these countries, however, a perpetuation of social and economic crises can be witnessed. Here and there, islands of successful modernization show up in a sea of underdevelopment, and the relative security of state socialism has disappeared from the life of tens of millions in those countries. Since those regions cannot be isolated from the participants in the next EU enlargement, their crises will strongly affect the future of the accession countries too.

The dilemma of catching up or falling behind, and the search for the road ahead between the chances of joining Western modernity and the threat of falling back to the Eastern periphery, will determine the agenda of the next few decades of Hungarian society as well as the shaping of the political system. Dahrendorf, Fukuyama and others have outlined one possible outcome of the transition. Based on the experience of the 1990s, however, we can find a number of independent variables that still make our political future uncertain. Alternative constellations of these variables could result in different scenarios for the first decades of the twenty-first century.

Determinants of the Political Future

The factors that influence Hungary's political future can be summarized in terms of three major groups: international politics, domestic economics and political demography.

In determining the trajectory of economic and social development in East-Central Europe, the main question is the progress of European integration and the state of the Atlantic coalition. Apart from these issues, the consolidation of the new regime in Russia is also an important independent variable. This dual foreign political determination, which can be seen as a tradition that has lasted for at least a century in Hungary's case, is itself embedded into the broadest world-political developments—namely, the rivalry of the three main capitalist centers of the world economy on the one hand, and the open and latent contradictions of centers and peripheries on the other. Recent developments in this area are embodied in the phrase "globalization," although the application of that word raises tremendous controversies in politics and social science.

For domestic politics in small states, economic prosperity can also be seen as an independent variable. In an age of economic openness, the governments of such small states have very little room for maneuver with respect to influencing economic developments. On the other hand, economic performance is a key factor underpinning social cohesion and affects the quality and quantity of domestic political conflicts.

There is in East Central Europe today an intimate, but highly complex, set of reciprocal relations between democratization, economic reform and security. Economic reform, including marketisation and privatisation, will facilitate the emergence of more vibrant civil societies, which alone can sustain pluralist democracies. On the other hand, economic reform (particularly of the shock-therapy type applied in Poland and elsewhere) involves considerable short-term economic dislocation. It also tends to deepen existing social inequalities. Economic reform can therefore place severe strains on societal cohesion and community spirit, thereby making it harder to achieve the consensus building and compromise which are the lifeblood of democratic politics. [Hyde-Price 1996: 277]

In the medium term, some subjective factors of politics can also be treated as independent variables. Every major transformation or epoch creates its own political generation, which has its particular needs and historic tasks. The political generations that emerge in times of change are inherited by those in future decades. In our circumstances, we can expect a major change to be completed soon after the turn of the century because of the controversial demography running alongside the political changes.

The first parliament of the transition was dominated by people who had developed their political views and attitudes in the late 1940s or in 1956. By the end of the 1990s they had disappeared from the front line of Hungarian politics, and the stage will now be dominated by a middle generation and the youth of 1989. The latter, however, who were socialized in either the Communist youth organization or in the alternative youth movements, are likely to preserve their positions in the higher state offices. The relations between these forces will determine whether the ideological doctrines of 1989 or a more pragmatic attitude will dominate the political agenda in Hungary.

The culture and institutions of politics, as well as the set of government policies, are shaped by these independent variables. The alternative outcomes of these variables could result in at least four different scenarios for the political future of Hungary.

European Integration with Balanced Economic Development

Although we must approach the rhetoric of the 1990s with a sense of criticism, the chances of an optimistic scenario cannot be excluded entirely. However, such would largely depend on external factors. It would require the rivalry of the great powers to continue in a peaceful way (which means it would also require the continuation of their cooperation). In an ideal case, the strengthening of the UN system would also have such an impact. For this reason, the way in which global organizations will function in the future is not irrelevant for Hungary's prospects. These organizations might help the process of European integration remain in a civilized and balanced framework.

If West European integration does not fall too short of the planned agenda and economic and monetary integration does not hurt the social and political stability of the member and associated states too much, the reforms of the 1990s may lay the foundations for a lasting and balanced economic recovery. Such a trajectory would have an extremely beneficial impact on the associated countries, not only in the narrowly defined economic sphere but also with respect to general social, cultural and political developments.

If Hungary can be integrated into the European Union soon after the millennium, then Western Europe could have a very strong cultural and political impact on Hungary in the subsequent decades. The strong embeddedness of Hungary into the frameworks of capitalist economy and liberal democracy would prevent possible domestic attempts to remove Hungary from the family of European democracies.

Balanced economic growth and stable international linkages could secure the survival of the political system that emerged in Hungary during the systemic change. The latter constitutes the basis for the new democracies of East-Central Europe in their pursuit of the norms and values represented by the Council of Europe and the United Nations. Thus, in such a case we can expect moderate forces to dominate the domestic political landscape. This moderate character does not depend on the existence of a large liberal bloc—parties can preserve their moderate attitudes even if the liberal segment of domestic politics shrinks even more than it did in 1998.

One step further, we may assume that if Hungary's integration and consolidation become successful in the European Union, it is not only the moderate parties in general that will dominate the scene but particularly social democracy, which is represented in Hungary by the Hungarian Socialist Party. On the peripheries of Europe we can observe the lasting hegemony of social democracy, not just because of the need to preserve common European social norms but also to represent the political interests of labor and continental redistribution. The system of permanent redistribution—that is, common regional and agricultural funds—requires those political parties to be in power whose political philosophy fits the needs of such economic policies. Thus in Hungary the MSZP may become a kind of natural party of government and may tie itself to government offices and authorities for decades, with all the advantages and drawbacks of such a development.

Contrary to recurring accusations, the hegemony of social democrats would not pose any threat to the operation of the market economy and multinational corporations. We can interpret modern social democracy as a compromise between, and coalition of multinational capital and the local working class. In such cases multinational capital has a much greater influence on domestic policies than do national capitalist groups, but for the sake of the maintenance of the ruling coalition this would go along with the compensation of much of the working population, mainly in the forms of subsidies and redistribution.

On the European periphery we can find diversions from the social democratic model, especially where the national question remains unresolved and causes acute crises—such as in Ireland and to a lesser extent in Greece. It cannot be excluded that, in the case of Hungary, due to the situation of minority Hungarians abroad, the national problem will remain on the agenda and have a strong impact on domestic politics. Similarly, we cannot assume that the EU accession of neighboring countries would automatically resolve the problems of minority Hungarians. The case of Austria shows that EU membership on its own does not necessarily eliminate or even diminish aggressive nationalist and racist tendencies and may even amplify them.

Peripheral Development with Recurring Social Crises

If the European integration process—and particularly eastward enlargement—suffers a significant delay, the suspicion will be that the European Union made easy promises in the early 1990s and irresponsibly generated illusions among the former socialist countries. This would not necessarily mean that the associated countries would turn their backs on Western Europe, but the current modernization cycle would certainly appear to be unbalanced again. Achievements in one area would be accompanied by symptoms of tension and crisis in another.

Society would again feel its peripheral status, even if EU accession were to take place according to schedule, because the new Eastern members would remain as a second-rate and openly discriminated-against group. Such a danger is apparently realistic if new members are denied access to certain redistribution funds tapped by Western EU members. The sense of national failure would thus emerge not only with the delay but also with the accomplishment of accession, and may generate new types of "politics of grievance." On the basis of nationalist disaffection, and with the support of the nationalist middle classes—small entrepreneurs, the peasantry and the bureaucracy—extremist forces may acquire significant parliamentary representation, albeit in this scenario without sufficient power to set the agenda of parliamentary politics.

If crisis situations occur repeatedly, the political elite may feel the need for centralizing measures. Further centralization of the governmental system would by definition take an antidemocratic character, though it would be possible to justify such measures by pointing to the needs of modernization and the duties deriving from European and Atlantic integration. The slogans of a European future would, in this case, clearly function as weak palliative factors of economic and social adjustment, yet without removing the burden of adjustment from the defenseless layers of society.

At the end of the 1990s, Hungarian parliamentary politics found itself not far from such a path. After the 1994 elections, the press celebrated the victory of moderate forces; however, a significant opposition party, the Smallholders, brought back into parliament a style that hardly fits the so-called European norms. Later a smaller right-wing party, the Christian Democrats, also displayed improper attitudes for which their Western partners expelled them from the international organization of Christian Democratic parties.

The failures of modernization, as well as various problems stemming from social tension, may also accelerate the degeneration of parliamentary parties, and subsequent elections may not necessarily be able to exclude improper behavior from the parliament. A lasting right-wing challenge to established institutions may create grounds for a symmetrical radicalization on the political left. The situation, however, is rather more complicated in the latter case. The Hungarian Socialist Party functioned as a disciplined and stable ruling party between 1994 and 1998. It is possible, however, that if regional disparities increase and social cleavages deepen, the MSZP would split, or another and more radical left-wing party may enter parliament. Relegation into opposition and strong right-wing attacks could accelerate such a process.

The two parties that have presented themselves as alternatives to the MSZP in the 1990s—the Workers' Party and the Social Democratic Party of Hungary— have not displayed a great capacity to renew and adjust themselves to new challenges, partly because of the high proportion of elderly among their members and also their failure to attract young people. Nevertheless, the emergence of a new left-wing party in Hungary cannot be excluded in the early 2000s.

The formation of a new left-wing party would become a possibility if the MSZP were to remain uncritical of aggressive NATO politics and a free-market version of European accession, in particular with regard to the concept of Euro-Atlantic integration. In such a case Hungary, like many other countries of the continent, would perceive various social conflicts and difficulties as European problems. A popular critique of European integration can indeed create grounds for radical socialist parties that feed on the communist, Trotskyist, pacifist and environmentalist legacies, similarly to what has happened in Mediterranean countries or in Scandinavia.

Whether relatively small and radical parties can enter parliament also depends on the electoral system, regardless of the objective social and political situation. In the Mediterranean and in Scandinavia, proportional representation makes it relatively easy for radicals to enter parliament, while in Hungary their representation has been deliberately limited by a mixed electoral system and the 5% threshold within the proportional mechanism.

Extreme Nationalism with the Threat of Military Conflicts

As Tismaneanu (1998) explains, it would be a mistake for the West to assume that liberalism will always triumph once Communism has lost its influence in Eastern Europe. Authoritarian nationalists continue to pose a serious threat to democratic forces and institutions. This is not only because they can always rely on tradition while liberalism has no deep roots in the region, but also because there is a permanent danger of liberal economics compromising liberal politics.

Analysts tended to see extreme nationalism as an immediate threat in Hungary in the first half of the 1990s, when the collapse of economic performance and the drop in the income levels of former socialist countries appeared to endanger political stability in the entire region. For some observers, the democratic achievements of postcommunist transition appeared temporary. This was the vision of "Weimarization," which suggested that it was not only the future of a few countries that was in danger, but the stability of the entire former Soviet bloc and, indirectly (comparably to the experience of the 1930s), the peace and security of the entire world.

The spectre of Weimarization increasingly occupied political discourse during the Yugoslav civil war, when Balkanization was seen as a factor that could influence the future of the region in the forthcoming era. When promises were made in the West to accelerate Euro-Atlantic integration, the fear of Weimarization or Balkanization diminished, but obstruction to the two enlargements may bring these dangers back onto the agenda again. Such a scenario would become likely not simply when economic development is derailed and lasting economic and social crises become apparent, but particularly if the great foreign powers release contradictory impulses toward the region. From this point of view, the Yugoslav war does indeed become a warning signal, since in that particular situation both factors—economic crisis and great power disarray—played a fundamental role in the emergence of military conflict.

The Paris peace treaties that gave rise to the Weimar republic of Germany and also determined its fate created an unstable state structure and a volatile zone between Germany and Russia. The situation that emerged after 1989 is worse, given that the collapse of the federal states—i.e. the Soviet Union, Czechoslovakia and Yugoslavia—has resulted in an even more fragmented state system. If economic and social crises occur, the latter may turn into a hotbed of international conflicts. In such situations, stability could be restored in one of two ways—either by the intervention of an external hegemonic power or by the balancing out of the influence of many rival great powers. In the first case, more small conflicts may arise, while in the second case the number of possible conflicts would be less; however, each of those conflicts would immediately threaten a clash of the great powers among themselves.

If the stability of East-Central Europe is based on the stabilizing effect of a few external great powers, the fragility of this arrangement could manifest itself if the power relations between these great powers change, or if such a change is anticipated by the governments of the region. More concretely, if German, U.S., French and Russian—and to a lesser extent British and Italian—interests balance each other out in East-Central Europe, the appreciation of German economic, political and military power, or even the anticipation of that, will encourage nationalist forces to seek alliance with Germany, particularly in Hungary and Croatia. If serious domestic political crises occur, such a perception of international developments would stimulate adventurous behavior among certain nationalist forces. The likelihood of such a scenario would be increased by the failure of the consolidation of the United Nations system; so far, the latter has been able to function as a balancing mechanism between great power interests.

In domestic politics, such a trajectory would mean that political forces that ignore parliamentary democracy and the norms of the peaceful coexistence of nations could frequently find themselves in dominant positions in the political system. Even if such forces do not occupy the major offices of government, their very presence could exercise pressure on the policies of the government, and they could make the ruling moderates retreat and give up their own policies. When governments lose popularity and extremists set the agenda, neither the free press nor the judiciary system can operate as sufficient brakes on the extremist endeavor. Centralization of the state may occur as a result of extremist activity or as a result of an attempt to prevent extremism.

In domestic politics, the rise of extremism does not simply mean that aggressive tendencies occupy a larger space in legislative and executive offices, but also that political extremism can endanger the institutional framework itself. The weakening of domestic legitimacy and the lack of external support could make the governing moderates captives of a demagogic opposition. In Hungary, nationalism might pretend to be a key to crisis management, and this could reactivate anti-Semitism and anti-Romany attitudes in official policy-making. Multinational capital might well become the target of xenophobia and intolerance, and such a campaign could easily be supported by major segments of domestic capitalist groups, the middle classes and to some extent the workers as well.

In Hungary, a real threat of military conflict cannot be conceived without external great-power intervention or the emergence of a mutually provocative relationship with the neighboring states, or both. Based on the experience of the 1990s, we cannot tell which factors represent a real threat and which are imaginary. What is certain, however, is that a number of issues are still on the table, and that, if mismanaged, they can lead to various forms of nationalist outburst—speed of enlargement, composition of new member groups, minority rights, Shengen, and so forth.

Revolutionary Crisis with Radical Democratization

The reform and crisis periods of state socialism, the triumphalism of the systemic change and the collapse of the Soviet Union apparently buried the chance for another socialist experiment in Eastern Europe. The events may justify Fukuyama's judgment about the end of history. Nevertheless, "never say never" is a general rule not only in politics, but also in history.

What disappeared after 1989 was the immediate and direct threat of a systemic alternative to capitalism. What is left is the immanent contradictions of the system and its cyclically reproduced cleavages and crises. These manifest themselves not only in the former socialist countries and in some more miserable parts of the world, but also in the strongest and dominant states of global capitalism. Forty million people without social security in the United States and five million unemployed in Germany is enough to illustrate that not even the strongest market economies can satisfy the needs of the entire population. The marginalized groups of these societies have good reason to seek a systemic alternative, even if they lack ideas, resources and organizational power.

Before the crash of 1929, not many believed that the contemporary institutions of Western capitalism were built on sand. The following collapse and the threat of various totalitarian alternatives convinced politicians of all different tendencies that radical projects could become part of the agenda in the West too, and thus reform was made inevitable if they wanted to avoid even greater changes in their lifestyles. Radical or revolutionary projects must be taken into consideration, therefore, not only if we want to imagine what a postrevolutionary situation might look like, but also because the existence of such projects might play a role in encouraging and enforcing moderate reforms.

Radical movements could have a strong impact on European politics if the decision-making system of the European Union were to become so distant from civil society that a general and widespread sentiment of despair were to take shape. The Maastricht process—that is, the creation of the single currency—is itself a factor that contains the possibility of such a degeneration. In the case of a revolutionary situation, however, concentrated state power faces not a weak but a strong civil society, which is capable of resisting the decisions of the official parliamentary structure. In such cases, civil organizations go beyond the realms of cultural activities and become alternative organs of power—they may even build up their own military power, demanding the takeover of certain functions of state power from the official institutions.

When decision-making becomes very distant from civil society, radical democratization becomes a legitimate political demand, focusing not only on the perfection of the existing political institutions but also the establishment of social control over the economic process. Such demands may break through various forms of civic disobedience organized by local or international political movements. Such movements and demonstrations can, after a certain point, come into open conflict with the legal state power. A dual control may emerge, when society becomes divided over the fundamental questions of state sovereignty and political loyalty. Potential or actual civil war may follow, although actual armed struggle may be avoidable.

A revolutionary situation manifests itself not only in the strengthening of radical tendencies within parliament but in a situation when parliament, together with the executive power, becomes marginalized as an influence over actual social and economic developments. Alternative decision-making fora emerge, and these may take an anarchistic character for a while. The agenda of politics becomes dominated by the street, and the options of the existing legislative and executive powers become limited to either following the directly expressed demands of the masses or trying to resist those. If Eastern Europe becomes Latin-Americanized, a local version of the Chiapas phenomenon cannot be ruled out.

The information age provides a number of new techniques for social resistance and civic disobedience. This, however, does not necessarily mean that we have to imagine a revolutionary situation without old-fashioned rallies and street gatherings of the masses. In the United States, for instance, it was exactly the most recent period in the 1980s and 1990s that created the need and the opportunity for unprecedented series of demonstrations with hundreds of thousands of participants. Thus the epoch of technological change, with the broadening of cyber space, has not provided a substitute for mass demonstrations—rather, it makes the latter easier from the point of view of organization, implementation and public relations.

In Hungary, among the existing political and social organizations there is not one that could become the basis for such a radical initiative for democratization or which would be capable of undertaking open conflicts in a sharp situation. Hence, a precondition of such a scenario is the emergence of new movements, probably as a consequence of the Euro-Atlantic integration process. If such forces emerge in the next decade in a primitive form, they could accumulate sufficient political and moral capital from critique of European and Atlantic integration and thus demand a leading role in a situation of future crisis—that is, when the idea of a different social order becomes a legitimate claim again.

In the case of a revolutionary situation, the political forces that emerged during the systemic change would not only be weakened, but their final disintegration would also become a reality. This would be more likely if their international networks—their various international and other alliances—were to fall into a crisis. Instead of the earlier (and still existing) international organizations, some new global organizations could appear on the scene. They could be rivals that would set alternative political ideologies against each other in a globalized conflict.

Without a transformation of international and global structures, we should not expect a revolutionary scenario in Hungary and other countries of the region. In national or regional isolation all revolutionary initiatives are doomed to failure. We should not expect a revival of radical movements in the FSCs until three or four decades after the systemic change unless major OECD countries face similar crises too, particularly in Western Europe. The likelihood of such a scenario does not look very great at the moment, but, since the ingredients may realistically emerge, the possibility cannot be ignored.

Closing Remarks

The future of liberal democracy in Central and Eastern Europe depends on the developments of other dominant segments of the world system, and particularly on the conditions that prevail in the European Union. We thus have to see the FSCs as "dependent democracies," not just because of the direct influence of greater—Western—powers, but also because the survival of their newly established political institutions depends on developments in the "paternal" states of the core of the world capitalist system.

Official political analyses, however, avoid discussion of serious crises and radical social alternatives. It is the nature of liberal politics to target the best possible results and describe them to society as realistic and achievable. If achievements fall short of promises and expectations, unforeseen circumstances and domestic political opponents could be held responsible. This study has attempted to show that transition and integration are typical areas where a distinction must be made between official political rhetoric and social reality; this is because the latter may raise certain barriers to the activities of communities while politicians do not necessarily want to talk about those.

In Hungary, just as in other ECE countries, the systemic change and the beginning of accession negotiations to the European Union and NATO triggered off very high promises and expectations. The political elite feels compelled to preach about the coming of a peaceful, happy, democratic and prosperous Europe. In conclusion, we only need to mention two fundamental problems in relation to this somewhat romantic vision.

First, it seems that in Hungary the image of Europe we find in the political pictures of the future still feeds on the European conditions of the 1970s or 1980s, instead of the union that is to come about as a result of the reforms of the 1990s. Europe itself is changing day by day, and this fact can divert the evolution of Hungarian politics and society from the trajectory assumed by official as well as popular expectations.

The second problem is that even the best possible outcome of European integration will not be able to help Hungary reach the level of development found at the core of the European Union. During the lifetime of the active generations of our time, Hungary will remain a part of the European periphery, even if the country gains membership in certain organizations. In the second quarter of the twenty-first century the country may appear very similar to that of the 1990s in terms of average living standards and political and economic power relations. Although the prevailing political discourse always predicts definite and significant improvements in present conditions, in a less favorable constellation of external circumstances significantly worse and more unstable conditions are equally likely to emerge.

Appendix 1
Acronyms and Abbreviations

ÁPV Rt.	Állami Privatizációs és Vagyonkezelő Részvénytársaság (State Privatization and Holding Company)
ÁVÜ	Állami Vagyonügynökség (State Property Agency)
BIS	Bank of International Settlements
BWIs	Bretton Woods Institutions
CAP	Common Agricultural Policy
CC	Central Committee (before 1989)
CC	Constitutional Court (after 1989)
CEFTA	Central European Free Trade Agreement
CEI	Central European Initiative
CIB	Central European Investment Bank
CIS	Commonwealth of Independent States
CMEA or COMECON	Council for Mutual Economic Assistance
COCOM	Coordinating Committee for Multilateral Export Controls
CPSU	Communist Party of the Soviet Union
CSCE	Conference on Security and Co-operation on Europe
CSU	Christian–Socialist Union (Germany)
DEM	Deutsche Mark
DNP	Demokrata Néppárt (Democratic People's Party)
EBRD	European Bank for Reconstruction and Development
EC	European Community
ECE	East–Central Europe
ECSC	European Coal and Steel Community

EEC	European Economic Community
EIB	European Investment Bank
EKA	Ellenzéki Kerekasztal (Opposition Round Table)
EMS	European Monetary System
EPU	European Payments Union
ÉSZT	Értelmiségi Szakszervezeti Tömörülés (Trade Union Alliance of Academics)
EU	European Union
Fidesz	Fiatal Demokraták Szövetsége (Alliance of Young Democrats)
Fidesz–MPP	Fidesz–Magyar Polgári Párt (Fidesz–Hungarian Civic Party)
FKGP	Független Kisgazdapárt (Independent Smallholders' Party)
FSC	Former socialist country
FSZDL	Független Szakszervezetek Demokratikus Ligája (Democratic League of Independent Trade Unions)
FTC	Ferencvárosi Torna Club (Ferencváros Athletic Club)
GAM	Gazdaságstratégiai Munkacsoport (Working Group for Economic Strategy)
GATT	General Agreement on Tariffs and Trade
GDR	German Democratic Republic
HNF	Hazafias Népfront (Patriotic People's Front)
IGC	Intergovernmental Conference
ILO	International Labor Organization
IMF	International Monetary Fund
KDNP	Kerszténydemokrata Néppárt (Christian Democratic People's Party)
KP	Köztársaság Párt (Republican Party)
LDC	Less developed country
MDF	Magyar Demokrata Fórum (Hungarian Democratic Forum)
MDNP	Magyar Demokrata Néppárt (Hungarian Democratic People's Party)
MDP	Magyar Dolgozók Pártja (Hungarian Party of Labor)
MFIs	Multilateral financial institutions
MIÉP	Magyar Igazság és Élet Pártja (Party of Hungarian Justice and Life)
MKDSZ	Magyar Kereszténydemokrata Szövetség (Hungarian Christian Democratic Alliance)
MLSZ	Magyar Labdarúgó Szövetség (Hungarian Soccer Association)
MNC	Multinational corporation
MP	Member of Parliament
MSZDP	Magyar Országi Szociáldemokrata Párt (Social Democratic Party of Hungary)
MSZMP	Magyar Szocialista Munkáspárt (Hungarian Socialist Workers' Party)

MSZOSZ	Magyar Szakszervezetek Országos Szövetsége (National Federation of Hungarian Trade Unions)
NATO	North Atlantic Treaty Organization
NDSZ	Nemzeti Demokrata Szövetség (National Democratic Alliance)
NEM	New Economic Mechanism
NGKM	Nemzetközi Gazdasági Kapcsolatok Minisztériuma (Ministry of International Economic Relations)
NKA	Nemzeti Kerekasztal (National Round Table)
NPP	Nemzeti Parasztpárt (National Peasant Party)
OECD	Organization for Economic Cooperation and Development
OFA	Országos Foglalkoztatási Alap (National Employment Fund)
OSCE	Organization for Security and Cooperation in Europe
PIT	Personal income tax
PSBR	Public sector borrowing requirement
SFOR	Strategic Force
SI	Socialist Internationale
SIMIC	Severely indebted middle-income country
SZDSZ	Szabad Demokraták Szövetsége (Alliance of Free Democrats)
SZEF	Szakszervezetek Együttműködési Fóruma (Cooperation Forum of Trade Unions)
SZOT	Szakszervezetek Országos Tanácsa (National Council of Trade Unions)
TDDSZ	Tudományos Dolgozók Demokratikus Szakszervezete (Democratic Trade Union of Scientific Workers)
TNC	Transnational Corporation
UN	United Nations
USSR	Union of Soviet Socialist Republics
VAT	Value Added Tax

Appendix 2
Statistical Tables

TABLE 1. Main macroeconomic indicators

Year	GDP[1]	Inflation[1]	Unemployment[1]	Employment[2]
1981	+2.9	3.6	—	5,701
1982	+2.8	6.9	—	5,678
1983	+0.1	7.3	—	5,676
1984	+2.7	8.3	—	5,616
1985	−0.1	7.0	—	5,373
1986	+1.5	5.3	—	5,361
1987	+4.1	8.6	0.1	5,371
1988	−0.1	15.5	0.2	5,329
1989	+0.7	17.0	0.3	5,278
1990	−3.5	28.9	0.5	5,251
1991	−11.9	35.0	2.0	5,153
1992	−3.1	23.0	8.2	4,940
1993	−0.6	22.5	13.9	4,753
1994	+2.9	18.8	14.0	4,514
1995	+1.5	28.2	12.0	4,313
1996	+1.3	23.6	11.7	4,240
1997	+4.4	18.3	11.4	4,206
1998	+5.1	14.3	11.0	4,211

[1] In percentages.
[2] In thousands.
Source: Central Statistical Office.

TABLE 2. Foreign trade between 1990 and 1998 (in millions of U.S. dollars)

	1990	1991	1992	1993	1994	1995	1996	1997	1998
Exports	9,588	10,187	10,705	8,906	10,700	12,867	15,703	19,637	20,749
Imports	8,647	11,382	11,079	12,530	14,554	15,466	18,144	21,371	22,870
Balance	941	−1,195	−373	−3,623	−3,853	−2,599	−2,440	−2,134	−2,701
Balance[1]	2.9	−4.0	−1.0	−9.4	−9.3	−5.1	−5.4	−4.7	−5.7

[1] Balance as percentage of GDP.
Source: National Bank of Hungary.

TABLE 3. The debt service between 1990 and 1998

	1990	1991	1992	1993	1994	1995	1996	1997	1998
Gross foreign debt	21.3	22.7	21.4	24.6	28.5	31.7	27.6	23.8	26.8
Net foreign debt	15.9	14.6	13.1	14.9	18.9	16.4	14.2	11.2	12.3
Foreign exchange reserve	1.2	4.0	4.4	6.7	6.8	12.0	9.8	8.4	9.2
Debt service[1]	4.2	4.0	4.7	4.9	6.2	8.2	9.3	9.1	7.6
Early repayment	0.04	0.3	0.6	0.7	1.0	9.6	1.7	1.6	1.7
Gross interest payment	1.6	1.6	1.6	1.6	1.9	2.4	2.3	2.3	2.0
Net interest payment	1.4	1.3	1.2	1.1	1.3	1.6	1.2	1.0	0.9

[1] In billions of U.S. dollars.
[2] Medium-term credit amortization plus gross interest payment.
Source: National Bank of Hungary.

TABLE 4. The balance on the current account between 1990 and 1998

	1990	1991	1992	1993	1994	1995	1996	1997	1998
Balance[1]	127	267	324	−3,455	−3,911	−2,480	−1,678	−981	−2,298
Balance[2]	0.4	0.8	0.9	−9.0	−9.4	−5.3	−3.7	−2.2	−4.9

[1] In millions of U.S. dollars.
[2] Balance as percentage of GDP.
Source: National Bank of Hungary.

TABLE 5. The structure of imports and exports by country

Country	1990	1991	1992	1993	1994	1995	1996	1997	1998
A. The share of major foreign trade partners in Hungarian exports[1]									
USSR[2]	20.2	13.4	13.2	15.2	7.5	6.4	5.9	5.1	2.9
Germany[3]	20.0	26.8	27.8	26.6	28.2	28.6	29.0	37.3	36.6
Austria	7.5	10.9	10.7	10.1	10.9	10.1	10.6	11.4	10.6
Italy	5.9	7.6	9.5	8.0	8.4	8.5	8.0	6.1	5.8
Yugoslavia[4]	4.7	3.7	3.6	2.8	—	—	1.1	0.8	n.a.
Czech Rep.[5]	4.1	2.2	2.7	3.3	1.9	1.6	2.2	1.7	1.6
France	2.7	2.9	3.2	3.3	3.5	4.0	3.7	3.8	3.8
U.K.	2.0	2.0	2.0	2.3	4.3	3.0	2.9	3.2	3.6
Switzerland	1.9	1.8	1.9	1.8	1.5	1.4	1.3	1.1	1.6
U.S.A.	3.5	3.2	3.2	4.3	4.0	3.2	3.5	3.2	4.5
Netherlands	1.5	2.1	2.0	2.3	2.6	2.9	2.6	2.8	4.7
Belgium	1.2	1.4	2.3	1.8	1.9	2.0	2.1	2.4	2.6
Poland	1.7	2.0	1.3	1.8	2.0	2.6	2.9	2.7	2.3
B. The share of major foreign trade partners in Hungarian imports[1]									
USSR[2]	19.1	16.3	16.8	22.2	12.0	11.8	12.4	9.2	6.5
Germany[3]	23.3	21.2	23.5	21.6	23.4	23.5	23.6	27.0	28.2
Austria	10.0	13.2	14.3	11.6	12.0	10.7	9.4	10.6	9.6
Italy	4.1	7.2	6.3	6.0	7.0	7.9	8.1	7.3	7.6
Yugoslavia[4]	2.3	1.3	1.3	1.0	—	—	0.2	0.3	n.a.
Czech Rep.[5]	4.7	4.0	4.3	3.9	2.4	2.3	3.1	2.4	2.2
France	2.1	2.6	3.1	3.2	3.4	3.9	4.3	4.3	4.9
U.K.	2.1	2.4	3.0	2.6	4.0	3.1	3.3	3.4	3.4
Switzerland	3.1	3.2	3.0	2.7	2.6	2.3	2.1	1.7	1.7
U.S.A.	2.6	2.6	3.0	3.9	3.1	3.1	3.5	3.8	3.9
Netherlands	2.1	2.7	3.0	2.7	3.1	3.1	3.2	2.6	2.5
Belgium	1.7	1.3	1.9	1.9	2.1	2.4	2.4	2.3	2.5
Poland	2.3	1.9	1.6	1.2	1.3	1.6	1.8	1.7	1.8

[1] In percentages.

[2] Soviet Union: CIS after 1991, Russia after 1994.

[3] Germany: FRG and GDR together in 1990.

[4] Yugoslavia: in 1992 and 1993 with successor states, after 1993 Serbia and Montenegro only (two-year embargo indicated).

[5] Czech Republic: until 1993 Czechoslovakia, or Czech and Slovak Republic.

Source: Central Statistical Office.

TABLE 6. The share of foreign ownership among Hungarian companies with double-entry bookkeeping

Year	Total[1]	Foreign employed[1]	Share[2]
A. Share in employment			
1992	2,508	183	7.3
1993	2,002	225	11.2
1994	2,026	268	13.2
1995	1,896	324	17.1
1996	1,973	360	18.2

Year	Total[3]	Foreign-owned companies[1]	Share[2]
B. Share in value added			
1992	1,305	128	9.8
1993	1,475	242	16.4
1994	1,838	379	20.6
1995	2,335	629	26.9
1996	2,824	911	32.3

[1] In thousands.
[2] In percentages.
[3] In billions of forints.
Source: Hungarian Statistical Yearbook.

TABLE 7. The inflow of foreign working capital annually and cumulated[1]

Year	Annual capital inflow	Cumulated capital inflow
1990	311	311
1991	1,459	1,770
1992	1,471	3,241
1993	2,339	5,580
1994	1,146	6,726
1995	4,453	11,279
1996	1,983	13,262
1997	2,085	15,347
1998	1,935	17,282

[1] In billions of U.S. dollars.
Source: Central Statistical Office.

TABLE 8. The exchange rate of the forint against the U.S. dollar[1]

Year	Average mean exchange rate	Change from 1989[2]
1989	59.1	100.0
1990	63.2	106.9
1991	74.8	125.7
1992	79.0	133.7
1993	92.0	155.7
1994	105.1	177.8
1995	125.7	212.7
1996	152.6	258.2
1997	186.8	316.1
1998	217.7	368.4

[1] 100% = 1989.
[2] In percentages.
Source: National Bank of Hungary.

TABLE 9. Living standards indicators

Years	Cars[1]	Computers[1]	Automatic washing machines[1]	Infant mortality[2]	Life expectancy at birth[3]	
					Male	Female
1990	39	5	31	14.8	65.1	73.7
1991	39	6	34	15.6	65.0	73.8
1992	37	6	36	14.1	64.6	73.7
1993	35	6	38	12.5	64.5	73.8
1994	36	6	40	11.5	64.8	74.2
1995	35	6	37	10.7	65.3	74.5
1996	37	8	44	10.9	66.0	74.7
1997	36	9	45	9.9	66.4	75.1

[1] In percentages of households.
[2] Number in 1,000 births.
[3] In years.
Source: Hungarian Statistical Yearbook.

TABLE 10. The results of parliamentary elections

Party	Share of votes on county lists[1]			Share of mandates[1]		
	1990	*1994*	*1998*	*1990*	*1994*	*1998*
MDF	24.7	11.7	2.8	42.8	9.8	4.7
SZDSZ	21.4	19.8	7.6	24.4	17.9	6.2
FKGP	11.4	8.8	13.2	11.4	6.7	12.4
MSZP	11.0	33.0	32.9	8.6	54.1	34.7
Fidesz	8.6	7.0	29.5	5.7	5.2	38.1
KDNP	6.5	7.0	2.3	5.4	5.7	—
MIÉP	—	1.6	5.5	—	—	3.6

[1] In percentages.
Source: National Election Committee (OVB).

TABLE 11. The Maastricht criteria and related indicators of associated countries

Country	Inflation[1]	Interest rates[1]	Budget deficit[2]	Public debt[2]
Poland	7.0	10.50	2.5	49
Hungary	9.5	9.70	3.9	59
Czech Republic	4.5	7.95	2.0	26
Slovenia	6.9	8.20	1.0	23
Estonia	4.5	8.70	1.5	28
Greece	2.6	6.20	2.0	105
Maastricht Criteria[3]	2.2	6.45	3.0	60

[1] In percentages.
[2] As percentage of GDP.
[3] Based on current EU levels of inflation and interest rates; the figures for ECE countries are those planned for the year 1999.
Source: Erste Bank and Central European Economic Review, July–August 1999.

TABLE 12. The popularity of EU accession[1]

Opinion	Hungary	Czech Republic	Poland
In favor	68	45	55
Against	14	25	26
Does not know	18	30	19

[1] In percentage of the population.
Source: CBOS, IVVM, Tárki and Népszabadság, August 14, 1999.

TABLE 13. Attitudes to EU-membership according to party sympathy at the end of 1996[1]

Party sympathy	In favor	Against	Uncertain
MSZP	74	12	14
SZDSZ	70	8	22
Fidesz–MPP	64	22	14
MDF	57	14	29
FKGP	55	23	22
KDNP	51	21	28

[1] In percentages.
Source: Navracsics (1997).

Bibliography

Ágh, Attila (1994). Organisational change in the Hungarian Socialist Party. *Budapest Papers on Democratic Transition*, No. 76.

Ágh, Attila, and Kenneth Janda (1994). Hungarians look to future, not past. *Chicago Tribune*, May 12.

Ágh, Attila, László Szarvas and László Vass (1995). The Europeanization of the Hungarian polity. In Attila Ágh and Sándor Kurtán (Eds.), *The First Parliament (1990–1994)*. Budapest: Hungarian Center for Democracy Studies.

Allison, Christine, and Dena Ringold (1996). *Labor Markets in Transition in Central and Eastern Europe, 1989–1995*. Washington, DC: World Bank.

Amsden, Alice H., Jacek Kochanowicz and Lance Taylor (1994). *The Market Meets Its Match: Restructuring the Economies of Eastern Europe*. Cambridge, MA: Harvard University Press.

Anderson, Ronald W., Erik Berglöf, Kálmán Mizsei, Lorand Ambrus-Lakatos and Mark E. Schaffer (Eds.) (1997). *Banking Sector Development in Central and Eastern Europe: Forum Report of the Economic Policy Initiative (No. 1)*. Washington, DC: Center for Economic Policy Research.

Andor, László (1994a). Capitalism in Eastern Europe: New concepts of development are needed in the new Europe. *New Economy, 1* (2: Summer).

Andor, László (1994b). The Hungarian Socialist Party. *Labour Focus on Eastern Europe* (Autumn).

Andor, László, and Martin Summers (1998). *Market Failure. A Guide to the East European "Economic Miracle."* London: Pluto Press.

Balázs, Péter (1996). *Az Európai Unió külkapcsolatai és Magyarország*. Budapest: KJK.

Bartlett, David L. (1997). *The Political Economy of Dual Transformations: Market*

Reform and Democratization in Hungary. Ann Arbor, MI: The University of Michigan Press.

Bayer, József (1998). Új felvonás, új szerepek. *Népszabadság*, 11 July.

Bebler, Anton A. (Ed.) (1997). *Civil–Military Relations in Post-Communist States: Central and Eastern Europe in Transition*. Westport, CT: Praeger.

Békesi, László (1994). *The HSP Economic Policy Plan*. Mimeo, 17 February.

Berend, T. Iván (1986). A historical evolution of Eastern Europe as a region. In Ellen Comisso and Laura D'Andrea Tyson, *Power, Purpose, and Collective Choice: Economic Strategy in Socialist States*. Ithaca, NY: Cornell University Press.

Blanchard, Oliver J. (1997). *The Economics of Post-Communist Transition*. Oxford: Oxford University Press.

Blanchard, Oliver J., Kenneth A. Froot and Jeffrey D. Sachs (1994). *The Transition in Eastern Europe*. Chicago, IL: University of Chicago Press.

Blejer, Mario I., and Marko Skreb (Eds.) (1997). *Macroeconomic Stabilization in Transition Economies*. New York: Cambridge University Press.

Böröcz, József (1992a). Dual dependency and the informalization of external linkages: The case of Hungary. *Research in Social Movements, Conflicts and Change, 14*.

Böröcz, József (1992b). Dual dependency and property vacuum: Social change on the state socialist semiperiphery. *Theory and Society, 21*.

Böröcz, József (1999). From comprador state to auctioneer state: Property change, realignment and peripheralization in post-state-socialist Central and Eastern Europe. In Dorothy J. Solinger, Steven Topik and David A. Smith (Eds.), *The State Still Matters*. New York: Routledge.

Bozóki, András, András Körösényi and George Schöpflin (Eds.) (1992). *Post-Communist Transition: Emerging Pluralism in Hungary*. London: Pinter.

Bresser Pereira, Luiz Carlos, José María Maravall and Adam Przeworski (1993). *Economic Reforms in New Democracies: A Social-Democratic Approach*. Cambridge: Cambridge University Press.

Brew, Jo (1997). EU aid or asset-stripping? *Spectre, 2*.

Brown, J. F. (1991). *Surge to Freedom: The End of Communist Rule in Eastern Europe*. Durham, NC: Duke University Press.

Bruszt, László, and David Stark (1998). *Postsocialist Pathways: Transforming Politics and Property in East Central Europe*. New York: Cambridge University Press.

Campbell, John L., and Ove K. Pedersen (Eds.) (1996). *Legacies of Change: Transformation of Postcommunist European Economies*. New York: Aldine de Gruyter.

Carter, Frank W., and W. Maik (1998) *Shock-Shift in an Enlarged Europe: The Geography of Socio-Economic Change in East–Central Europe*. Brookfield, VT: Ashgate.

Chang, Ha-Joon, and Peter Noland (Eds.) (1995). *The Transformation of the Communist Economies: Against the Mainstream*. New York: St. Martin's Press.

Clague, Christopher, and Gordon C. Rausser (Eds.) (1992). *The Emergence of Market Economies in Eastern Europe*. Oxford: Blackwell.

Comisso, Ellen, and Laura D'Andrea Tyson (1986). *Power, Purpose, and Collective Choice: Economic Strategy in Socialist States.* Ithaca, NY: Cornell University Press.

Comisso, Ellen, and Paul Marer (1986). The economics and politics of reform in Hungary. In Ellen Comisso and Laura D'Andrea Tyson, *Power, Purpose, and Collective Choice: Economic Strategy in Socialist States.* Ithaca, NY: Cornell University Press.

Crawford, Keith (1997). *East Central European Politics Today.* Manchester, U.K.: Manchester University Press.

Csaba, László (1997). A kibővülés dinamikája. *Külpolitika, 3* (1).

Dahrendorf, Ralf (1990). *Reflections on the Revolution in Europe, in a Letter Intended to Have Been Sent to a Gentleman in Warsaw.* New York: Times Books.

Dallago, Bruno, and Giovanni Pegoretti (1995). *Integration and Disintegration in European Economies.* Brookfield, VT: Dartmouth.

Denton, Nicholas (1993). Hungary set for austerity before election. *Financial Times,* 18 May.

Dési, András (1998). Az EU-joganyag nem vita tárgya. *Népszabadság,* 27 June.

Dobrinsky, Rumen and Michael Landesmann (Eds.) (1995). *Transforming Economies and European Integration.* Brookfield, VT: Edward Elgar.

Dupcsik, Csaba (1997). Az európai régiók és a Közép-Európa-vita a nyolcvanas években. *2000, 9* (8: August).

East, Roger, and Jolyon Pontin (1997). *Revolution and Change in Central and Eastern Europe.* New York: Pinter.

Economist, The (1998). Is Central Europe, along with Hungary, turning right? 30 May.

Elster, Jon (1989). *Solomonic Judgements: Studies in the Limitations of Rationality.* Cambridge: Cambridge University Press.

Estrin, Saul, Kirsty Hughes and Sarah Todd (1997). *Foreign Direct Investment in Central and Eastern Europe.* London: Pinter.

Faini, Riccardo, and Richard Portes (Eds.) (1995). *European Union Trade with Eastern Europe: Adjustment and Opportunities.* London: Centre for Economic Policy Research.

Falk, Richard, and Tamás Szentes (1997). *A New Europe in the Changing Global System.* New York: United Nations University Press.

Fassmann, Heinz (1997). Unemployment in East-Central Europe and its consequences for East–West migration. In Hans H. Blotevogel and Anthony J. Fielding (Eds.), *People, Jobs and Mobility in the New Europe.* New York: John Wiley and Sons.

Fáy, László (1997). *"Ha majd a bőség kosarából . . ."* Budapest: Belvárosi Könyvkiadó.

Felkay, Andrew (1997). *Out of the Russian Orbit: Hungary Gravitates to the West.* Westport, CT: Greenwood Press.

Fishlow, Albert (1986). The East European debt crisis in the Latin American mirror. In Ellen Comisso and Laura D'Andrea Tyson (1986), *Power, Purpose, and Collective Choice: Economic Strategy in Socialist States.* Ithaca, NY: Cornell University Press.

Friedman, Harriet (1998). Warsaw Pact socialism: Detente and disintegration of the Soviet bloc. In Allan Hunter, *Rethinking the Cold War*. Philadelphia, PA: Temple University Press.

Gianaris, Nicholas V. (1996). The question of enlargement. In George A. Kourvetaris and Andreas Moschonas (Eds.), *The Impact of European Integration: Political, Sociological and Economic Changes*. Westport, CT: Praeger.

Goldgeier, James M. (1998). NATO expansion: The anatomy of a decision. *The Washington Quarterly, 21* (1: Winter).

Goldman, Minton F. (1997). *Revolution and Change in Central and Eastern Europe*. Armonk, NY: M. E. Sharpe.

Gowan, Peter (1990). Western economic diplomacy and the new Eastern Europe. *New Left Review, 182* (July/August).

Gowan, Peter (1995). East Central Europe's headless hegemon. *Labour Focus on Eastern Europe* (Spring).

Gowan, Peter (1997a). The dynamics of European enlargement. *Labour Focus on Eastern Europe, 56.*

Gowan, Peter (1997b). The post-Communist socialists in Eastern and Central Europe. In Donald Sassoon (Ed.), *Looking Left: Socialism in Europe after the Cold War*. London: The New Press.

Gowan, Peter, and Perry Anderson (Eds.) (1997). *The Question of Europe*. London: Verso.

Grabbe, Heather, and Kirsty Hughes (1998). *Enlarging the EU Eastwards*. London: Pinter.

Grancelli, Bruno (Ed.) (1995). *Social Change and Modernization: Lessons from Eastern Europe*. New York: Walter de Gruyter.

Greskovits, Béla (1998). *The Political Economy of Protest and Patience*. Budapest: CEU Press.

Gross, Daniel, and Alfred Steinherr (1995). *Winds of Change: Economic Transition in Central and Eastern Europe*. New York: Longman.

Habsburg, Otto von (1996). Nő a fa, avagy bizalom a jövőben. *Népszabadság, 6* (September).

Hagen, Jürgen von, Andrej Kumar, Elzbieta Kawecka-Wyrzykowska, Lorand Ambrus-Lakatos and Mark E. Schaffer (Eds.) (1996). *Coming to Terms with Accession: Forum Report of the Economic Policy Initiative (No. 2)*. Washington, DC: Centre for Economic Policy Research.

Halm, Tamás (Ed.) (1995). *Magyarország úton az Európai Unióba*. Budapest: Aula.

Ham, Peter van (1995). *The EC, Eastern Europe and European Unity: Discord, Collaboration and Integration since 1947*. London: Pinter.

Heinrich, Hans-Georg (1986). *Hungary: Politics, Economics and Society*. Boulder: Lynne Rienner Publishers.

Harris, Laurence (1995). Financial fragility in the transition to market economies (Ch. 7). In Ha-Joon Chang and Peter Nolan (Eds.), *The Transition of the Communist Economies*. London: Macmillan.

Henderson, Anne (1992). The International Monetary Fund and the dilemmas of adjustment in Eastern Europe: Lessons from the 1980s and prospects for the 1990s. *Journal of International Development, 4* (3).

Héthy, Lajos (1995). Hungary. In John Thirkell, Richard Scase and Sarah Vickerstaff (Eds.), *Labor Relations and Political Change in Eastern Europe: A Comparative Perspective*. Ithaca, NY: Cornell University Press.

Hitchens, D.M.W.N., J. E. Birnie, J. Hamar, K. Wagner and A. Zemplinerová (1995). *Competitiveness of Industry in the Czech Republic and Hungary*. Brookfield, VT: Ashgate.

Hobsbawm, Eric J. (1994). *Age of Extremes: The Short Twentieth Century, 1914–1991*. London: Michael Joseph.

Hoensch, Jörg K. (1996). *A History of Modern Hungary 1867–1994*. New York: Longman.

Horváth, Gábor (1992). Hiba lenne túl gyorsan belépni az EK-ba: Katona Tamás előadása a magyar kül- és belpolitikáról. *Népszabadság*, 17 April.

Huffschmid, Jörg, et al. (1997). Full employment, social cohesion and equity for Europe, alternatives to competitive austerity [in Hungarian]. *Eszmélet*, 35.

Hunter, Allan (1998). *Rethinking the Cold War*. Philadelphia, PA: Temple University Press.

Hutton, Will (1995). *The State We're In*. London: Jonathan Cape.

Hyde-Price, Adrian (1996). *The International Politics of East Central Europe*. Manchester, U.K.: Manchester University Press.

Inotai, András (1995). From association agreements to full membership? The dynamics of relations between the Central and Eastern European countries and the European Union. *Working Papers, 52*. Budapest: Institute for World Economics.

Inotai, András (1997). *Útközben. Magyarország és az Európai Unió*. Budapest: Belvárosi Könyvkiadó.

Kaldor, Mary, and Ivan Vejvoda (Eds.) (1998). *Democratisation in Central and Eastern Europe*. London: Pinter.

Kapstein, Ethan, and Michael Mandelbaum (Eds.) (1997). *Sustaining the Transition: The Social Safety Net in Postcommunist Europe*. New York: Council on Foreign Relations.

Karatnycky, Adrian, Alexander Motyl and Boris Shor (1997). *Nations in Transit: Civil Society, Democracy and Markets in East Central Europe and the Newly Independent States*. New Brunswick, NJ: Transaction Publishers.

Kocsis, Györgyi (1998). Az elfolyó idő. EU-csatlakozási tárgyalások. *Heti Világgazdaság*, August 1.

Kornai, János (1989). *Indulatos röpirat a gazdasági átmenet ügyében*. Budapest: HVG RT.

Kornai, János (1990). *The Road to a Free Economy*. New York: Norton.

Kornai, János (1993). *A szocialista rendszer. Kritikai politikai gazdaságtan*. Budapest: HVG Kiadói Kft.

Kornai, János (1995). *Highway and Byways: Studies on Reform and Post-Communist Transition*. Cambridge, MA: MIT Press.

Kourvetaris, George A., and Andreas Moschonas (Eds.) (1996). *The Impact of European Integration: Political, Sociological and Economic Changes*. Westport, CT: Praeger.

Kovács, János Mátyás (1994). *Transition to Capitalism? The Communist Legacy in Eastern Europe*. Hadleigh, NJ: Transaction Publishers.

Kovács, László (1997). Time and space. *The Hungarian Observer, 10* (1).

Krausz, Tamás (Ed.) (1998). *Rendszerváltás és társadalomkritika.* Budapest: Napvilág Kiadó.

Kuti, Éva (1996). *The Nonprofit Sector in Hungary.* Manchester, U.K.: Manchester University Press.

Lazear, Edward P. (1995). *Economic Transition in Eastern Europe and Russia: Realities of Reform.* Stanford, CA: Hoover Institution Press.

Léderer, Pál (1998). Másfél évtizedes halasztás? *Népszabadság,* August 19.

Lendvai, Ferenc L. (1997). *Közép-Európa koncepciók.* Budapest: Áron Kiadó.

Lomax, David (1986). *The Developing Country Debt Crisis.* London: Macmillan.

L. Z. (1998). A magyar gazda várja az uniós csatlakozást. *Népszabadság,* 30 June.

Martonyi, János (1998). Polgárosodás és európai integráció. *Magyar Hírlap,* 28 January.

McBride, William L., and Yvanka Raynova (1998). *Philosophical Reflections on the Changes in Eastern Europe.* Lanham, MD: Rowman and Littlefield.

Michalski, Anna, and Helen Wallace (1992). *The European Community: The Challenge of Enlargement.* London: Royal Institute of International Affairs.

Michie, Johathan (1991). *The Economics of Restructuring and Intervention.* Aldershot, U.K.: Edward Elgar.

Michie, Jonathan (Ed.) (1991). *The Economics of Restructuring and Intervention.* London: Routledge.

Minc, Alain (1992). *The Great European Illusion: Business in the Wider Community.* Oxford: Blackwell.

Milenkovitch, Deborah (1991). The politics of economic transformation. *Journal of International Affairs,* 45 (1).

Mizsei, Kálmán (1995). Lessons from bad loan management in the East Central European economic transition for the second wave reform countries. In Jacek Rostowski (Ed.), *Banking Reform in Central Europe and the Former Soviet Union.* Budapest: Central European University Press.

Navracsics, Tibor (1997). *A Missing Debate? Hungary and the European Union.* Mimeo. Budapest: ELTE.

Niederhauser, Emil (1989). Körkérdés. *Századvég: különszám* [special edition].

Nove, Alec (1983). *The Economics of Feasible Socialism.* London: Allen and Unwin.

Oltay, Edith (1994). Hungarian socialists prepare for comeback. *RFE/RL Research Report, 3* (9: 4 March).

Perszynski, Maciej, Jan Kregel and Egon Matzner (Eds.) (1994). *After the Market Shock: Central and East-European Economies in Transition.* Brookfield, VT: Dartmouth.

Petras, James, and Steve Vieux (1995). *The Morbidity of Capitalism in the Former Soviet Bloc.* Mimeo.

Pinder, John (1991). *The European Community and Eastern Europe.* London: Pinter, Chatham House Papers.

Pitti, Zoltán (1998). Bejött, de mit hozott a tőke? *Társadalmi Szemle,* Vol. 53, No. 3 (March).

Plasser, Fritz, and Andreas Pribersky (Eds.) (1996). *Political Culture in East Central Europe.* Brookfield, VT: Avebury.

Pócs, Balázs, and Edit Inotai (1998). EU-tagság a dátumok bűvöletében. *Népszabadság,* 8 July.

Preston, Christopher (1997). *Enlargement and Integration in the European Union.* New York: Routledge.

Pridham, Geoffrey, Eric Herring and George Sanford (1997). *Building Democracy? The International Dimension of Democratisation in Eastern Europe.* London: Leicester University Press.

Przevorski, Adam (1993). Economic reforms, public opinion, and political institutions: Poland in the East European perspective. In Luiz Carlos Bresser Pereira, José María Maravall and Adam Przeworski, *Economic Reforms in New Democracies: A Social-Democratic Approach.* Cambridge: Cambridge University Press.

Radice, Hugo (1995). Organizing markets in Central and Eastern Europe: Competition, governance and the role of foreign capital. In E. Dittrich, G. Schmidt and R. Whitley (Eds.), *Industrial Legacies and Industrial Transformation in Europe.* London: Sage.

Ranis, Gustav, and Schultz, Paul (1988). *The State of Development Economics: Progress and Perspectives.* Oxford: Basil Blackwell.

Ránki, György (1985). Közép-Európa kérdéséhez—gazdasági szempontból. *Valóság,* November.

Raskó, György (1998). Mindig válság van. A búzamizéria okairól és a megoldásról. *Magyar Narancs,* July 23.

Révai, József (1966). *Válogatott történelmi írások.* Budapest: Kossuth Könyvkiadó.

Romány, Pál (1998). Korszakváltások fél évszázada. *Népszabadság,* August 19.

Romsics, Ignác (1997). Közép- és/vagy Kelet-Európa. Egy terminológiai vita nyomában. *Rubicon,* 8 (69–70).

Rose, Richard (1996). *What is Europe?* New York: Longman.

Rostowski, Jacek (Ed.) (1995). *Banking Reform in Central Europe and the Former Soviet Union.* Budapest: Central European University Press.

Sadler, David, and Swain, Adam (1994). State and market in Eastern Europe: Regional development and workplace implications of direct foreign investment in the automobile industry in Hungary. *Trans. Inst. Br. Geogr.* NS 19.

Sassoon, Donald (Ed.) (1997). *Looking Left: Socialism in Europe after the Cold War.* London: The New Press.

Socialist Bulletin (1994). *No. 1. and No. 2. PR Publication.* Hungarian Socialist Party.

Stiglitz, Joseph E. (1994). *Whither Socialism?* Cambridge, MA: The MIT Press.

Struyk, Raymond J. (Ed.) (1996). *Economic Restructuring of the Former Soviet Bloc: The Case of Housing.* Washington, DC: Urban Institute Press.

Swain, Nigel (1992). *Hungary: The Rise and Fall of Feasible Socialism.* London: Verso.

Szabó Pelsőczy, Miklós (Ed.) (1996). *Fifty Years after Bretton Woods: The New Challenge of East–West Partnership for Economic Progress.* Brookfield, VT: Avebury.

Szakolczay, György (1993). Az alapelvek módosítása elkerülhetetlen. *Figyelő,* 4 February.

Szentes, Tamás (1972). *Elmaradottság és fejlesztés. Az elmaradottság leküzdésének kérdései Afrikában.* Budapest: KJK.

Szőnyi, István (1997). Az Egyesült Államok és az unió bővítése. *Külpolitika,* 3 (1).

Szűcs, Jenő (1981). *Vázlat Európa három történeti régiójáról.* Budapest: Magvető Kiadó.

Tamás, Gáspár Miklós (1996). Az európázás kétes gyönyörei. *Magyar Narancs,* 10 October.

Taylor, Rogan and Klara Jamrich (Eds.) (1997). *Puskas on Puskas: The Life and Times of a Footballing Legend.* London: Robson Books.

Thirkell, John, Richard Scase and Sarah Vickerstaff (Eds.) (1995). *Labor Relations and Political Change in Eastern Europe: A Comparative Perspective.* Ithaca, NY: Cornell University Press.

Tismaneanu, Vladimir (1998). *Fantasies of Salvation: Democracy, Nationalism and Myth in Post-Communist Europe.* Princeton, NJ: Princeton University Press.

Tiusanen, Tauno (1996). *Post-Communist Capitalism and Capital: Foreign Investors in Transitional Economies.* Commack, NY: Nova Science Publishers.

Tong, Yanqi (1997). *Transitions from State Socialism: Economic and Political Change in China and Hungary.* Lanham, NJ: Rowman and Littlefield.

Townsend, Peter (1995). Poverty in Eastern Europe: The latest manifestation of global polarization. In G. Rodgers and J. Von Der Hoeven (Eds.), *New Approaches to Poverty Analysis and Policy—III: The Poverty Agenda: Trends and Policy Options.* Geneva: International Institute for Labour Studies.

Turnock, David (1997). *The East European Economy in Context: Communism and Transition.* New York: Routledge.

Ulman, Lloyd, Barry Eichengreen and William T. Dickens (Eds.) (1993). *Labor and an Integrated Europe.* Washington, DC: The Brookings Institution.

Vásárhelyi, Mária (1994). . . . és mi lesz, ha nem jönnek vissza? *Kritika,* June.

Vass, László (1992). A Magyar Szocialista Párt. In Mihály Bihari (Ed.), *A többpártrendszer kialakulása Magyarországon.* Budapest: Kossuth Könyvkiadó.

Wainwright, Hilary (1993). *Arguments for a New Left: Answering the Free-Market Right.* Oxford: Blackwell.

Weidenfeld, Werner (Ed.) (1995). *Central and Eastern Europe on the Way into the European Union: Problems and Prospects of Integration.* Gütersloh: Bertelsmann Foundation Publishers.

White, Stephen (1993). *Eastern Europe after Communism.* In Stephen White, Judy Batt and Paul G. Lewis (Eds.), *Developments in East European Politics.* Durham, U.K.: Durham University Press.

White, Stephen, Judy Batt and Paul G. Lewis (Eds.) (1993). *Developments in East European Politics.* Durham, U.K.: Durham University Press.

Wiener, György (1998). A 98-as választási paradoxon. *Népszabadság,* 29 June.

Wightman, Gordon (Ed.) (1995). *Party Formation in East-Central Europe: Post-Communist Politics in Czechoslovakia, Hungary, Poland and Bulgaria.* Brookfield, VT: Edward Elgar.

World Bank (1996). From plan to market. *World Development Report.* New York: Oxford University Press.

Wyzan, Michael L. (Ed.) (1995). *First Steps Toward Economic Independence: New States of the Postcommunist World.* Westport, CT: Praeger.

Zecchini, Salvatore (1997). *Lessons from the Economic Transition: Central and Eastern Europe in the 1990s*. Boston, MA: Kluwer Academic Publishers.

Zon, Hans van (1991). East European debt: A comparative perspective. In Johathan Michie, *The Economics of Restructuring and Intervention*. Aldershot, U.K.: Edward Elgar.

Zon, Hans van (1996). *The Future of Industry in Central and Eastern Europe*. Brookfield, VT: Ashgate.

Zwass, Adam (1995). *From Failed Communism to Underdeveloped Capitalism: Transformation of Eastern Europe, the post-Soviet Union and China*. Armonk, NY: M. E. Sharpe.

Index

ABOUT THE AUTHOR

LÁSZLÓ ANDOR is an Associate Professor, Department of Economic Policy, Budapest University of Economic Sciences. A former Visiting Fulbright Scholar at Rutgers University, Professor Andor has published widely in scholarly journals. His latest English-language book is *Market Failure: A Guide to the East European Economic Miracle*, with Martin Summers (1998).

ISBN 0-275-96394-2